Cuban American Theater

edited by

Rodolfo J. Cortina

Arte Publico Press
Houston
Texas
1991

ents

This volume is made possible through a grant from the National Endowment for the Arts, a federal agency.

The editor gratefully acknowledges the invaluable assistance of the following persons and institutions: for the preparation of the typescript and some textual editing, María Elena Cros, Mercedes Boffill, Soledad Díaz, Sandra Bergeson and Catherine Barry; for financial support in terms of editing, Florida International University's Department of Modern Languages; for the financial support for translation, Arte Publico Press; for translation in record time, David L. Miller, and for other translation assistance and editing, Lynn E. Rice Cortina; for bibliographic suggestions and research, Nicolás Kanellos, and for running down one of these items in New York, Alberto Moncada.

Arte Publico Press
University of Houston
Houston, Texas 77204-2090

Cover design by Mark Piñón

Cuban American theater / edited by Rodolfo J. Cortina.
    p.   cm.
    Contents: Martínez / by Leopoldo M. Hernández — Your better half / by Matías Montes Huidobro — Birds without wings / by Renaldo Ferradas — With all and for the good of all / by Uva Clavijo — A little something to ease the pain / by René R. Alomá — Once upon a dream / by Miguel González-Pando
    ISBN 1-55885-020-1
    1. American drama—Cuban American authors.   2. Cuban American drama (Spanish)—Translations into English.   3. Cuban Americans—Drama. I. Cortina, Rodolfo J.
PS628.C82C83 1991
812'.5408097291–dc20   91-9898
                                        CIP

For Olivia Augusta, whose very own play she writes, she directs, and she acts in the simultaneity of her experience.

Contents

INTRODUCTION

Definition and Periodization

Cuban literature, Cuban exile literature, Cuban American literature: where does one end and the other one begin? It is in the midst of these thorny questions that the issue of definitions arises. In the case of the other U.S. Hispanic literatures such as that of Mexican, Mexican-American and Chicano literature, the demarcations are more clearly observed, though there are moments in the aftermath of the Mexican Revolution of 1910 that exile Mexican literature enters the U.S. Cuban literature has been traditionally written both on the island and abroad. The cases of Heredia, Avellaneda, Casals, Merlin, Martí, Florit, Carpentier, Sarduy, Arenas are but a few examples of this phenomenon. So then, if Cuban literature has often been written in exile, is there a difference between the literature of exile and that of the homeland? The answer, of course, is no, as long as the writer is considered both as a national author and as an exile after his or her death.

Cuban American literature, on the other hand, requires other considerations. For instance, the very nature of the context makes it difficult to make perfect analogies with other U.S. Hispanic literatures. Should Cuban American authors be born in the U.S.? Should they write only in English or, at least, in alternating codes? Should they write only about their immigrant experience? To some degree, whereas the questions are legitimate, they are not irrelevant, but impertinent. It seems to me that if José Martí lived in New York for fifteen years, he was to an extent a Cuban writer, an exile writer, but also a Cuban American writer. There is no law that forbids literary historians from including the same figure in several categories, or even in distinct groupings that are based on nationalist definitions, when the author lives a transnational reality.

It is my preference to view Cuban American authors as those who live in the U.S. and write about whatever topics may interest them (home country, new country, other places, peoples or things), and to place them in generational cohorts for ease of classification. Hence, in the case of theater, it would be better if we were to group authors in the following scheme: a Romantic generation, a Realist generation, a Naturalist generation, an Impressionist generation (corresponding to *Modernismo*), an Avant-Garde generation, an Existentialist generation, a Revolutionary generation, and a Postmodern generation. These groupings correspond, roughly, to the nineteenth century for the first three, turn of the century for the next group, and the twentieth century for the final four groups. The difference between both centuries lies in the fact that both Romanticism and a significant Cuban presence in the U.S. did not begin in 1800, but almost thirty years later. This general classificatory scheme also serves another very useful purpose: besides creating a mechanism for ordering the facts that we now know about the Cuban American writers whose persons and works have received some attention, it prepares the way for other newly researched facts to fit into the outline, or to demand changes in it.

Themes and Genres

In addition to the general issues of definition and periodization which have been addressed above, there are problems of genre which demand our attention. Perhaps some of the best work on Cuban theater history regarding the issue of genre has been in the major identification which has existed since Aristotle's *Poetics* in dividing tragedy from comedy.[1] The very nature of classifying across this gulf marked by laughter and tears is not in itself a problem; the notable exception is that theater that is not funny, becomes serious, and, therefore, more important. This, obviously has more to do with class prejudice than with anything else: the lords act tragically, the servants, comically.

Some scholars of French seventeenth century theater have very ingeniously availed themselves of approaches to communication theory designed as such by Roman Jakobson in order to elucidate the Aristotelian distinction even further. By identifying comedy with the emotive, poetic and conative functions, and farce with the referential, phatic and metalinguistic functions, they have managed to clarify not only the source of humor, but also the shape of its dramatic presentation.[2] This is helpful to those who would continue the verticality of judgement, making comedy superior to farce in the general esthetic scale of value. Thus, one could conclude from these general exercises on dramatic genre definition, Cuban theater would be ranked as follows: serious theater, comedy, *teatro frívolo*, and *teatro bufo*, the latter being gradations of comedic drama. But what appears logical in the deductive realm is contradicted by an investigation of historical experience.

The origins of Cuban American theater are intimately tied to a tradition of theater in Cuba which marked Cuban theatrical tastes, dramatic possibilities, and artistic aspirations for actors, artists, playwrights, and entrepreneurs.[3] They are also inextricably connected to the dimension of exile literature which brings together the twin preoccupations with the homeland as a lost paradise, and the new land as an alien place.[4] For Cuban American theater, therefore, the major themes will cluster around the political and the social lives of the exile and the immigrant communities, respectively. But these are not the only divisions, as we have been discussing above. Likely as not, Cuban American theater will tend to follow the dichotomy imposed by a similar dramatic schizophrenia in the late nineteenth and early twentieth centuries when the Cuban theater separated the popular slapstick from the elite dramaturgy. Spanish colonial censorship forbade the serious treatment of Cuban nationalist themes in the theater. This led playwrights who preferred working the serious side of the stage to imitate Spanish drama. Thus, serious Cuban colonial theater became a servile imitator of the Spanish stage. This took place not only in Havana, but also in Tampa, the exile capital of Cuban independence patriots, where theater flourished.[5] The only authentic Cuban themes were left to the genres of comedy and farce. So much so is the case that the general division has included a range of subgenres of comedy such as *juguete, juguete cómico de costumbres, juguete histórico-dramático, alta comedia, apropósito, sainete, sainete provincial, pieza cómica, comedia mundana, ajiaco bufo-lírico bailable, pasillo cómico-lírico, disparate cómico, disparate bufo-lírico, pasatiempo cómico, paso de comedia, película cómica, capricho cómico, humorada lírica, episodio lírico-cómico, esperpento cómico-bufo, descarrilamiento cómico, zarzuela bufa,* and *disparate catedrático.*[6]

With a few exceptions that took place in the twenties and thirties when labor and other social topics were introduced to the stage, this has remained true since then, practically to this day. Cuban American serious theater during the Revolutionary period for the first twenty-five years struggled to survive. Meanwhile, the comic theater continues to blossom.

Another important circumstance that affected Cuban and Cuban American theater, as it has most theaters, was the advent and growth of the radio, film and television industries. These technological innovations have made theater an art of the masses in new ways, but have left traditional stagecraft as a more marginal enterprise. Entrepreneurs have, therefore, catered to the mass appeal of comedy, and to some extent to the musical comedy. Such are the cases of Miami, New York and Tampa in our day, where serious drama continues to lose ground to comedy.[7]

A Bit of History

It is in the latter part of the 1820s that New York boasted two Spanish language newspapers, *El Mensajero Semanal* and *El Mercurio de Nueva York*, which carried news as well as literary artifacts.[8] These consisted mostly of poetry and stories, but already in their pages there appeared actual dramatic literature from Spain. By the second half of the century, the Hispanic publishing industry was including drama among its titles on all manner of subjects. Some books like Francisco Javier Balmaseda's *Los confinados a Fernando Poo*, which was issued in 1869, are political tracts that took advantage of the venue for free expression, leaving their creative work for publication in their homeland. But others who had either fled permanently or happened to have a passing connection with the U.S. did entrust their work to the stateside publishers. In his *A History of Hispanic Theater in the United States: Origins to 1940* (Austin: University of Texas Press, 1990) Kanellos makes reference to Orman Tu-Caes (which he suspects is a penname) as having had his play published by the Granja firm *El hermano generoso* in 1840. I agree that it is a pseudonym used to hide the author's name whose four-act prose work probably contained unflattering allusions to the Spanish government. Others like José Francisco Broche were not so lucky. Broche had one drama, *Mendoza*, refused for publication in 1841 by the Spanish colonial authorities. And in 1842 he managed to get another one in print in Havana, *El Juglar*, a prose and verse five-act ponderous piece. The government forbade its distribution immediately. This was also the case with Nicolás Cárdenas y Rodríguez whose historical four-act prose drama, Diego Velázquez, was denied publication, and Isaac Carrillo O'Farrill whose sonnet addressed to Isabel II cost him some prison time. Orman Tu-Caes established a trend that Broche's obstinacy confirmed: publish political works abroad.

Beside those obviously political works, there were others which dealt with just plain nationalist themes. This in itself was offensive to the colonial establishment and made it easier for some to avoid the tortured language necessary to escape censorship. In this category we can place some of the Realist theater of manners following the more political Romantic dramas. Among them, Justo Eleboro's *El rico y el pobre*, a three-act play which appeared in New York in 1864. Two other important literary figures of the time had their plays published in New York: (1) José María Heredia, whose *Abufar o la familia árabe* saw the light in 1854, though it had been written in 1826 and staged in 1833 and (2) Gertrudis Gómez de

Avellaneda, whose play *Baltasar*, which had been published both in Madrid and in Bogotá in 1858, was reissued in New York in 1908 as one of the early Hispanist versions for the Hispanophiles of the time. The New York version contained an introduction, notes, and vocabulary by Carlos Bransby, making this Biblical four-act verse drama an important title for the American Book Co.

Other Cuban American plays of the time include José Jacinto Milanés's *Obras*, reissued by Juan F. Trow y Cia. in one volume in New York in 1865; Luís García Pérez's *El grito de Yara* published in New York by Hallet & Breen in 1879; Diego Tejera's *La muerte de Plácido*, a dramatic play on the death of the celebrated Cuban Romantic poet, appeared in New York under the imprint of Imp. Ponce de León in 1875. Meanwhile in Key West Félix R. Zahonet saw his two-act *zarzuela* printed by the Imp. de la Revista Popular in 1890 with the title of *Los amores de Eloísa o Heroicidades de una madre*. Two plays by Francisco Sellén also saw the light in New York: *Hatuey*, a 147 page five-act dramatic poem, was published by A. Da Costa Gómez in 1891, and *Las apuestas de Zuleika*, a 33 page one-act prose piece, was offered by M.M. Hernández in 1901. In 1892 G. Gómez y Arroyo had a one-act satirical, burlesque, comical, lyrical *juguete* entitled *Polilla regional* released by Conner in New York. Desiderio Fajardo Ortiz's *La fuga de Evangelina*, a one-act *juguete* in four scenes, written to celebrate Evangelina Cossío's sensational escape from political Spanish imprisonment in Havana, was dated in 1898 by Howes upon publication in New York. With Mario F. Sorondo's *Locura repentina*, published by The Speranto [sic] Student in Rutherford, N.J. in 1909, we may bring the nineteenth century to a close.

The history of twentieth century Cuban American theater prior to the Revolution is no less rich, but the information is just as scanty and the documentation is no less spotty. Thanks to José Luís Perrier and to Nicolás Kanellos there is some sense of what may have taken place in the U.S. urban areas where Cubans and theater intersected. In his *Bibliografía dramática cubana* (New York: The Phos Press, 1926), Perrier provides an accounting of Cuban and Cuban American dramatic publishing and production. (He also includes Puerto Rico and Santo Domingo in the book.) But Perrier's information is offered within a context of abundant periodical commentary by newspapers and magazines of the time in New York. Much of this material is lost or in recondite collections of difficult access for most. What Kanellos has done in his *A History of Hispanic Theater in the United States: Origins to 1940* is to painstakingly unearth some of that lost history. In two key chapters of his book (chapters 4 & 5 covering New York and Tampa respectively) he offers careful reconstruction of the context of the times by utilizing old newspapers and magazines, looking for theater chronicles, reviews, announcements and advertisements. This task is made more difficult for him because of a most peculiar characteristic. In Tampa and in New York the Hispanic communities were that, Hispanic. They consisted of Spaniards, Cubans (in Tampa), plus Mexicans, Puerto Ricans, Argentines, Venezuelans, Dominicans, etc. in New York. It is sometimes difficult, if not impossible, to distinguish a particular writer's background. Here Perrier is invaluable, and Kanellos, relying on both Perrier and the periodical materials is able to detail what we will merely sketch very broadly here.

The twentieth century may be segmented as follows for the purpose of establishing some order to the facts: from 1898–1925, from 1926–1940, from 1941–1960, and from 1961–1991. These dates correspond roughly with the above mentioned generational scheme (Impressionist, Avant-Garde, Existentialist and Revolutionary). These labels are not meant to necessarily characterize (we know too little of the actual content and style of much of the production of those earlier years), but to orient ourselves in terms of the broader categories of literary history.

The first years are well set in Tampa where the institutions of the Hispanic (primarily Spanish and Cuban, though to some extent Italian) community were able to sustain a non-profit theater activity which had two interesting characteristic notes. First, it has left a legacy which continues to this day. In Tampa the children and grandchildren of the theater crowd of that time have continued, if somewhat diminished, a theatrical tradition. Second, it has had the distinct historical quirk of being the only Spanish-language Federal Theater Project supported by the government during the Depression years. Tampa's tobacco workers and their families were able to group together into seven mutual-aid societies: the Centro Español, the Centro Asturiano, the Centro Español de West Tampa, the Círculo Cubano, the Unión Martí-Maceo, the Centro Obrero, and L'Unione Italiana. Each of these societies had a show committee in charge of events, an amateur group, and a theater. The presentations ranged from light musical operettas (zarzuelas) at the Centro Español, the most conservative society, to the more liberal fare at the Centro Asturiano which, without giving up the *zarzuelas* themselves, added the ever present *bufos cubanos*, including the *negrito* and the *gallego* with the participation of directors like Manuel Aparicio and Rafael Arango, playwrights like

Cristino R. Inclán, and actors and actresses like Bolito (Roberto Gutiérrez), Alicia Rico and Luis Guerra, all veterans of the Cuban and Cuban American stage in Havana and in New York. At the Círculo Cubano and at the Unión Martí-Maceo it was easier to find the *bufos*, while at the Centro Obrero the more socially progressive protest plays and political satires could be enjoyed. Typical offerings in their various programs might include *La viuda alegre* at the Español, *Bodas de Papá Montero* at the Asturiano, the Círculo or the Unión, and *Justicia humana* at the Obrero. The Tampa-Ybor City audiences may have been working class, but they were not untutored. Through the institution of the *lectores* or readers, cigar workers got to listen to great literature while toiling in the factories. They also alternated amateur performances with those of professional traveling troupes which they invited to their theaters. This made Tampa theater better than could be otherwise reasonably expected at first glance. Cuban American theater has always had a very good home there.

The New York scene, much more complex because of the lack of clearly established Cuban or Hispanic theatrical centers throughout this period, contrary to the case of Tampa, does acquire a firmer foothold in the later part of the Roaring Twenties. During the 1926–1940 period, New York Cuban American theater history becomes a bit clearer. The first years of the century had seen some activity by groups like the Club Lírico Dramático Cubano and later the Compañía de Bufos Cubanos. But until theaters like the Dalys, the Apollo, the San José (later Variedades), and the Campoamor (later Cervantes, and still later Hispano) provide solidity to the varied theatrical boom of the period, Cuban American theater cannot take hold in the Big Apple. In addition to the establishments themselves, there appeared an important group of playwrights and actors. Among the playwrights are several mentioned by Perrier, such as Alberto O'Farrill, the editor of *El Gráfico*, a newspaper devoted to the theater and entertainment world which began publication in 1927. O'Farrill, a well-known blackface actor of Cuban farce, penned plays like *Los misterios de Changó, Un doctor accidental, Un negro en Andalucía, Kid Chocolate,* and *La viuda como no hay dos,* all presented at the Apollo during 1926. Another dramaturg is Juan C. Rivera, also an actor who played the *gallego* roles opposite O'Farrill's *negritos*; he authored *Terremoto en Harlem* and *Cosas que pasan,* two *zarzuelas bufas* also presented at the Apollo in the same year. The most prolific of these playwrights was the famous Afro-Cuban singer Arquímides Pous who created over two-hundred (200) of these *obras bufas cubanas,* among which one might mention *Pobre Papá Montero* or *Las mulatas de Bombay*. Other authors like Guillermo J. Moreno (*Bronca en España, De Cuba a Puerto Rico*, both premiered at the Apollo in 1927) had works produced at the Teatro Campoamor (like *De la gloria al infierno*) as late as 1936. The *Cuba bella* revue which was presented at the Teatro Hispano dates to 1937. But with few exceptions Cuban American theater appears to go from a strong river to a smaller stream into the next period.

The fifties, which comprises the next period in the Cuban American stage, is the province of one very important playwright who practically on her own makes New York hospitable to Cuban American theater again. She spans the late fifties, sixties, seventies and has served in different capacities as model playwright, perspicacious commentator, generous teacher and ardent advocate of Cuban American, Hispanic and women's causes in the theater. But she has served it best by being the best. María Irene Fornés received critical acclaim in 1977 for her play *Fefu and Her Friends* in which eight women join each other for a weekend retreat during which they reveal their hopes, aspirations, frustrations, regrets and most of all their innermost selves. She has a varied repertoire among which we might mention *Promenade*, a light musical piece; *Mud*, an examination of dire poverty; *The Conduct of Life*, a consideration of the cruelties of a tyrannical dictator; and *Sarita*, set in the South Bronx in the 1939–1947 period, in which she follows the life of her protagonist from her age thirteen until age twenty-one when she enters a mental hospital. Though her work has merited her six OBIE awards, she has not reached the popularity with mass audiences in the past. Nevertheless, Fornés stands alone in the U.S. during a critical period for the Cuban American stage.

The Revolutionary period of the last thirty years or so, has brought many changes to the Cuban American theatrical experience.[9] According to Watson Espener, who prefers to separate the exile from the immigrant, there is now an incipient immigrant theater next to a dominant exile enterprise.[10] For Pottlitzer, Miami has not been easy on serious theater, because the first wave of Cuban exiles had not really been exposed to serious drama at home, only vaudeville and comedy revues.[11] But if we look carefully at the facts, we will see that in the late sixties and early seventies several Cuban American/Hispanic theatrical institutions came into being in various parts of the country. In New York Cuban refugees began to become involved in the theater during the sixties. Gilberto Zaldívar and René Buch founded the Repertorio Español in 1968. Buch had studied theater at Yale University and never went back to Cuba. Zaldívar was a Castro refugee who arrived in the U.S. in 1961. INTAR (International Arts Relations) was founded as ADAL in 1966, changing its name in 1972. It was the product of seven Cuban Americans and Puerto Ricans interested in the theater; among them was their current director, Max Ferrá. Their main contribution to it has been the development of new playwrights who write in English and the production of new material. One of their programs sponsored by the Ford Foundation under the direction of María Irene Fornés was their INTAR Playwrights in Residence Laboratory. Among the first interns was the late René Alomá. In Los Angeles, Margarita Galbán, a Cuban American, was one of the three founders of the Bilingual Foundation of the Arts (BFA) in 1973. Leopoldo Hernández's *Martínez* was produced by the BFA in Los Angeles. In Miami Teresa María Rojas founded Teatro Prometeo at Miami Dade Community College in 1972. By 1973 Mario Ernesto Sánchez had founded Teatro Avante. Salvador Ugarte and Alfonso Cremata opened in the late sixties two small theaters named "Las Máscaras" which are very financially successful by dealing with topics of adaptation within the genre of comedy known as *comedia bufa*. Plays like *Enriqueta se ha puesto a dieta*, for instance, address the ideal of feminine beauty in both cultural realms (Cuban/American) and explore the problems of culturally derived models of behavior.

The political dimension of theater in Miami has had not so much to do with the content of the plays, but with the views of the playwright on issues alien to the stage. Such was the case with Dolores Prida (*Coser y cantar, Beautiful Señoritas, Savings, Pantallas*) and her brush with censorship in Miami in 1986 or even the case of Rafael de Acha's New Theater whose county funds were jeopardized because of questions, similarly alien to the stage, of local politics. While Tampa continues since 1959 with the Spanish Lyric Theater, now under the direction of René González, Miami has seen other theaters and theater groups flourish: Mirella González's Teatro Bellas Artes, Pepe Carril's Teatro Guiñol, Judith Delgado who runs the Hispanic Program at the Coconut Grove Playhouse, Pili de la Rosa's Pro Arte Grateli, Marta Llovios's Chicos, Inc., María Malgrat's M.A.R.I.A., Ernesto Capote's Capote Enterprises, Inc., and Jordana Webster's Andromaca in Hollywood, Florida, within the Greater Miami area.

Among the new playwrights, one needs mention, Iván Acosta, whose play, *El super*, has also not only been well received by the critical establishment, but through León Ichaso's film it has received mass distribution. In English Julio Matas has distinguished

himself with *Penelope Inside Out*, though he is better classified with
those authors who were educated in Cuba and who came to the
U.S. already with a literary profile. Also important in English (with
some Spanish) is Manuel Martín whose *Swallows* and *Union City
Thanksgiving* are very interesting plays. Of the younger generation,
Omar Torres's *If You Dance the Rhumba* (still unpublished) and
Achy de Obejas (*Brisas de Marianao*) bear watching. Of the masters who were accomplished playwrights in Cuba, Matías Montes
Huidobro's work is of special importance, as is that of Leopoldo
Hernández. Montes Huidobro is also important because of his ed-
itorial efforts in promoting Cuban and Cuban American theater
through his Editorial Persona, which has allowed several authors
to see their work in print. Also worth mentioning are several exile writers like José Sánchez Boudy (*La soledad de la playa larga*),
René Ariza (*El hijo pródigo*), Tomás Travieso (*Prometeo desenca-
denado*), Celedonio González (*José Pérez, candidato a la alcadía*),
Carlos Felipe (*Un requiem por Yarini*), José Brene (*El gallo de San
Isidro*), Raúl de Cárdenas (*Recuerdos de familia, Los gatos*), among
others.

   This anthology presents a variety of plays from the Cuban American experience. It has plays that deal with the »Cuban problem,"
as is Clavijo's play, and in a more personal way, Alomá's. Others deal with life in the U.S., especially young people (Ferradas),
and their relationship to adults (González Pando). Hernández explores discrimination, as does Montes Huidobro, although the former does so experimentally and the latter metatheatrically. Nor
is the anthology as originally conceived: Acosta and Prida who
were to be in it got their own collections from Arte Publico Press,
while Achy Obejas has been impossible to reach, even by visiting
Chicago and speaking to friends and former employers. As usual,
the works of human beings are fraught with accident and accumu-
lation, rather than with design. I hope, however, that the collection
will open a door to the world of Cuban American theater.

Notes

[1]See Rine Leal, *La selva oscura* (Havana: Arte y Literatura, 1975).

[2]Anthony Ciccone, *Comedy of Language: Four Farces by Moliére* (Potomac, MD: Porrúa Turanzas, 1980).

[3]Rine Leal, *Breve historia del teatro cubano* (Havana: Letras Cubanas, 1980).

[4]See Maida Watson Espener's forthcoming book *Cuban Exile Theater* (Gainesville: University presses of Florida).

[5]See Nicolás Kanellos, *A History of Hispanic Theater in the United States: Origins to 1940* (Austin: University of Texas Press, 1990).

[6]See José Luis Perrier, *Bibliografía dramática cubana* (New York: Phos Press, 1926).

[7]See Nicolás Kanellos "Hispanic Theater," *Goodlife Magazine* (May, 1985), pp. 8–10; also his book *Hispanic Theater in the United States* (Houston: Arte Publico Press, 1980).

[8]See Nicolás Kanellos "Towards a History of Hispanic Literature in the United States," in Asela Rodríguez de Laguna, ed., *Images and Identities: The Puerto Rican in Literature* (New Brunswick, N.J.: Transaction Books, 1987).

[9]For the Revolutionary generation, see Matías Montes Huidobro, *Persona, vida y máscara en el teatro cubano* (Miami: Universal, 1973); Maida Watson Espener's articles "Teatro, mujeres e identidad," in R.J. Cortina and A. Moncada, eds., *Hispanos en los Estados Unidos* (Madrid: Ediciones de Cultura Hispánica, 1988), and "Ethnicity and the Hispanic American Stage: The Cuban Experience," in Nicolás Kanellos, ed., *Hispanic Theater in the United States* (Houston: Arte Publico Press, 1984); José Escarpenter's many articles, reviews and introductions, including his latest "El exilio en Matías Montes Huidobro y José Triana," *Linden Lane Magazine* IX, 4 (1990), pp. 63–64, and John C. Miller's two articles "Hispanic Theater in New York, 1965–1977," *Revista Chicano-Riqueña* VII, 9 (1978), pp. 40–59, and "Contemporary Hispanic Theater in New York," in N. Kanellos, ed., *Hispanic Theater in the United States* (Houston: Arte Publico Press, 1984).

[10]See note 4 *supra.*

[11]See Joanne Pottlitzer, *Hispanic Theater in the United States and Puerto Rico* (New York: Ford Foundation, 1988).

Martínez

by

Leopoldo M. Hernández

Martínez

About the Author

Leopoldo M. Hernández was born in Havana in 1921 and grew up in Cuba's capital city. His elementary education at the Colegio Marista Champagnot was followed by that of the secondary Instituto de Segunda Enseñanza de la Víbora, a Havana neighborhood. He became a lawyer, obtaining his doctorate in jurisprudence from the Universidad de La Habana in 1945. To that point Hernández had dabbled in the short story, a traditional Cuban genre, but at age twenty-six he began writing drama and thereafter he never ceased writing. The short story genre has yielded fourteen stories in English, all unpublished, and some sixty-three stories in Spanish. Twenty-three of these won the CCC literary prize and were published in a book entitled *Cuentos viejos, breves, minúsculos* (San Sebastián: CCC, 1977.) Others have appeared in *Bohemia* ("El niño cueruso" in 1959, and "La carretilla," "La décima," and "La sonrisa" in 1960), in Los Angeles' *Revista América* ("Danny" in 1971 and "La mica" in 1973) and in UCLA's *Mester* ("La montaña" in 1969). Hernández also has three unpublished novels ("Y salieron del humo," from 1975, Letras de Oro finalist in 1988; "Diario Cero" from 1974 and "Kiri" from 1974, this one a novella), and poetry together with other prose works. Of the later his most important is *Eric: viñetas sobre un ladrón chiquito*, Los Angeles, 1972. His one book, *"Carta a mi madre muerta" y "Carta a mi madre viva": Dos poemas*, appeared in Havana, 1960, in limited edition.

His production in Spanish and in English includes more than fifty plays (some forty-three conventional plays, nine monologues, and a fourteen scene tableau entitled *Extraño mundo nuestro*). His plays have been recognized with prizes and awards, staged and published. Those receiving awards in Cuba are "La pendiente," by Sala Arlequín in 1959, "El mudo," "Los huesos," and "El barquito de papel" (a children's play), all receiving government recognition in 1961, and "Martínez," which was recognized in 1980 and staged in Los Angeles a year later by the Bilingual Foundation of the Arts with Luis Ávalos playing the lead role. Published plays include a book written under the pseudonym of Karlo Thomas entitled *Teatro de la Revolución* (Mexico, 1957), which collects three plays ("La espalda," "La consagración del miedo" and "Los hombres mueren solos"), "Sombras" which appeared in *Diario Libre*, October, 1959, "Mañana, el sol" in *Mestre* I, 1 (1981); "La Pendiente" appeared in 1959 and merited the praise of Frank Dauster in his *Historia del teatro hispanoamericano*; he credits him with reflecting the spiritual mutilation of modern man. *Siempre tuvimos miedo* (Honolulu: Editorial Persona, 1988) appeared with a very valuable study by Matías Montes-Huidobro and *Piezas cortas* (Honolulu: Editorial Persona, 1990) collects "Sombras" (1957), "El infinito es negro" (1959), "En el parque" (1961), "Mañana, el sol" (1963), "El mudo" (1961), "Infierno y duda" (1967), "No negocie, Sr. Presidente" (1977), "Cheo" (1975), and "Los pobres ricos" (1979) with a useful introduction by José A. Escarpenter.

Besides "Martínez," the following plays have either been read, staged or produced in a full fledged production: "El mudo" and "Los huesos" in 1961, as part of the Festival Obrero y Campesino, "Guáimaro: lección de historia," "940 S.W. Segunda Calle" and "Liberación" in 1969 (the latter an experimental piece accompanied with Afro drums) presented in Monterey Park, "Hollywood 70" written for the opening of the theater Pro Arte of Hollywood, and produced by 6 Actores in Hollywood in 1970, "Ana" in 1971. "Hollywood" was presented in 1973, "Do not negotiate, Mr. President" in 1983, the former at Pro Arte and the latter at the Bilingual Foundation of the Arts. In 1987 Florida International University's theater program produced "We Were Always Afraid," following a dramatic reading the year before at the Coconut Grove Playhouse. An abridged English version by Rafael de Acha was staged by New Theater during Florida International University's First Symposium on Cuban Theater in the United States. "Sombras" was read at the University of Miami in 1988. In 1987 his play "Tres azules para Michael" makes the final list for Letras de Oro, and "Tipit" receives honorable mention in the Concurso Gala de 1988.

Even though his prodution seems large, he has nevertheless lost over twenty plays confiscated by the Cuban government when he left in 1961. Hernández, according to Montes-Huidobro, places his characters between responsibility and commitment, pushing for an ethical stance. His existentialism, as explained by Escarpenter, does not marry his theater to the techniques of Realism. Rather, Hernández avails himself of a variety of dramatic strategies making his theater an eclectic and effective mixture of styles ranging from Naturalist, Symbolist, Expressionist, Brechtian epic theater and others. This varied repertoire of styles is also present in his monologues. These are true soliloquies in Escarpenter's view, but even though they are a difficult sub-genre of drama, Hernández manages to center them on marginal characters of society who are subjected to enormous pressure to reveal their innermost selves. Their need to communicate stands in an unbearable tension with their need to preserve their own dignities. Their need to connect with the other is confronted with indifference and hostility.

In "Martínez" all these problems are explored in a context of linguistic markedness and socioeconomic need with the added factor of ethnic rejection. The need to speak is an existential need to be, to exist, and a denial of that possibility is a denial of the self by preventing its being. The central conflict is rooted in such fundamental preoccupations by the author that it would be very easy to slip away from dramatic convention into ranting and raving on stage. Instead Hernández, unforgiving and uncompromising in his characterizations, explores the psyche before him by utilizing all manner of very useful and contemporary techniques of fiction which slowly reveal the raw battle raging in the soul.

CHARACTERS IN ORDER OF APPEARANCE

MARTÍNEZ
FRIEND
FOREMAN
PROSTITUTE BOUNCER
MARRIAGE COUNSELOR PRIEST
BUREAUCRAT
GIRL
POLICEMAN
SERGEANT
IMMIGRATION OFFICIAL
APARTMENT OWNER
OFFSTAGE VOICES

PLACE

A city in the United States

TIME

The present

ACT I

At rise: Dim lights let us see a young man in his early 30's sitting in a chair in a vacant apartment. There is a window at the rear with the shade down. The man's dark complexion as well as the shiny black hair and thick moustache indicate that he is a Latin. He is dressed in dark pants and a white shirt half open.

MARTÍNEZ: My name is Martínez, and I have an accent. (*His accent is not as heavy as that of certain people from Central Europe, but it is heavy enough to be detected immediately. His eyes wander, scrutinizing the audience as if he were trying to find a reaction to his first sentence. There is, however, a certain aloofness in his manners, as if he couldn't care less anyway.*) An accent is like an illness. At least it hurts like one. You see, I have been looking for an apartment since I was asked to leave from the one I live in, probably because of my accent (*Pause.*) and I have not found one as yet because of my accent. (*Makes an ample gesture which embraces the empty living room.*) See this? The owner wants two hundred and seventy dollars for this crappy room. He doesn't know that I know that these apartments rent for $200. He is overcharging me $70 a month, that is to say $840 a year for my accent. Which means that if I did not have an accent and I moved in here, in ten years I would have saved enough money to buy a brand new Ford or a used Cadillac. That is a hell of a price to pay for an accent. Of course, he will never admit that he is punishing me for that, but I know. You see, Johnny, the black guy that works with me, lives in this building and he said to me, "you may try to rent here but the owner doesn't like foreigners. He will overcharge you." "How much do you pay? I asked him, "$200," he answered. (*Talking rapidly.*) Then I come and the owner says "$270. Just for you." And I realize that Johnny was right and I can feel my blood rushing to my head and I wanna say "shove it up your ass" but instead, because I'm a gentleman, I use the only word in the English language that I can say without an accent: (*Pause, looks at the audience.*) Bullshit. But then he pretends not to hear me and offers me this chair so I can sit here and take my time deciding if I will pay $270 or tell him to shove it. And I really start to get pissed off, because I am sure that the bastard dislikes blacks as much as he dislikes accents, and yet he rents to Johnny for $200 because he is afraid of blacks, but he is not afraid of foreigners that can be deported easily if he complains to immigration, and so he takes advantage. Like my boss does. On top of everything else he does, he says to me: "Why don't you get rid of your accent?" And I should have said: "Why don't you get rid of your blue eyes?" But instead I smiled, and said, "I might just do that." (*Pause.*) If you are a foreigner, either you shut your mouth when un blanquito talks to you like that, or you let him have it and mess up your chances for citizenship. I would hate to get busted because I talked back to some fat-headed son of a bitch. I get so much steamed off in my head when somebody tries to screw me. See, I let go. I feel better now. (*A* VOICE *is heard on the other side of the apartment wall.*)

VOICE: Keep that noise down.

MARTÍNEZ: What are you talking about? I don't put out noise.

VOICE: What do you mean—keep out my nose?

MARTÍNEZ: I don't say nose, I say noise.

VOICE: Same to you, buddy.

MARTÍNEZ: I resent to be told that I do not understand English. What I cannot understand is the English that Americans speak. (*Pause.*) Back in my country I was taught the language of Shakespeare, which is not the same as the language of Frankie from the Bronx. I was taught to say (*Pronounces each word slowly and clearly.*) "When do we eat" (*Pause.*) Therefore I hardly know what the hell Frankie means when he asks, "Whendwit?" The same thing happens to a poor Anglo-Saxon that learns Spanish here and tries it in the first Latin American country he visits by saying: (*Pronounces each word slowly and clearly.*) "¿Dónde está el caballero de la triste figura?" which is what he read about Don Quixote, and a little bastard like myself answers: (*Rapidly.*) "Déjate de eso mi socio que la cosas no tan pa tanta legancia ni tanta fulastrería." (*Pause.*) On the other hand there are some things in English that make no sense to me regardless who says them or with what accent. (*Pause.*) The prepositions kill me. I tend to say the bread is in the table when I mean on the table because in

Spanish you say "en" which is in and by the same token I will say the bread is on the oven meaning in the oven. Also, instead of "tear it up" I say "tear it down," I chew people up instead of chewing them out, and for exercise I do twenty-five "sit-ins" every morning. (*Pause.*) Sometimes when I get confused—you're confused as to why I am confused, but the confusing thing is what you said to begin with. Like for instance, "come over" to you is a simple invitation to your place or to your bed if you are a woman, but the goddam preposition gets me every time and I say: "come over what?" because I am picturing myself coming over you. I have many problems with some words in your language. For example, I had this talk with a friend the other day:

FRIEND: (*Entering.*) Hello, buddy, what are you up to?

MARTÍNEZ: I am up to my ears in hamburgers and questions that I do not understand.

FRIEND: That's not what I meant.

MARTÍNEZ: It is what I wanted to say, damn it.

FRIEND: Why do you blow your top so quickly?

MARTÍNEZ: What top? (Points at the ceiling.) That top?

FRIEND: I better go home.

MARTÍNEZ: Take it easy.

FRIEND: You bet.

MARTÍNEZ: I bet what? A hundred? A thousand? What do I bet?

FRIEND: Forget it. Your fly is open.

MARTÍNEZ: I don't have a fly. Flies fly, they don't belong to people. Nobody has a fly.

FRIEND: Goddam spic.

MARTÍNEZ: Hijo de la gran puta. (FRIEND *exits.*)

MARTÍNEZ: It is a pity. You see? We like each other. It is just that we cannot communicate. Mostly because of the funny way you Americans speak English.

VOICE: (*Through the wall.*) You think you speak so good?

MARTÍNEZ: I no talking to you.

VOICE: Well, I'm talking to you, shorty.

MARTÍNEZ: (*Examines the wall to see if there is a hole.*) How do you know if I'm short . . .

VOICE: Just shut up. I'm trying to get some sleep.

MARTÍNEZ: (*Helpful and friendly.*) Oh—a siesta?

VOICE: What fiesta? My big fiesta is working all night—so keep it down and let me get some shut-eye.

MARTÍNEZ: You know there is another thing that bugs me. You don't understand "la siesta." Americans will never understand how back home you can rush from work at noon, take a battered bus with passengers hanging from the door like bananas, reach home forty-five minutes later, have a beer, soup, lots of French bread, a juicy steak with eggs and white rice and plantains and custard for dessert, go to sleep for exactly ten minutes and get so much rest in those ten minutes that you have the energy to jump back into a bus full of sweat and strange odors, make a pass or two at a female passenger who is forgotten immediately after, and reach the office to put four more hours in yelling over the phone. You will never understand that. (*Pause.*) You would understand however to work in downtown Manhattan and live in Connecticut and take the car at 5:45 a.m. and rush to the station to get the 6:45 on time and travel fifty-two miles standing while munching burnt toast, then take the subway to the final destination in which you work for eight hours with no siesta, get back into the subway and defy death while trying to get into the 5:20 along with a tribe of cavemen and eventually reach home where your wife tells you that the plumber never came and then you remember that you have to pee in the patio like yesterday. And you have suffered all the goddam day without a siesta. Which is beyond comprehension for any Latin lover and even those that are not lovers. (*Pause.*) By the way, I'll tell you a little secret: we are no better in loving matters than Americans, but we talk better while making love. We talk a lot in her ear. She likes that. (*Pause.*) What was I talking about? Oh, yes. The language and the custom in the country are a big problem to me. Here are some conversations I have had in just one day that represent poor communication that lead to misunderstanding on both sides. Round one: (*Bell.*) Martínez looks for a job. (*The* FOREMAN *enters wheeling in a table. He sits behind it.*)

FOREMAN: What can I do for you?

MARTÍNEZ: I need a job.

FOREMAN: So do I.

MARTÍNEZ: I do everything.

FOREMAN: So do I.

MARTÍNEZ: Could you give me one?

FOREMAN: One what?

MARTÍNEZ: A job.
FOREMAN: I guess so.
MARTÍNEZ: I cannot eat a "guess so."
FOREMAN: I guess so.
MARTÍNEZ: Couldn't you be more specific?
FOREMAN: I guess so.
MARTÍNEZ: Will you please stop the guessing?
FOREMAN: I guess I should.
MARTÍNEZ: I don't think you understand.
FOREMAN: (*Rising.*) I guess I don't. And either you leave fast or
      I'll kick your ass.
MARTÍNEZ: Okay. I leave.
FOREMAN: Fast.
MARTÍNEZ: I guess so. (*The* FOREMAN *exits with the table.*)
      So I left fast and went to a house of ill repute to reassert
      my manliness. Round two: (*Bell.*) Martínez commits a
      sin. (*Enters a* PROSTITUTE *whose make-up and dress
      are typical of the New York hooker. She is small and thin.*)
MARTÍNEZ: The "madama" probably did not understand my En-
      glish. You are not the one I was expecting.
PROSTITUTE: Why?
MARTÍNEZ: You are not much of a woman. I am sorry.
PROSTITUTE: (*Staring at* MARTÍNEZ'*s body.*) You are not much
      of a man, either. And I am not sorry.
MARTÍNEZ: Perhaps we can converse for a while.
PROSTITUTE: Did you say converse?
MARTÍNEZ: Yes.
PROSTITUTE: Twenty dollars an hour. Begin talking and make
      it long, son. The longer the better.
MARTÍNEZ: How much if we converse five minutes.
PROSTITUTE: Twenty dollars, anyway.
MARTÍNEZ: That is not fair.
PROSTITUTE: Look, little man. I came here to do my job, not
      to converse. If you want me to make you big, I'll do it
      in ten minutes. If you want to converse, I'll do that, too.
      But I want bread above all. That will be twenty dollars,
      either to do my job or to converse. I, personally, couldn't
      care less which one you choose.
MARTÍNEZ: I'll give you a kiss and two dollars. How does that
      strike you?
PROSTITUTE: Strike me! I'll show you someone who knows
      about striking. (*Shouting.*) Monster! (*A huge* BOUNCER
      appears and approaches them both.)

BOUNCER: What's the problem?

PROSTITUTE: He wants to pay two dollars.

BOUNCER: (*Getting* MARTÍNEZ *by the armpits and lifting him.*) You want trouble, son?

MARTÍNEZ: (*Terrified.*) No trouble whatsoever. Put me down.

BOUNCER: (*Putting him down.*) Give her her twenty goddam dollars.

MARTÍNEZ: (*Trying to get the money out of his pocket.*) At once.

BOUNCER: (*Shouting.*) Quicker!

MARTÍNEZ: (*Shouting.*) Here! (*He gives some bills to the* PROSTITUTE.)

BOUNCER: (*Leaving.*) Have a good day, son.

PROSTITUTE: (*Leaving.*) Have a good day, lover. (PROSTITUTE *exits, laughing.*)

MARTÍNEZ: (*To the audience.*) So I was taken and abused by a monster and half a girl, and it all happened because the madam did not understand what I asked for. I said to her, "Get me a dame," and she probably understood "shame" because that's what I got. Anyway, I was so confused that I went to a marriage counselor in spite of the fact that I am not married. A marriage counselor is one of those guys that tells you how to solve your problems, which are usually the same problems he has and he does not know how to solve himself. Round three: (*Bell.*) Martínez asks for advice. (*Enter a man with thick glasses pushing a table. He sits behind it.*)

COUNSELOR: Tell me your problems, son.

MARTÍNEZ: I asked for a dame and got a shame.

COUNSELOR: Are you talking about your wife?

MARTÍNEZ: You don't understand. It cost me twenty dollars.

COUNSELOR: Your wife?

MARTÍNEZ: The shame.

COUNSELOR: Your shame?

MARTÍNEZ: Instead of the dame.

COUNSELOR: What dame?

MARTÍNEZ: She made me give it to her.

COUNSELOR: She made you give it to her?

MARTÍNEZ: Yeah, twenty dollars.

COUNSELOR: That is exactly my fee.

MARTÍNEZ: I don't have twenty dollars.

COUNSELOR: (*Shouting.*) Monster! (*The same* BOUNCER *of the previous scene enters.*)

MARTÍNEZ: Oh, shit! (*The* BOUNCER *and the* COUNSELOR *exeunt.*) So I left and went to church. Round four: (*Bell.*) Martínez confesses his sins. (*The* PRIEST *enters and sits in the chair.* MARTÍNEZ *kneels to the right of him.*)
PRIEST: Let me hear your sins, son. (MARTÍNEZ *laughs.*) I do not hear your sins, son. (MARTÍNEZ *laughs louder.*) Are you laughing, son?
MARTÍNEZ: My sin, father.
PRIEST: Did you say sin, son?
MARTÍNEZ: I said sin—sin.
PRIEST: Sing-sing, son?
MARTÍNEZ: Simply sin.
PRIEST: Let me hear them, son.
MARTÍNEZ: I cursed and used the word goddam 143 time last week.
PRIEST: Very bad. What else, son?
MARTÍNEZ: I just laughed at your words.
PRIEST: What words, son?
MARTÍNEZ: Sin, son.
PRIEST: Did I say sin, son?
MARTÍNEZ: (*Laughing.*) And I laughed.
PRIEST: Why did you laugh?
MARTÍNEZ: (*Laughing.*) Because it reminded me of sing-sing and King-Kong.
PRIEST: (*Begins laughing too.*) Why?
MARTÍNEZ: (*Still laughing.*) I don't know.
PRIEST: (*Laughing.*) King-Kong?
MARTÍNEZ: (*Really laughing.*) Sin, son.
PRIEST: (*Really laughing.*) Sing-sing?
MARTÍNEZ: Sin, son.
PRIEST: (*Stopping the laugh suddenly.*) Stop the goddam laugh. (*The* PRIEST *exits.*)
MARTÍNEZ: So I left very ashamed of myself and sad because I meant to ask him if God could be a Latin. See? I cannot picture a God with an angry moustache. (*Pause.*) So then I decided to go to the IRS and ask some questions about my return. Round five: (*Bell.*) Martínez and the government. (*A* BUREAUCRAT *enters with a table with a calculator on it. He sits behind the table.*)
BUREAUCRAT: May I help you?
MARTÍNEZ: (*With a silly grin.*) Yes, please.
BUREAUCRAT: What will it be?
MARTÍNEZ: Two fried eggs.

BUREAUCRAT: I beg your pardon?
MARTÍNEZ: (*The grin is sillier.*) I mean ... I am sorry.
BUREAUCRAT: Forget it. So?
MARTÍNEZ: (*Silly smile.*) No.
BUREAUCRAT: What do you mean no?
MARTÍNEZ: (*The same silly smile.*) You said so.
BUREAUCRAT: So?
MARTÍNEZ: And I said no.
BUREAUCRAT: So?
MARTÍNEZ: I don't know.
BUREAUCRAT: Then?
MARTÍNEZ: When?
BUREAUCRAT: When what?
MARTÍNEZ: A cat. (*To the audience.*) You see, being fascinated
     by the sounds of English words I look for words that sound
     the same. The problem is, it never makes sense.
BUREAUCRAT: What do you mean a cat?
MARTÍNEZ: I meant that.
BUREAUCRAT: (*To the audience.*) I wanted to answer "the hat,"
     but I refrained myself. (*The* BUREAUCRAT *exits with
     the table.*)
MARTÍNEZ: So I drifted toward the park and met a girl. Round
     six: (*Bell.*) Martínez finds romance. (*The* GIRL *enters
     and sits on the chair. She opens a small book and reads.*
     MARTÍNEZ *sighs.*) I am always inclined towards girls
     who read a lot. They tend to be romantic or at least ap-
     preciate a pass made by a romantic jerk. (*He crosses to
     right of her.*) Hello. (*He crosses to left of her.*) Hello. (*She
     does not acknowledge him.*) I read too.
GIRL: (*Looking at him for only a moment.*)
MARTÍNEZ: (*Silly grin.*) No.
GIRL: (*Astonished.*) What do you mean no?
MARTÍNEZ: (*The same silly grin.*) You said so.
GIRL: So?
MARTÍNEZ: And I said no.
GIRL: So?
MARTÍNEZ: I don't know.
GIRL: Then?
MARTÍNEZ: Do you work for the IRS?
GIRL: No.
MARTÍNEZ: Do you know some words other than so, no and
     then?
GIRL: Yes.

MARTÍNEZ: What words

GIRL: Beat it, you creep.

MARTÍNEZ: (*Sitting next to her.*) It is not bad, not bad at all. (*Counts with his fingers.*) Yes, beat, it, you creep, in addition to so, no and then. Eight words. I'm impressed. (*Kneels.*) You deserve a kiss. (*He goes to kiss her hand.*)

GIRL: (*Shouting.*) Help!

MARTÍNEZ: What's wrong?

GIRL: (*Rising and dropping the book.*) Rape.

MARTÍNEZ: (*Rising.*) What do you mean rape? (*The* GIRL *knees him in the groin.* MARTÍNEZ *doubles over in pain. A* POLICEMAN *enters.*)

POLICEMAN: What is going on?

GIRL: (*Picking up book.*) He tried to rape me.

POLICEMAN: (*Grabbing* MARTÍNEZ.) You are under arrest.

MARTÍNEZ: (*Still in pain.*) Thank you. You saved me. Take her away.

POLICEMAN: What do you mean "Take her away"? She is not under arrest. You are.

MARTÍNEZ: (*Still bending.*) Why?

POLICEMAN: Because you are a dirty rapist.

MARTÍNEZ: She is unrapable.

POLICEMAN: We take her word for it.

MARTÍNEZ: Why?

POLICEMAN: Because you have an accent.

MARTÍNEZ: What the hell does the accent have to do with a rape?

POLICEMAN: Well ... in our minds we associate foreigners with rape.

MARTÍNEZ: So what? In my mind I associate your mother with a whore. That does not mean that your goddam mother is a whore. (*The* POLICEMAN *pulls* MARTÍNEZ's *arms behind him and shoves him down stage. The* POLICEMAN *and the* GIRL *exit.*) The only thing I remember after that is standing before the sergeant, handcuffed and aching all over. I also remember thinking: "Oh, boy, there goes my chance to be a citizen," although by that time I wasn't sure if I wanted to be a citizen. Round seven: (*Bell.*) Martínez meets law and order.

SERGEANT: (*Enters with a clipboard.*) Your name?

MARTÍNEZ: Martínez.

SERGEANT: (*Writing it down.*) Martínez?

MARTÍNEZ: No, I said Martínez.

SERGEANT: So I said.

MARTÍNEZ: You said Martínez.
SERGEANT: So what?
MARTÍNEZ: A cat.
SERGEANT: A what
MARTÍNEZ: Like that.
SERGEANT: It makes no sense.
MARTÍNEZ: The tense.
SERGEANT: The what?
MARTÍNEZ: The present tense
SERGEANT: Are you some kind of nut.
MARTÍNEZ: No, but ...
SERGEANT: You talk funny.
MARTÍNEZ: Like a bunny.
SERGEANT: Stop it, damn it.
MARTÍNEZ: Yes, sir.
SERGEANT: I am no sir.
MARTÍNEZ: No, sir.
SERGEANT: I am a sergeant.
MARTÍNEZ: Yes, Sergeant.
SERGEANT: You mean sergeant.
MARTÍNEZ: You called me Martínez so I will call you sergeant.
SERGEANT: You will call me sergeant, Martínez.
MARTÍNEZ: I'll call you sergeant unless you call me Martínez.
SERGEANT: This is stupid.
MARTÍNEZ: Do you have a brother who works for the IRS?
SERGEANT: (*Sitting.*) No.
MARTÍNEZ: Are you the father of an unrapable girl?
SERGEANT: No.
MARTÍNEZ: So?
SERGEANT: What do you mean, "So"?
MARTÍNEZ: You said no.
SERGEANT: So?
MARTÍNEZ: And I said so.
SERGEANT: So what?
MARTÍNEZ: A cat.
SERGEANT: (*Rising, shouting.*) Shut up!
SERGEANT: A cat.
MARTÍNEZ: It makes no sense.
SERGEANT: The tense. (*Tremendous howl.*) What am I saying?
MARTÍNEZ: I don't know.
SERGEANT: I hope they give you ten years!
MARTÍNEZ: In Sears?
SERGEANT: (*Shouting.*) Captain! (*The* SERGEANT *exits.*)

MARTÍNEZ: (*To the audience.*) The captain and I did not understand each other either. I was then sent to court where in addition to the charge of rape, I was made to answer the additional charge of making fun of a sergeant of which I am innocent also inasmuch as I am Martínez and sergeant was accusing Martínez. (*Two actors appear at opposite sides and along with* MARTÍNEZ *are isolated in spotlights for the "trial."*)

VOICE #1: You?

MARTÍNEZ: Yes

VOICE #2: Him?

MARTÍNEZ: Sí

VOICE #1: What?

MARTÍNEZ: That

VOICE #1: No

VOICE #2: No?

MARTÍNEZ: Yes

VOICE #1: So?

VOICE #2: Go

MARTÍNEZ: What?

VOICE #1: Hat

VOICE #2: Louder

MARTÍNEZ: Powder?

VOICE #1: Rape

MARTÍNEZ: Grape?

VOICE #2: Brat

MARTÍNEZ: Sat

VOICE #1: Fat

MARTÍNEZ: Sergeant

VOICE #1: Sergeant

MARTÍNEZ: Sí

VOICE #2: My God!

MARTÍNEZ: que cosa

VOICE #1: qui casa?

VOICE #2: No

VOICE #1: So?

MARTÍNEZ: Sí (*The two actors exit, the lights come back up.*) I think they dismissed my case because nobody knew what was going on. I walked out free, thinking of all the misunderstandings in just one day and went home and found this nasty note ordering me to vacate the premises prior to the end of the month, which means tomorrow, and all because of my accent. Oh, shit! I better make a decision to rent this crappy place or I'll be in the streets by tomorrow pushing a little cart with my belongings. (*He sits in the chair.*) But right now I'm too tired to worry about it. It would be so nice to take a little nap, and who knows, I might even (*Slows down.*) dream ... of better ... luck ... and all that ... and sleep. (MARTÍNEZ *goes to sleep. Fade out.*)

ACT II

A spotlight comes up on MARTÍNEZ. *He is still asleep in the chair. The dream that follows is performed with the help of voices coming from backstage.* MARTÍNEZ *begins talking in his sleep.*

MARTÍNEZ VOICE: (*Tape.*) Sir ... Sir ...
VOICE #1: (*Tape.*) What do you want?
MARTÍNEZ VOICE: (*Tape.*) Una visa.
VOICE #1: (*Tape.*) Have passport?
MARTÍNEZ VOICE: (*Tape.*) Sí.
VOICE #1: (*Tape.*) Twenty dollars.
MARTÍNEZ VOICE: (*Tape.*) Cuánto?
VOICE #1: (*Tape.*) Plus stamps.
MARTÍNEZ VOICE: (*Tape.*) Stamps?
VOICE #1: (*Tape.*) Plus vaccinations.
MARTÍNEZ VOICE: (*Tape.*) Needles?
VOICE #1: (*Tape.*) Several.
MARTÍNEZ VOICE: (*Tape.*) Hurt.
VOICE #1: (*Tape.*) Many times.
MARTÍNEZ & MARTÍNEZ VOICE: (*Tape.*) (*Together.*) It hurts
        (MARTÍNEZ *opens his eyes while dreaming.*) Sir ... Sir
        ...
VOICE #1: Is it you again?
MARTÍNEZ: My needles.
VOICE #1: What about?
MARTÍNEZ: They hurt. (*Pause.*) Sir ... Sir ... How many times?
        I have died many times.
VOICE #1: Who cares?
MARTÍNEZ: Each death is different.
VOICE #1: Ja, ja, ja.
MARTÍNEZ: It hurts. (*Pause.*)

Béseme, por favor, béseme madre
comprenda, madre
tengo que irme
debo hacerlo
no llore, madre, please mother, don't cry
a telegram?
madre ... vieja ... (*Yells.*)
Vieja!
She is gone
like me
like all
gone. He spoke
I don't understand
priests
nor saints
life is ... (*Pause.*)
you've got to have a job.
VOICE #2: Two million unemployed.
MARTÍNEZ: Don't give me that.
VOICE #2: Two million.
MARTÍNEZ: It is a lie.
VOICE #2: Two million.
MARTÍNEZ: A nightmare.
VOICE #2: Two million.
MARTÍNEZ: A nightmare.
VOICE #2: Two million.
MARTÍNEZ: Stop the goddam lie.
VOICE #2: Two million.
MARTÍNEZ: Like everything else a very bad dream. (*He moves
    nervously, clears his throat, still sleeping. Sings in a low
    voice, like a mother singing to her baby. He sings "Anda
    Jaleo."*)
Yo me subí a un pino verde
por ver si la divisaba
por ver si la divisaba
y sólo divisé el polvo
del coche que la llevaba
del coche que la llevaba
Anda jaleo, jaleo;
ya se acabó el alboroto
y ahora empieza el tiroteo
y ahora empieza el tiroteo (*Moistens his lips like a thirsty
    person.*)

Where is she?
I couldn't see her
Why?
Don't know
she just left
yes
and disappeared
I guess
like the wind
I mean
the wind
that blows
away
my life (*Sighs deeply.*)
A ship
sailing
no port in sight
no captain
my ship
foundering
like everything else
amid orgasms of love
and friendship
and above all
of hate
foundering
like the life of every cursed foreigner
damn the foreigner (*Kicks the floor.*)
damn the bastard (*Kicks the floor.*)
because of this accent
and the blackness
and the dark eyes
and the permanent tan
damn the ship (*Kicks the floor.*)
sailing
toward despite
and despite (*Kicks the floor.*)
and despite (*Kicks the floor, sighs again.*)
me voy a los Estados Unidos
te amo
enviaré por ti tan pronto triunfe (*Sighs.*)
success is a mirage
you sink your lips into the water

that does not exist
not a drop
of water
just vinager
while my English
gets its words into my
Spanish
no lo hablas ya
I don't
si lo hablaras
I can't
tienes que hablarlo
they pay me in dollars not in pesos (*Kicks the floor.*)
they accuse me in English (*Kicks the floor.*)
they screw me in English (*Kicks violently.*)
I can't beg in Spanish
then
I lose my identity
and speak English with a lousy accent
and I am rewarded
with a little job
two dollars an hour
perhaps
and with a little compassion
a smile perhaps
and with a kiss
a whore perhaps
and all is very strange
beyond the island
that floats
and sails
from my heart to my small intestine
and all is mighty sad
within my bedroom
without the smell of mangoes
the salty breeze of the Caribbean
the noise of waves that break
and die
upon the bloody sands
stained the death
of my brothers
slaughtered by a score of small Hitlers
millions of brothers

millions that hate me
because I beg
y no suplico en español
and love
y no me enamoro
and die
y no confieso mis pecados
que llamo sins
y al cura priest
y no sé cómo escribir mis cartas en español
and I don't know how to write my letters in good En-
    glish
y no soy
and I am not
español ya
nor American
but casi
español casi
American
that is to say un poco
of each
representando la miseria
of each
la pequeñez
of each
the solitude
del medio hombre
half a soul
that I am
wrapped in a flag
sin colores
stains of grease
quizá
of waste
the flag
of the anti-hero hero
very pale
my heroes
triste
neither future
nor history
poor hero
that I am

mierda in my language
in your language
shit
because of la visa.
VOICE #2: You want a visa?
MARTÍNEZ: Sí.
VOICE #2: You are too young.
MARTÍNEZ: Cinco años.
VOICE #2: Too small.
MARTÍNEZ: Soy grande.
VOICE #2: Too fool.
MARTÍNEZ: Muy grande.
VOICE #2: Go home.
MARTÍNEZ: No tengo

    and it goes on
    todo
    goes on
    and on
    and on
    the same face always
    enseñando los dientes.

VOICE #2: ¿Estudios?
MARTÍNEZ: Some.
VOICE #2: Skills?
MARTÍNEZ: None.

    and it goes on
    and on
    and on
    the same eyes
    flaming.

VOICE #2: Have a record?
MARTÍNEZ: No.
VOICE #2: Have experience?
MARTÍNEZ: No.

    and it goes on
    and the face
    and the teeth
    and the eyes
    look and bite and freeze
    when you demand
    and later on, smile
    when you beg

and all goes on
and on
and on
while you chain smoke
or masturbate
which they don't mind
because nobody gives a damn
if you have a lonely erection
and a horrendous need to embrace somebody
because nobody
gives a damn
if your insomnia
is caressed by your hunger
or your emptiness
it just goes on
and on
and on
till you show your own teeth
under your flaming eyes
and pull a knife
and make a mess of yourself
across the desk
where they concoct a crucifixion
between the penal code and the morals
but otherwise
it just goes on
and on
and on
like:
VOICE #1: You cannot enter.
MARTÍNEZ: What do you mean no puedo entrar?
VOICE #1: You are not dressed.
MARTÍNEZ: And you look at your shirt with maps of sweat
           at your worn out pants with maps of grease
           and the two holes exactly at your knees
           look back at you with sorrow
           and you suddenly realize that he is right
           because you are naked
           and you don't dare to enter
           even if he invites you to enter
           which is a dream anyway
           and todo goes on
           and on

and on
the dream
the illusions
at the bottom of a deep and empty
pocket wrapped in a flag
sin colores
while all goes on
and on
and it is sinister
the voice
you hear
from a cave
somewhere in the back
of your own head
a cave
the voice
an echo
vuélvete
an echo
go back
vuélvete
así en inglés
y en español
go back
poor bastard
vuélvete hijo de nada
y uno casi se vuelve
and cries a little
and suddenly remembers
that there is nothing
I say nothing to go back to
except
the same misery
500 years old
and the same sadness
4,000 years old
no longer the smell
of mangoes
and the breeze
and the land
that understood no English
no longer
the desire to seek a life

that does not exist abroad
let alone
at home
that does not exist
under the teeth stained of Chesterfields
under the filthy nails full of the filthy dead skin of filthy
    Latins
that like to die for two dollars an hour
a whole life
for two dollars an hour
because they know
"necesito dinero"
because they know
"no hay futuro en mi tierra"
because they know
"my battered pride for una visa"
and they show their long teeth
through short smiles
and dance around machines with odd smiles
and cry a lot because they can't afford
the two dollars they pay
and kick our balls
while smiling and calling us "son"
or "my son"
or simply "my boy"
while putting together stacks of dollar bills
and counting them
and counting them
every Saturday night
while sharpening their nails and their teeth
for Monday
when they will conduct themselves as perfect sons of
    bitches
that we are
too
while smiling
at them
and thanking them
and congratulating them
thus conducting ourselves
as perfect sons of bitches and todo goes on
and on
and on

between the visa and the death
a narrow span of life
above a sea of sweat
and blood
and vomit
in which we eventually fall
and drown
or simply swim
and breathe
the stinky breath of death
no flowers at the end
like in those movies
with priests and maidens
and a devoted wife crying
no children singing in the choir
no lover saying words like (*Affectation in the voice.*)
"I want to go with you,
come oh, sweet death"
no dignified man dying
while saying words like (*Affectation in the voice.*)
"I love you all, my son
farewell ... I have been happy,"
no dignity at the end
for us
just a lot of crawling
and yelling
and urinating in our pants
and shitting all over
amid insults of the nurses
in the ward for the poorest
of the hospital for the poor
in the borough where all the poor live
and die
without dignity
no flowers
no priest
not even a tiny God around
to see us to the exit
from a tiny life
and then the little devils
all of them blonde
all of them with thin noses
and blue eyes

smiling from the gates
whatever gates
of hate
smiling
with their long tridents
and their tails
popping out of a forest of red hair
the little demons
smiling at us
and calling us "son"
or "my son"
or simply "my boy"
while coming toward us
from the gates
whatever gates
of hate
to kick our balls
which they do (*Still sleeping—covers his groin with both
     hands.*)
very efficiently
they do
and it hurts (*Yelling and bent as in pain.*)
when they kick
and it hurts (*Howls—bends more.*)
when they kick
very efficiently
they kick (*Howls again, bends even more.*)
right in the spot
they kick (*Shouts with a deep voice of pain.*)
where it hurts
very efficiently
where it really hurts (*Cries.*)
hurts
really
hurts
goddam it (*Loud.*)
hurts. (MARTÍNEZ *sinks into the chair and opens his
     eyes. The dream lights disappear.* MARTÍNEZ *hears
     banging on the wall.*)

VOICE: (*Through the wall.*) It's going to hurt a lot more if you
     don't shut up!

MARTÍNEZ: ¿Qué pasó? I must have been dreaming. A hell of
     a nightmare. All those demons. The tridents and the

tails. (*Pause.*) God! I thought they were going to fuck me. (*Lights up in the apartment.*)

MARTÍNEZ: I must have talked in my sleep. I always do. (*Pause. He looks around.*) As usual. Bare walls. (*Pause.*) If I could only remember a single time in which somebody really listened to me. They are usually too interested in the accent to pay attention to the thoughts within the words. (*Raises his voice.*) "Say, you, the guy with the accent, come here." (*Low voice now.*) Something to play with. (*Raises his voice.*) "Say, talk to me, I like to hear your accent. It's cute." (*Low voice again.*) What can you do? Swallow it. Have a little pain. Try to forget. Which is difficult because the damn accent gets worse with the years. Never improves. And the jokes directed at you will be funny, too funny sometimes. Then heavy, too heavy sometimes. Burning inside your ears, and strangely pleasant sometimes, and filled with prejudice all the time. Secret, perhaps, unknown to the bearer, but prejudice anyway. (*Pause.*) Anyway ... I better take care of business and decide about the apartment. I should talk to the owner. The son of a bitch. The minute I came, he began throwing at me the only Spanish word he knew, to prove that he likes Latins: "grazia," which sounded like Italian to me because the Spanish word he was trying to say is "gracias." Then I added: "How much?" and he replied "$270, grazia," and I said "What do you mean, grazia? I haven't given you a damn thing," and he smiled and said "grazia." (*Pause.*) I guess you cannot expect too much of guys like him other than to overcharge rents and screw poor bastards like me, which is easy, since we will not fight him, for fear of being deported. Not that we should be afraid. After all, our contribution to this country is enormous. Whenever I hear: "If you don't like to answer, I'll tell you why. Because if I go along with all the mejicanos, argentinos, peruanos and so forth, there will be a massive losing of restaurants and a tremendous crisis in the fields, which will force the poor white Americans to bend under the sun eight hours a day to pick strawberries. That's why." You see? We might even say that we don't go back to our countries because we feel obligated to feed you and do the dirty work for you, which is a way to remind you that you need us as much as we need you. This I would love to say face to face to an American some day. Now

I do not because of fear of deportation. Shit! I better make a decision about the apartment. The question in my case is not the classic "to be or not to be" but the "do I let the bastard screw me or do I tell him to shove it?" (*Takes out a pack of cigarettes, puts one in his mouth and looks in his pockets for a match. He pulls out an envelope instead; puts cigarettes away.*) What the hell is this? It's the letter I got from the mail box when I left my place. I didn't even look at it. (*Reads envelope.*) United States Department of Justice. Immigration and Naturalization Service. (*Opens the envelope, sits in the chair and reads the letter.*) Dear Mr. Martínez: (*Raises his voice.*) Please come to our offices on October 15, at 9:30 a.m. (*Growing excitement.*) You will be tested on your knowledge of the government of the United States and its history. You will also be tested on your ability to read, write and speak English. (*Raises his head and looks at the audience.*) This is it. (*Hits the paper with his hand.*) Goddam it, this is it.

VOICE: (*Through the wall.*) You're not kidding, this is it. You keep it up—and I'll not only throw you out of this building, I'll have you thrown out of the country, too.

MARTÍNEZ: I'm going to be an American. Not that I really want to be an American that bad, but damn it, after becoming one I will be able to tell all kinds of creeps that they are creeps without fear of deportation and ... (*Stops.*) Shit! I forgot the test. (*Reads the letter again.*) "You will be tested on your knowledge of the history of the United States." (*Looks at the audience.*) That's bad. I don't even remember the independence date. Was it the fourth of July, 1789? I always get confused with the French Revolution, which was ... let me see ... 14th of July, 1789, yes, the Bastille, a lot of heads chopped off, so the American Revolution cannot be in 1789. I used to find a way to remember, association of ideas, the spirit ... let me see ... the spirit of '76, that's it, the orange ball gyrating on top of a pole and the blond guy saying: "Fill it up, sir" with American independence. All I have to do is to remember the ball and I won't have to go back to my country fighting cockroaches. Not that you don't have cockroaches here. I have seen them in New York and Miami by the millions. The difference is that ours are bigger and they fly. Then there is the problem of amendments. There is no way I can remember twenty-five, or is it twenty-six? You

never know. There is always a senator from Arkansas trying to hand another one to the Constitution. You see?
They don't like foreigners either and they figure the more
amendments, the less foreigners. Let me see. (*He climbs
the chair and perches on the edge of the back.*) I used
to have also some association of ideas to remember the
amendments.

VOICE: (*Through the wall.*) You're just another goddam radical!

MARTÍNEZ: Radicals—radicals use a certain freedom to destroy
that freedom. What would that be? Let me see. Freedom of ... speech ... that's it ... freedom of speech.
(*The person on the other side of the wall slams a door.
MARTÍNEZ aims at the audience with his index finger,
pointing it like a revolver.*) Right to bear arms. Soldiers
messing my house and chasing my wife. "No soldier shall
be quartered in my house without my consent." If they
search me on Saturday night after a wild party, I will be
deported. "Right of the people to be secure against unrea-
sonable searches." Poor Pérez was tried thirty-two times
for the same offense, which is, of course, smoking mar-
ijuana, and the trials lasted too long. "Due process of
law and right to a speedy trial." (*He counts with his fingers.*) One, two, three, four, five, six—there are others.
But that's all I remember. Six. Damn it. On the other
hand, they might ask some questions about the government of the United States. I know that some policemen
take money from the whores exactly as the ones back in
my country. What else? I don't think that immigration
will appreciate my knowledge of Watergate. That's about
the only two things I know pretty well in regards to the
system. (*Pause.*) It always happens. Little kids learn the
word fuck before they are capable of saying the word flag.
It is sad. I better learn to say flag or I'll be sent back to
the flying cockroaches. I am not going to flunk the silly
test. No way. Okay. Let me practice. (MARTÍNEZ *snaps
his fingers and the lights change, spotlighting* MARTÍNEZ
and the IMMIGRATION OFFICIAL, *who has entered to
the down left corner of the stage.*)

OFFICIAL: Martínez!

MARTÍNEZ: I am Martínez, para servirle.

OFFICIAL: Pera what?

MARTÍNEZ: It is a way we have to say we like you.

OFFICIAL: You don't have to like me. All you are required to do is to answer the questions.

MARTÍNEZ: The spirit of '76.

OFFICIAL: What's that?

MARTÍNEZ: Nothing. I just answered a question.

OFFICIAL: I did not ask any as yet.

MARTÍNEZ: Es lo que te digo.

OFFICIAL: I don't quite understand.

MARTÍNEZ: I don't understand, either.

OFFICIAL: May I proceed with the exam?

MARTÍNEZ: Yes, ma'am.

OFFICIAL: I am no ma'am, I am a man.

MARTÍNEZ: It is funny. Both sound the same to me.

OFFICIAL: This is ridiculous.

MARTÍNEZ: Superman.

OFFICIAL: What?

MARTÍNEZ: I am talking to myself.

OFFICIAL: Will you tell me when the United States attained its independence?

MARTÍNEZ: (*Impetuously.*) Fill it up with regular, son.

OFFICIAL: I beg your pardon!

MARTÍNEZ: The spirit of '76.

OFFICIAL: I think you are under the influence.

MARTÍNEZ: But it is a fact that the ball gyrates on top of a pole.

OFFICIAL: The ball? What ball?

MARTÍNEZ: The orange one. It is a riot.

OFFICIAL: I don't want to flunk you. Be serious.

MARTÍNEZ: Like a dead body. Just ask me the Amendments.

OFFICIAL: Talk to me about the First.

MARTÍNEZ: (*Yelling.*) Radicals use it. Mafia people use it. It is a shame.

OFFICIAL: Good for you. That's exactly what is happening.

MARTÍNEZ: Es lo que te digo.

OFFICIAL: You passed the exam.

MARTÍNEZ: Let me talk about the Second.

OFFICIAL: I said you passed the exam.

MARTÍNEZ: I did?

OFFICIAL: You will be sworn in a month from today in the Music Center.

MARTÍNEZ: What orchestra will we have?

OFFICIAL: Orchestra? What do you mean, orchestra?

MARTÍNEZ: You said the Music Center.

OFFICIAL: I said the Music Center. So what?

MARTÍNEZ: I better go.

OFFICIAL: You are weird.

MARTÍNEZ: I am weird.

OFFICIAL: That's what I said.

MARTÍNEZ: It is sad.

OFFICIAL: What is sad?

MARTÍNEZ: The word flag.

OFFICIAL: You are nuts.

MARTÍNEZ: Yes, an American nut.

OFFICIAL: (*To himself.*) This is unbelievable. I don't understand why I still like the son of a bitch. (*As he exits down left.*) You are ... (*The lights cross fade up on the apartment as the* OFFICIAL *exits.*)

MARTÍNEZ: (*Rising.*) ... an American. Come October 15, I'll be an American citizen. I am going to tell him that I do not want the apartment because it is filthy, good only for foreigners, not for a soon-to-be American like me. (*He crosses up left, calling.*) Sir! (*Stops.*) Why the hell "sir?" (*Calling.*) Óyeme tú. (*Calls again.*) Mr.! (*The* APARTMENT OWNER *enters up left.*)

OWNER: (*Warm and friendly.*) Did you make up your mind, Sinor Martínez?

MARTÍNEZ: (*Accentuating the error.*) Yes, Sinor, I most certainly have.

OWNER: (*Smiling; it is obvious that he enjoys the company of* MARTÍNEZ.) I love the way you pronounce words. I love accents.

MARTÍNEZ: (*Mistrusting.*) You do?

OWNER: I would prefer to have foreigners renting all my apartments. They are hard working people who take nothing for granted.

MARTÍNEZ: Is that the way you think?

OWNER: Sure do.

MARTÍNEZ: Really?

OWNER: I have decided to reduce your rent 50 dollars. It is an incentive to help you make up your mind.

MARTÍNEZ: Are you not kidding?

OWNER: No, Sir.

MARTÍNEZ: I don't understand.

OWNER: There is nothing to understand. The apartment is yours for $50 less if you decide to rent it.

MARTÍNEZ: (*Reacting.*) I'll rent your beautiful apartment.

OWNER: I hope this is the beginning of a beautiful friendship. (*They shake hands.*)

MARTÍNEZ: I hope so, too.

OWNER: (*Exiting.*) Grazia, grazia.

MARTÍNEZ: (*Calling after the owner.*) De nalgas ... de nalgas ...
(*To the audience, smiling.*) I am beginning to sound like a
son of a bitch myself. I guess I am already a full fledged
American. (MARTÍNEZ *looks around the room, then adjusts the position of the chair. He looks at the window, goes
to it and raises the shade. The view out the window is of
a brick wall. He looks at it for a moment, then turns the
chair to face the window and sits down. The lights fade to
blackout.*)

Your Better Half

by

Matías Montes Huidobro

Translated into English by

David Miller and Lynn E. Rice Cortina

Your Better Half

About the Author

Matías Montes Huidobro was born in Sagua la Grande in the province of Havana in 1931. There he attended several private elementary schools. At the capital he studied at the Instituto No. 1. de La Habana. Montes Huidobro went on to the Universidad de La Habana where he obtained a doctorate in education in 1952. It was while at the university that he began to get involved with the theater. In 1950 his play "Las cuatro brujas" placed as a finalist in the Prometeo National Play Contest that year. By the next year he had won First Prize at the same competition for his play "Sobre las mismas rocas," which was also produced by Prometeo as a result of the contest. From 1959 to 1961 he wrote theater pieces free lance for *Lunes de Revolución*. He became the Drama Review Critic for *Periódico Revolución* from 1960 to 1961, a role he also played on TV Revolución in Havana. From 1964 to the present he has taught Hispanic theater at the University of Hawaii, with occasional visiting professor stints at Arizona State University, Swarthmore College and the University of Pittsburgh.

Montes Huidobro is the author of over one hundred (100) articles published in the newspapers mentioned above as well as in monthly magazines. They are related to the theater or to literature in general on varied topics such as *Hamlet*, Juan Antonio Ramos, Paddy Chayefsky, Arthur Miller, Tennessee Williams, Beijing Opera, Cervantes, Chekov, *Las pericas*, Stanislavski, Cuban authors such as Piñera, Felipe, Ferrer, Ferreira, Camps, Parrado, González de Cascorro, Alonso, Millán, Triana, Álvarez Ríos, Cuqui Ponce, José Martí; Spanish and Latin American authors like Lorca, Calvo Sotelo, Llopis, Mihura, Salinas, Ruíz Iriarte, Neville, Buero Vallejo, Lope de Vega, Boch, and from other countries such as Moliere, Anouilh, Sartre, Ionesco, Pirandello, Williams, Inge, Brecht y Chekov. He has also written two major books on theater: *Persona: vida y máscara en el teatro cubano* (Miami: Ediciones Universal, 1975), and *Personas: vida y máscara en el teatro puertorriqueño* (Puerto Rico: Centro de Estudios Avanzados de Puerto Rico y del Caribe, 1986).

His creative work in drama, however, has brought him wide acclaim. He is the author of some twenty plays. Three of them, including "Your Better Half" in this anthology, *Ojos para no ver* (Miami: Ediciones Universal, 1979) and "La sal de los muertos" in *Teatro contemporáneo hispanoamericano III* (Madrid: Escelicer,

1971) have not been staged. Others, published and unpublished, have all been produced, read, or have received awards. "El tiro por la culata" was included in *Teatro cubano revolucionario* (Marianao: Ediciones del Municipio de Marianao, 1961); it was produced by the Teatro Nacional in Havana in 1960 and by the Teatro Estudio in Marianao that same year, by the Festival de Teatro Obrero y Campesino in Havana in 1961, and adapted for television for CMBF in Havana by the author in 1961. "Gas en los poros" appeared in *Teatro cubano en un acto* (Havana: Ediciones Revolución, 1963) Two years before, however, it was produced by Prometeo in Havana and much later at CUNY in 1987 and at Drew University also in 1987. A television version by the author was shown in CMBF-TV Revolución in Havana in 1961, and a reading was done in Córdoba, Argentina in 1989 at the ILYCH International Conference. "The Guillotine" was chosen for *Selected Latin American One-Act Plays* (Pittsburgh: University of Pittsburgh Press, 1975) In its Spanish version it was produced at the Contemporary Theater Symposium and Festival at Queensborough Community College, CUNY, 1976; at the Hispano Festival II of New York's Mercy College also in 1976; by Prometeo at the New York Café Teatro El Portón in 1976. In its English version it was staged at the Marquette University Symposium on Alienation and Revolution in Milwaukee in 1980; at the University of Wisconsin Superior in 1981; at Florida International University's First Symposium on Cuban Theater in the United States by New Theater in 1987, and it received a reading at Teatro Campesino in California in 1988.

The other plays remain unpublished, but some have been produced, read or awarded a prize. Among them are "Las cuatro brujas" and "Sobre las mismas rocas" already reported above, and others such as the following: "Los acosados" produced by the Asociación Pro-Arte Dramático in Havana in 1960, and a television production called Pueblo y Cultura for CMBF in Havana in 1961. "Las vacas" received a First Prize in the José Antonio Ramos National Play Contest in Havana in 1960, and the next year it was staged in the Palacio de Bellas Artes. "Exilio" received dramatic readings as at the Coconut Grove Playhouse in Miami in 1986 and at El Portón by the Latin American Theater Ensemble del Barrio in New York in 1987. It was produced by the Museo Cubano de Arte y Cultura in Miami in 1988 and placed as a Finalist in the Letras de Oro literary contest in Miami in 1987. "La navaja de Olofé" was produced by Teatro Nuevo at the Primer Festival de Teatro Hispano in Miami in 1986. "Hablando en chino" was produced at Milwaukee's Marquette University in 1988. This is a version of "Ojos para no ver" and of "Funeral en Teruel" which appeared in *Escolios* in the Spring of 1977. "Las paraguayas," a Letras de Oro finalist, received the Lilla Wallace Foundation Award for a workshop production by Teatro Campesino in San Juan Bautista in California in 1988, where it was read in 1989. A monologue from the play "La Diosa de Iguazú" was read at the Taller Literario of the University of Hawaii in 1989.

Other works mentioned by his critics, some of which have received no prizes or have remained unpublished, are nevertheless important artifacts of great artistic merit and of significant documentary value. Among them are "Sucederá mañana," "La puerta perdida," "El verano está cerca," "Las caretas" and "La botija." Some of them have been published by *Revista Casa de las Américas* in 1960 and produced by the Sala Arlequín, by the Asociación Pro-Arte Dramático in 1960 and later in Guanabacoa, Matanzas and several other cities in the rest of the island. He has received the acclaim of critics of the caliber of Max Henríquez Ureña, Rine Leal, Ramón Gainza, Orlando Rodríguez-Sardiñas, Carlos Miguel Suárez Radillo, Francesca Colecchia, Julio Matas and Leon Lyday.

"Your Better Half" is a very suggestive play rich in inventive dialogue and fond of interior duplication. Montes Huidobro crafts the kind of play which encodes its different levels of meaning not from his symbolic language, such as he does with allegory in "Las paraguayas," for example. Rather it is imbued with metatheatrical discourse which brings a multidimensionality to the texture of the play. This is a remarkable achievement.

CHARACTERS

RAÚL, (*who pronounces his name English-style*) thirty-five years old, looks like twenty-five, very good looking Latin type.

BOB, about ten years older than Raúl, a shapeless sort of appearance.

SAM, fifteen years older than Raúl, kind of heavy and uncouth; could be confused with a longshoreman.

JUDY, at least two years older than Sam, attractive and with a figure worthy of Penthouse, looks like fifteen years less.

SARA, thirty-five years old, blond, somewhere between sporty and elegant.

MARÍA, around twenty-five years old, Latin type, insignificant looking.

THE DRUNK

PLACE

The play takes place in the living room of a New York penthouse that overlooks Central Park, the afternoon and evening of a Spring day. In the background, the door to the apartment; it must be wide. To one side a glass door that leads into the balcony. To the other side a door that leads into the bedroom. In the front of the stage a sofa, some armchairs, a coffee table and an end table with a phone, etc.

ACT I

As the curtain opens the stage is completely lit. Very visible, with its back to the audience, is a chair with a jacket. The telephone rings. RAÚL enters barefoot, with a robe on. He picks it up and answers slightly agitated. He looks toward the interior of the bedroom, the door to which remains open.

RAÚL: Hello! Yes, of course it's me. Raúl. Who else could it be? No, no, I wasn't sleeping ... Well, maybe I sound like I was sleeping, all right ... Yes, I finished the first act ... I've changed lots of the things and I've given it an unexpected twist, you'll see ... While I was writing, things kept occurring to me that I hadn't thought of when I spoke to you ... No, you don't need to come right away. I'd rather you heard it later, when everyone is here. That way everyone reads their part ... No, no don't come over now ... We'll leave time for that another time, don't you think? (*Lowers voice*). Of course, I want to ... Yes, but right now ... It would be better not to ... We'll see each other tonight anyway ... Yes, of course, I know that is something else ... Okay, whatever you want ... Yes, around two as usual ... No, nothing weird is happening ... Anyway, with the traffic it will take you more than two hours to get here ... We won't have time to do anything ... Okay, whatever you say ... later. (*He hangs up a little annoyed. He looks at the bedroom door. You can hear a toilet flush. BOB enters in short sleeves tying his tie. He dresses conservatively and elegantly.*)

BOB: Who was it?

RAÚL: Your wife.

BOB: My wife? What'd she want?

RAÚL: She wanted to know what time the dinner was.

BOB: Dinner! Raúl, you've made answers for everything! ... First dinner ... Then the reading of the first act ... and when we finish, we go to the awards ceremony ... It's a little too much, don't you think?

RAÚL: I told you not to come today.

BOB: Well, it's Tuesday, isn't it?

RAÚL: No reason to be so punctilious.

BOB: I don't know how you got that dinner thing in your head. In a couple of hours I'll have to be back here again.

RAÚL: You know that I have that commitment.

BOB: With whom?

RAÚL: With all of you.

BOB: With us? You don't have any obligations toward me.

RAÚL: I owe you a lot. If it hadn't been for you, *Your Better Half* would never have gotten on stage.

BOB: Don't exaggerate. You could have at least chosen another day.

RAÚL: Don't think it's so easy. I have a family-complicated schedule. Each day brings different obligations.

BOB: And that idea about reading the first act ...

RAÚL: It won't take long, I promise.

BOB: Anyway, there was no need for this invitation. You don't owe me anything. I've told you a hundred times.

RAÚL: I owe you everything that I am.

BOB: I owe more to you.

RAÚL: I also owe a lot to your wife.

BOB: In what way?

RAÚL: Don't forget she was the first to recognize my talent, before you even knew it existed.

BOB: That's true. But don't forget it was my idea to have Sara direct the play.

RAÚL: Besides, she has a grudge against me.

BOB: Who put that idea in your head?

RAÚL: You both did.

BOB: Both of us?

RAÚL: Both.

BOB: But that was a long time ago. When she was jealous of you.

RAÚL: You don't think she's jealous anymore.

BOB: No. That was in the beginning, when we spent a lot of time together, working, and Sara didn't feel like I paid enough attention to her ... That when we got all involved in our projects, I'd forget about everything else. Remember?

RAÚL: Of course I remember! Thanks to that we finished a few scenes of *Your Better Half.* Sara played an important part in the whole thing. In the long run it was fun.

BOB: Have you told her?

RAÚL: No, of course not. Did you?

BOB: Certainly not, but I think Sara suspects. In any case, I don't think she cares very much.

RAÚL: In any case. She used to hold a grudge against me.

BOB: That's strange, I just remembered she thought the same thing.

RAÚL: What?

BOB: That you held a grudge against us.

RAÚL: Why?

BOB: Because you're Hispanic. She said that you thought that we discriminated against you.

RAÚL: And wasn't it true?

BOB: I have proven to you that that isn't the case.

RAÚL: (*With an almost imperceptible smile touched with disdain.*) Do you really think so?

BOB: Please, Raúl, stop talking garbage.

RAÚL: And her, didn't she discriminate against me?

BOB: No, what happened was that Sara thought that you believed yourself to be the typical "Latin Lover," and that drove her nuts. I found it amusing.

RAÚL: I don't get it.

BOB: Really! Don't make me laugh. From the first day you came to see us ...

RAÚL: I came to bring you the first act.

BOB: Exactly. I had something to do, I can't remember what, and Sara received you ... From then on she started with the Latin Lover routine ... You know, now and again I've thought ...

RAÚL: She'd have her reasons.

BOB: ... It's still amusing.

RAÚL: Maybe you think the same ... that I'm the typical Latin Lover. (*Pause. They look at each other fixedly for a moment.* BOB *looks away.*)

BOB: Anyway, when the three of us began working together and I told her that she should direct the play ...

RAÚL: At my insistence.

BOB: What do your mean at your insistence?

RAÚL: Don't you remember? If Sara had always directed your plays, it was only reasonable that now that we were writing together that she would be the one to direct it.

BOB: You're dead wrong. Sara in those days had become unbearable and very suspicious. I had to get her busy doing something. Sometimes she talked too much, and other times she was too vague.

RAÚL: Maybe, it was Sara's idea and we haven't realized it. You know how that is.

BOB: What do you man to say with that "you know how that is?"

RAÚL: I don't mean to say anything, but it seems to me that if
the three of us were in agreement ...

BOB: The three of us?

RAÚL: What's your problem? Why are you so suspicious?

BOB: I don't know. I'm sorry.

RAÚL: Well, it hasn't turned out badly. After all, Sara has left you
alone.

BOB: I was thinking ... if on that day ... when you brought the
script ... you came to see me or Sara?

RAÚL: You, I spoke with you on the phone.

BOB: But you knew that Sara had directed all my plays.

RAÚL: Everyone knows that, Bob. Or are you going to take away
importance from the work that Sara has been doing all
these years? You know very well that they say that she
puts the finishing touches on what you write. Which is
reasonable, because she is the one that puts them to the
stage. She is the one that directs them. (*Pause.*) Maybe
... Maybe even before you write them. (*Both remain pensive.*)

BOB: Meaning?

RAÚL: She's directed *Your Better Half* too. (*Pause.*)

BOB: Which doesn't answer my question. Maybe, since the very
beginning, you were coming to see Sara.

RAÚL: All of which is beside the point. The order of events
doesn't alter the outcome.

BOB: Anyway, she no longer has any reason to say that I don't
spend any time with her. Really, you spend ... (*Pensive.*)
Which is more or less the same. You spend a lot of time
together.

RAÚL: If Sara is going to direct the play, it's better if we talk
from the very beginning. Later come the changes. Take
that out. Put this in over there. We agreed on this, right?
That's why we've spent days, months I'd say, working together. In the end, I have to confess, that I've made so
many changes that I've ended up doing everything on my
own.

BOB: You think? You never know. You've said it yourself. Maybe,
without you even realizing, she's been writing it all for
you, if she's done it to me ...

RAÚL: I think it's different. There are situations in the play that
not even Sara con imagine.

BOB: Nor can I, I suppose.

RAÚL: I want to surprise you.

BOB: I hope you're doing the same with the audience. And not laying a trap for us, Raúl.

RAÚL: It's too bad you don't know everything. It's not my fault that you didn't want to work together on *Forbidden Games.*

BOB: But wasn't it called *Rules for Conduct?*

RAÚL: That's what you wanted, you're the moralist. You dislike calling things by their name.

BOB: That's exactly why I had to leave you on your own. You have insisted on calling a spade a spade, and that is the most _dangerous thing there is. I thought that with the success of *Your Better Half* you'd realized, well, anyway ... If you insist ... It was impossible for us to reach an agreement.

RAÚL: That's what Sara told me. That we'd never come to an agreement.

BOB: She told you that?

RAÚL: That you liked rules for conduct, but that I preferred forbidden games.

BOB: But we did agree on *Your Better Half.* Even though it probably could never pass for more than a quarrel. I thought that it had gone well for us, right? (BOB *looks fixedly at* RAÚL. *The latter does not answer the question.*)

RAÚL: I had to change the title. And Sara was in agreement there. She thought that right now forbidden games would sell better than rules for conduct. Don't forget your wife is an expert when it comes to sales.

BOB: But in the long run everything depends on the quality of the merchandise.

RAÚL: You'are miffed, Bob. The thing is you're jealous of the time your wife and I spend together. But that doesn't make any sense. Deep down, she has always considered me an opportunist, a johnny-come-lately ... (*Very violently.*) That's what she understands for Latin Lover. That's what she's wanted to say since the first day we laid eyes on each other. Don't think for a moment that I have any illusions. And it's very possible that you think the same, I've already told you. Deep down, don't worry, you two will always finish in agreement.

BOB: Now you're the one that's jealous.

RAÚL: You're confusing jealousy with class struggle.

BOB: Oh, so that's what it's called now?

RAÚL: You mean you didn't know?

BOB: You're angry.

RAÚL: You are, because with this play I began working on my
         own. Even though Sara didn't think I should; that's true.
         According to her she always wanted us to write it together
         in order to stabilize our relationship.

BOB: Stabilize our relationship? What did she mean by that?

RAÚL: I don't know. I didn't want to ask.

BOB: Whose relationship?

RAÚL: Maybe she was talking about the three of us.

BOB: But she is working with you.

RAÚL: But not in the same way.

BOB: Yeah, I know.

RAÚL: Don't get like that. You're in a bad mood and you feel as
         if we ... as if I ... have displaced you ... But for Sara
         ... for me ...

BOB: She wanted the exact opposite. You don't know Sara.

RAÚL: Are you sure?

BOB: I know my wife better that you, don't forget. I have lived
         with her for fifteen years.

RAÚL: Maybe that's a good reason to not know her.

BOB: Since she came to see me when she was twenty years old,
         I've known very well what Sara wanted.

RAÚL: Apparently you're very sure.

BOB: In the end she is "my better half" and not yours.

RAÚL: I thought ... I thought that she was something like the
         exact opposite for you ... You surprise me, Bob ... That
         is at least what you had given me to understand ... What
         you wrote ... What we wrote ... in *Your Better Half.*

BOB: Half and half. Don't forget this is nothing more than a play.

RAÚL: I think it's time for you to go, Bob. This conversation is
         going nowhere and we're only irritating each other.

BOB: I don't remember the exact moment that Sara changed her
         point of view or why she did.

RAÚL: What point of view?

BOB: Her point of view regarding you.

RAÚL: Just ask her.

BOB: She would tell me the exact opposite.

RAÚL: It would be one way of knowing, don't you think?

BOB: It's always difficult to find the truth, much more so by saying
         the opposite. Or a fraction of what one thinks. Well, you
         know that as well as I do, after you're a playwright too.
         Even though you prefer to be more explicit.

RAÚL: She changed her mind when she read what I had written.

BOB: No, no it was much later.

RAÚL: She read the entire thing one night when she couldn't sleep and you were snoring.

BOB: She told you that?

RAÚL: She said she thought it was a work of art. And that it wasn't anything else that you had written.

BOB: Don't be ridiculous.

RAÚL: It's true that the first act just wouldn't gel. Nevertheless . . .

BOB: You were good raw material.

RAÚL: If you intend to speak badly about me to your wife . . . who is after all, the one who directs what I write . . .

BOB: Why do you think that she wanted me to work with you?

RAÚL: Do you want me to tell you something that she told me?

BOB: If you want to run me down to my wife, remember that no one should interfere with man and wife. That is a strictly forbidden topic.

RAÚL: I think it would be best if you left. You're impossible.

BOB: I'll get out when you tell me *everything* she told you.

RAÚL: I'll tell you when you tell me *everything* she said about me.

BOB: That you'd never get anywhere, because you were an inhibited Hispanic, a typical empty-headed Latin Lover that thought he could solve everything with what he had between his legs, and that what you had written was shit.

RAÚL: Then, why did she insist that we work together?

BOB: She didn't insist. I was the one that wanted to.

RAÚL: You're lying, Bob.

BOB: And you've told the truth right along?

RAÚL: You're right. We've only told a pack of lies. (*A key is heard in the door of the apartment. RAÚL and BOB stay still for a moment, looking at the door. SAM enters, he looks rude and sort of brutal, different. He dresses badly and untidily. He is robust and not at all refined.*)

SAM: (*To BOB.*) Ah, you're here?

BOB: I was leaving. See you later, Raúl.

SAM: I didn't ask you if you were leaving. I asked you if you were here.

BOB: That question makes no sense, Sam. It should be an exclamation.

RAÚL: It's obvious that he was here, Sam.

SAM: Don't get smart, Raúl. Don't give me lessons or make me feel as though I were stupid. We already know that you are one of the authors of *Your Better Half.* Why don't you let the other half have his say?

BOB: Okay, Sam. Let's drop this stupid conversation. I was here, but now I'm leaving.

SAM: Not because I arrived. (*To* RAÚL.) See how easy it is? Even Bob knows how to say his part. There was no reason to get so upset (*To* RAÚL.) Why don't you fix me a drink? (*To* BOB.) Later, Bob. See you tonight, right? Give my love to Sara. (RAÚL *prepares a drink. SAM sits in a chair, stretching his legs and somewhat rudely putting them on the table in the center.* BOB *goes to the door. He opens it, remains pensive and turns around.*)

BOB: (*To* SAM.) I didn't know you had a key to the apartment.

SAM: Why do you need to know?

BOB: No reason. But it was strange. You walked in like you owned the place, Sam.

SAM: I do, Bob. After all, I am the owner of the apartment. Raúl is nothing more than a renter. And I give him a really good deal on the rent. Right, Raúl?

RAÚL: A real bargain.

SAM: The least he can do is let me have a key so I can come in and inspect when I feel like it, so I can see how things are. (RAÚL *brings* SAM *a drink. Without saying another word* BOB *closes the door and leaves.*)

SAM: What's the matter with him? Why's he in a bad mood?

RAÚL: I thought you were the one in the bad mood.

SAM: I'm not talking about mine. I'm talking about Bob's. What did he want?

RAÚL: He isn't happy with the title of the play. He prefers *Rules for Conduct.*

SAM: That's all? I thought you were writing that play by yourself.

RAÚL: Yes, but nevertheless Sara directs it, Judy acts in it and you produce it. Bob can't be kept out. This is a pentagon, Sam.

SAM: A state secret. They all were and nobody looked it. Spy against spy.

RAÚL: Don't trust anyone, Sam. You've never trusted me. Like keeping the apartment key so you can inspect it once in a while.

SAM: You're too big for your britches. Don't forget ...

RAÚL: I don't forget anything, it isn't necessary for you to continually remind me. I remember who removes the thorns and who puts them in. The apartment business was in poor taste.

SAM: What was I gonna say? After all, I told the truth.

RAÚL: It would have been simpler to knock on the door.

SAM: So now I have to ask permission to come into my own house?

RAÚL: This isn't your own house. Your house is the one you live in with your wife.

SAM: You're getting uppity, you know it? Give a finger, they'll take your hand. I don't know if Bob realized it.

RAÚL: Maybe I've become a revolutionary.

SAM: You? If one who truly is one hears you, you'll be sent before a firing squad for giving revolutionaries a bad name. And they wouldn't be totally incorrect, I warn you.

RAÚL: Watch it, you're becoming quite disagreeable.

SAM: I didn't know you cared.

RAÚL: Did you want something?

SAM: (*Taking his feet off the coffee table and putting the drink on it.*) I'm choking on this drink.

RAÚL: If you want something, let's have it out fast. I don't have any time to waste. I have people coming to dinner. As you know, you're one of the guests.

SAM: What's this dinner for?

RAÚL: Today is the 200th performance of *Your Better Half.* Most likely we will be given an award tonight, you included, for having been the producer and we'll leave with a little statue under our arms. There are lots of reasons to celebrate. We've come a long way. Besides, I want to express my gratitude to you all.

SAM: To whom do you wish to express your gratitude?

RAÚL: To you, I know that I owe you.

SAM: There are better ways to do it than that.

RAÚL: I know you risked a large amount for "your better half."

SAM: With Judy in the cast there was no way to lose. It's the surest investment I've ever made. Don't get your hopes up, Raúl. I know what I do with my money.

RAÚL: I'm glad you realize how much your wife is worth, because I'm also grateful to her. Without her *Your Better Half* would have never gotten to its 200th performance, I have to acknowledge that.

SAM: It would have gotten to a lot less without my money, which was the half you didn't have.

RAÚL: I don't deny that, but you have gotten it all back with interest. You can't complain.

SAM: I don't guess you complain about anything. You've arrived where you least expected to. You are the first Hispanic to conquer Broadway.

RAÚL: With help from all of you. Why don't we leave to one side what Bob and Sara have given.

SAM: So they've given something too?

RAÚL: I know you've given your money, but Bob and Sara have given their talent and effort.

SAM: And my wife? Has she given anything else?

RAÚL: Well, your wife has given her beauty. As you know, it is half of her talent.

SAM: What else have Bob and Sara given?

RAÚL: What else do you expect them to give?

SAM: I don't know, but Bob's talent ... Well, you know where it's at. But you should know what each has contributed. After all, aren't you the one who pays the interest? Maybe they've given more than you have told me.

RAÚL: And why should I tell you?

SAM: I thought it was implicit in our contract.

RAÚL: Don't start up. With all your money and at this advanced stage, you know very well that there is nothing implicit in a contract. If it isn't stipulated in writing, then it doesn't count. This is a rent contract, temporary and purely a financial question. We'd be in a fix if we did things otherwise.

SAM: Well if Bob and Sara have only contributed effort and talent, their investment can't lose. Much better than mine, which was more generous, right?

RAÚL: Your interest rates are high Sam.

SAM: I thought you liked paying them.

RAÚL: No one likes to pay interest.

SAM: You never told me.

RAÚL: You never asked me. I don't know of anyone who ever got excited paying interest to a bank.

SAM: Judy has always paid with pleasure.

RAÚL: How do you know? Judy's a good actress. Everybody knows that. Or hadn't you heard? You are dense. After all this, you thought I paid with pleasure. Maybe your wife and I have more in common than you can imagine.

SAM: Yeah, me.

RAÚL: Or your money.

SAM: Birds of a feather.

RAÚL: Flock together.

SAM: Raise crows.

RAÚL: And they'll peck out your eyes.

SAM: You need guts for that. Neither you or her have any.

RAÚL: How do you know?

SAM: Because I know where you both came from.

RAÚL: You think your wife and I are playing the same role?

SAM: I don't know, but it sure looks that way.

RAÚL: Doesn't necessarily mean that it is.

SAM: I thought you were a straight talker. You've hung around Bob too long. Stop with the riddles. Why don't you call a spade a spade? Talk already.

RAÚL: Maybe it's you and your wife that have the same tastes.

SAM: Then it would be you that we have in common. Is that what you're saying.

RAÚL: Don't think so? The logic is the same, Sam. You just change the view point.

SAM: Go to hell, Raúl. You're pissing me off.

RAÚL: Cut the macho routine, for Christ's sakes. I know your weaknesses.

SAM: Talk, once and for all, and say what's on your mind.

RAÚL: It's over. Give me the key.

SAM: So, you've found someone to give you loans at a lower interest rate. Bob, right? Is Bob the moneylender? I know your weaknesses too.

RAÚL: You don't know anything, Sam. You solve everything with a dollar sign.

SAM: A sign that everyone follows. They'll stuff themselves with money anywhere they can. When they find it difficult to swallow, they become repulsed by the smell. Those who don't reach that choking the point it's because they never have gotten enough. You're no exception, Raúl. The world is full of degenerates like you. (*The violence increases. As though they will come to blows.*)

RAÚL: Need and like are not the same.

SAM: Yeah, that's what the whores say, but who knows.

RAÚL: You think you can buy everything with money, corrupt everything.

SAM: Isn't that right?

RAÚL: You should be exterminated.

SAM: You don't have the balls for that.

RAÚL: You don't think so. I put this whole trick together with these balls.

SAM: You could regret what you're doing. So Bob has given his effort and his talent? Have you given him a key? Goddamn it! You gave him a key! You're a son of a bitch. You must have given the key to half of New York. It must be the key of public domain.

RAÚL: You are an idiot, Sam. You'll wreck everything. Judy was right.

SAM: This is between you and me. Leave my wife out of it. Don't bring her into this.

RAÚL: You didn't count on that. You didn't know I'd bring Judy into this. And she's in up to her neck.

SAM: Go to hell before I bust you in half.

RAÚL: I gave you the key, but now it's time for you to give it back. Give me the key.

SAM: Go to hell.

RAÚL: (*Screaming.*) Give me the key!

SAM: (*Screaming also.*) Listen you Fuck. I'll kill you first! (*The door to the hall opens. JUDY comes in. Loaded down with packages. She is a very attractive and beautiful woman, well preserved, thanks to make-up, exercise, diet and plastic surgery. Well dressed, but too flashy, a touch vulgar. She looks like a copy of Joan Collins.*)

JUDY: What a racket! Your screaming can be heard all the way to the elevator doors.

SAM: So you've got a key too.

JUDY: What key?

SAM: The one everyone's got, it seems. The one to this apartment.

JUDY: (*Looking at the key she was about to put in her purse.*) Oh, the key ... Were you arguing about that?

RAÚL: No, not exactly.

JUDY: (*To* RAÚL) But your screaming at him to give it back. (*Handing him the key.*) If you want me to give it ...

SAM: Why didn't you knock?

JUDY: Because I'd already taken the key out of my bag.

SAM: You walked right in as if it were yours.

RAÚL: You noticed.

SAM: I didn't know you were going to come here.

JUDY: Nor did I know you were going to. I'd promised Raúl some wine glasses for the dinner. If I'd known you were coming, I could have saved myself the trip.

RAÚL: See? Everything has an explanation, Sam.

SAM: (*To* RAÚL) So, you've given the key to my wife too.

JUDY: What do you mean, given me the key? I've had this key for a long time. Have you forgotten that we once lived here? When Raúl moved in, I kept a set of keys.

SAM: It would seem that half of New York has a key to this apartment, and it's very likely half again that many in the barrio. I'll have to change the lock.

RAÚL: Perhaps I'm the one that should change them. After all, Judy owns this house too, Sam. Furniture included. Don't forget this is a furnished apartment, everything in it.

JUDY: Oh, Raúl, don't talk nonsense. You know I hate to talk about money. Money was made to spend, dear. That's all he's interested in.

RAÚL: Sam, everything should be shared in life.

SAM: You talk like this is a commune.

RAÚL: Money and capital in particular.

SAM: Especially if it is not your capital.

RAÚL: Don't be so sure.

SAM: Money has to be sweated for, Raúl.

RAÚL: I don't know one capitalist with B.O.

JUDY: What an innocent you are, Raúl! I've met some.

RAÚL: Well, maybe if they're dirty, but not because they've had to sweat.

SAM: So now it's class struggle. You gotta have nerve.

RAÚL: Don't forget, I'm the one that's sweated.

JUDY: This is ridiculous. What stupidity are we talking about? Everything has to be shared in life, Sam. (*To* RAÚL.) That's why when this apartment was empty and you started working on *Your Better Half* and you didn't have a good place to do it, I thought it was a good idea for you to live here. You needn't think that capitalists are ogres, Raúl. We might not be communists, but we like to share what we have. Isn't that right, Sam?

RAÚL: But I thought that the business about the apartment had been Sam's idea. (*Turning around.*) At least that's what you told me.

SAM: It's mine, isn't it?

JUDY: (*To* SAM.) Did you say that?

RAÚL: Both of yours, Sam. Judy's and your's. Don't forget. It's what's called community property. (*To* JUDY.) And that's why you also have a key. It's part of the contract.

JUDY: What contract?

RAÚL: The rent contract.

JUDY: I didn't know there was a contract.

SAM: Of course, there is. Never give anything away. Everything should be paid for.

RAÚL: Sam doesn't give something for nothing, Judy.

JUDY: You don't have to tell me. For more than twenty-years I've paid high interest rates. You don't know Sam, Raúl.

RAÚL: Don't believe it, I'm finding out.

JUDY: After all, as you would say, I am "his better half." (*Sugary to* SAM.) Right?

SAM: (*Abruptly.*) Nevertheless, you should still have knocked ... You might have surprised Raúl.

JUDY: Surprised Raúl?

SAM: With a lover.

JUDY: A woman?

SAM: Of course. What do you think?

JUDY: That's not possible, Sam.

SAM: Why isn't it possible? After all, Raúl is a young, good-looking guy, that's made a big splash on Broadway, with a brilliant future and a penthouse on 5th Avenue. He's a nominee for Hispanic who made good.

JUDY: I already told you that your screams could be heard at the elevator. Sam. So it isn't likely that Raúl was with a lover.

RAÚL: Maybe your husband will end up saying that I'm a typical "Latin Lover" too.

JUDY: "Latin Lover?" But that's obvious. This isn't Rudolph Valentino's time! I'd say that Raúl is a good-looking yuppie.

SAM: With a bedroom papered with mirrors? Must be the exception that proves the rule. A barrio product that left from the starving Latin minority to the chosen minority.

JUDY: I don't see anything the matter with the bedroom.

SAM: But, have you seen it?

JUDY: You think I'm blind. Haven't you?

RAÚL: You have to go through it to get to the bathroom.

SAM: Mirrors of public domain.

JUDY: (*Moving close to* RAÚL, *sweetly.*) Raúl doesn't keep secrets from me or Sam. I'm his confidant. If he had a lover, he'd have told me. Isn't that right, Raúl?

RAÚL: (*Playing along.*) Yes, Judy, I don't keep secrets from you.

JUDY: Raúl tells me everything, Sam. He's not like you, you keep lots back. Right, Raúl?

RAÚL: Yes, I tell you everything, Judy.

JUDY: That's why I know he doesn't have a lover. He would have told me. (*Moving away from* RAÚL, *faking.*) But he never has wanted to tell me whose idea it was to have a bedroom papered with mirrors.

SAM: Must be a bedroom secret he doesn't even want to share with
 you. (*Mocking* JUDY.) Right, Raúl? (*Violently.*) Must
 have taken the mirrors from the barrio, out of some place
 where he or someone in his family was working. (RAÚL
 makes a violent gesture. JUDY *moves toward him again.*)

JUDY: Oh, no, don't pay any attention to him, Raúl. They're
 ideas Sam gets, but he gets over them. He's said the same
 to me. Deep down Sam is old fashioned. You'd think he
 was watching Mexican movies. Problem is Sam's jealous.
 Maybe he's got some harebrained idea in his head.

SAM: God damn it, Judy. Go to hell! (SAM *leaves violently.* JUDY
 and RAÚL *look toward the door of the room where* SAM
 has gone. SAM *is heard slamming the door to the bathroom.* JUDY *and* RAÚL *look at each other. Then they
 kiss passionately, but in a theatrical, movie sort of way.*)

JUDY: You don't mind if I tell you something.

RAÚL: What?

JUDY: Swear you won't get mad.

RAÚL: I swear.

JUDY: It's true ... you are a "Latin Lover." (*As they kiss again,
 a door opening and a toilet flushing can be heard. At the
 same time, the curtain slowly falls.*)

ACT II

*Shortly after the previous act. The stage is completely illumi-
nated, as in the first act. The telephone rings.* RAÚL *comes in
dressed in a tuxedo. He looks great, but he seems somewhat nervous and uncombed. He is frankly uneasy, but would not want to
appear to be so. He answers.*

RAÚL: Hello! Hello! What? No, no I don't understand. What did
 you say? Yes, yes that is the phone number ... On Fifth
 Avenue, yes ... No, no revolutionary lives here ... No,
 nor any terrorist. An attempt? What do you mean? No,
 I don't understand you, and maybe it is better that way.
 If I did I'd have to call the police ... No, I assure you we
 don't want to kill anyone ... Me? Who would want to kill
 me? Nor do I want to kill anyone ... It's true, maybe it's
 better that we don't agree. (RAÚL *turns. He notices that*
 SARA *is opening the door to the china cupboard.*) No, no

one here has ordered a pepperoni pizza ... Nor a dozen
tacos ... Look, why don't you stop screwing around? No,
I promise you, we haven't ordered anything ... Okay, I'll
see you. Good night. (RAÚL *hangs up, thoughtful and
a little disturbed. SARA comes in from the terrace with
a glass in her hand. Black evening dress, very elegant.
Perfectly made up, without exaggeration, she looks great.
Although she should look natural, she has a touch of femme
fatal.*)

SARA: Who was it?

RAÚL: Wrong number. Someone who wanted to bring us a pizza
covered with pepperoni.

SARA: A pepperoni pizza! How disgusting! He must want to kill
us with indigestion.

RAÚL: Maybe he is a revolutionary.

SARA: I doubt it. (*Brief pause.*) Why'd you say he was a revolutionary.

RAÚL: That's the impression I got.

SARA: Probably on drugs.

RAÚL: I couldn't understand very well. He talked about a bomb,
a terrorist act.

SARA: You've got something else on your hands? We've had
enough for one night.

RAÚL: Yes, must be a crazy dope addict, one of the many running
loose.

SARA: Maybe its a character that you didn't allow in the first act,
like you did with me.

RAÚL: Don't talk rubbish.

SARA: Think about it. Think hard, because if he had your phone
number ... maybe he knows your name ... and he might
come any minute.

RAÚL: No, that guy wasn't in character. He wouldn't fit in with
you guys.

SARA: With all of us, you mean. (*Irritated.*) After all, Bob, Sam
and you are dressed alike. You're the same as them.

RAÚL: Which is also like saying that I am the same as you.

SARA: Exactly. We have assimilated you.

RAÚL: You have assimilated me?

SARA: Yes, we have assimilated you. Hadn't you noticed? Did
you think you were like that guy that just called on the
phone? Well, maybe it was you, before. Because I remember it as if I were seeing it. You didn't arrive the

first time dressed in a dinner jacket. You looked like a
terrorist, a revolutionary, maybe a tiger.

RAÚL: Anyway, he'll be a character in a play that I've yet to write.

SARA: He'll be furious. He'll want to wreck everything, breaking down doors and smashing windows. But if he called
on the phone, then he's nothing but an absent character,
those kind that never get on stage. Like you did with me.
I warn you, not everyone is as patient as I've been.

RAÚL: You're in a bad mood. Like everyone else.

SARA: And what kind of a mood would you like us to be in? Don't
you realize what you've done? After you give everyone a
slap in the face, what kind of a mood do you expect us to
be in?

RAÚL: But I thought you were American, a little masochistic.

SARA: Masochistic, us? You don't understand us.

RAÚL: Possibly I haven't assimilated you enough.

SARA: You're an ingrate.

RAÚL: I thought you were objective. This is nothing but a theater piece. I have only written the first act of *Your Better
Half* to celebrate the 200 productions of *Rules of Conduct.* That's all. Fiction is only fiction. But, if you insist
on making reality from fiction, that's up to you.

SARA: You are going to say that it isn't us? With our first names
and almost last name? You wanted to humiliate us. You
are resentful. What right do you have to complain? You
have everything you could ever want.

RAÚL: Think for a moment about the resentment of others. Because there are many that do have a right to complain.
Remember, someone is calling on the phone.

SARA: You're not going to scare me with that foolishness. You've
gotten this into such a tangled mess, I don't know how
we'll ever get out. You've ruined everything! But do not
forget who you are and who we are. (*Pause.*) Not only
that, but to make matters worse, you made me an absent
character, like Judy ...

RAÚL: Ah, so that's it. A problem among women.

SARA: It would seem to be one among men too.

RAÚL: A comedy of errors, Sara, in which each one seems to put
on an item of clothing belonging to the others. Take it
like a spring night's dream in which each one is reborn to
what he is.

SARA: Interpret however you like, but there is nothing amusing
about being an absent character. You've made me put on

such a show, especially in front of Judy.

RAÚL: (*Moving closer. Satisfied.*) So ... so you're jealous too.

SARA: Of course, but it doesn't take the form that you think.

RAÚL: And how do I imagine it?

SARA: Like all men imagine it, regardless of circumstances. As if the issue between Judy and me was something between women ...

RAÚL: Then you didn't know about the Judy and Paul business ...

SARA: As if I were jealous of Judy because she is contending for the ... the love ... the love of a man ... Oh, God, how ridiculous this sounds, Raúl! Are you sure you aren't writing a soap opera?

RAÚL: With these ... episodes? No, no I don't think so! Perhaps we've fallen into one and haven't noticed. After all, it is the only merchandise that sells.

SARA: The thing is, since you hung up the telephone, I could see myself entering a scene from one minute to the next, waiting for my bit part to arrive.

RAÚL: I was considering it, but it seemed a little monotonous for her to open the door too.

SARA: She could have rung the bell.

RAÚL: No, she could not have done that because that would have placed you beneath all the rest, which indeed would have damaged you. It was indispensable that you would have had the key, because to the contrary ...

SARA: But indeed everyone seems to have that key.

RAÚL: Precisely ... You understand, Sara, I assure you that the more I thought about it, the idea of letting you enter at the beginning of the second act seemed better to me, as you have done at this moment. Because it would be a most intimate second act, between you and me, secret, about which the other characters would not find out. (*Taking her in his arms.*) Something ... something unique ... really different.

SARA: (*Separating herself from him.*) It doesn't interest me. You have calculated badly. And perhaps you have also given the key to him.

RAÚL: To whom?

SARA: To the terrorist. To that one who called you a few minutes ago. But perhaps he would not be more than an absent character anxious to say his small mouthful. What a joke! Thus he will be made a corpse from hunger, without a morsel to carry to his vocal cords. You are a coward, Raúl. The surest thing is that he won't appear here, the one whom you would not allow to show himself here.

RAÚL: Come on, don't get that way. As if you were an actress.

SARA: Aren't we that? We are always acting, Raúl. What happens is that at times we are so involved in this role, we cannot realize it. I might not be an actress, but it pleases me to interpret important roles, and in this case it is evident that Judy, with that final scene, is the one who steals the show.

RAÚL: But didn't you like that final "Latin Lover" scene of the first act? Judy seems enchanted with it.

SARA: Why wouldn't she be? You know her.

RAÚL: What do you mean?

SARA: That Judy has a soap opera mentality, and with endings such as those, these episodes conclude each day, with an expectation that is all "to be continued tomorrow." I fear that you are infected with all that foolishness. I never would have thought that now you were going to stoop to that type of theater. Without counting on the key business and the lock's keyhole. All very stale. That doesn't mean that people won't like it.

RAÚL: So it looks bad to you ...

SARA: I have not said that exactly.

RAÚL: For that matter, here no one says anything exactly.

SARA: You would know it better than I. But I warn you, it is the only way of saying it all exactly.

RAÚL: I believe that the one who is lowering herself to a soap opera is you. I could never have imagined that you would do such a thing. From Judy, it does not surprise me, but from you ...

SARA: In any event, a woman of her age getting kissed by a "Latin Lover" twenty years younger than she, is always enchanted with her role, although that role might be nothing but making a fool of herself.

RAÚL: Really, I never imagined you in that light. But it is possible that I intuited it, and it is for that reason that I did not let you enter in the first act. An encounter with Judy would have spoiled it all.

SARA: In spite of everything, we always know how to behave. Do not confuse us with one of those barrio Latinas.

RAÚL: I thought you had more class.

SARA: You shouldn't come to me with the story that that kiss at the end of the first act was faked. I assure you, Raúl, that you did it very well. Author and character. It's a good thing that Sam did not miss the sound effects and went to the bathroom. From any point of view, he would have had a bad moment.

RAÚL: Truthfully, now you are the one who is about to play the fool. It's better that you calm down, because the others may enter at any moment, and it would not be very elegant for them to find you this way.

SARA: You are a degenerate, Raúl.

RAÚL: And what are you?

SARA: At least I do not play on both sides like you. With one, I have more than enough.

RAÚL: Depends on how you look at it.

SARA: You don't know me very well, which at this point doesn't bother me. I believed ... Well, you don't know women very well. Not for nothing.

RAÚL: I did not think you were so conventional. I assure you that you seemed to me to be the total opposite. I am sorry. Apparently, we both were mistaken. Perhaps you are right, and perhaps *my* protagonist is Judy.

SARA: But do not believe that you are her first dramatist. Neither the first nor the last.

RAÚL: If I am not mistaken, the first playwright was your husband.

SARA: When you brought that libretto so that Bob would read it and you came to see him that day that he was not here, I thought that things would be different. But later ... Later you started to change the text.

RAÚL: You told Bob that what I wrote was of no use, that it was all shit.

SARA: Who told you this?

RAÚL: Bob told me.

SARA: Bob told you that Sara had said it, but you cannot know what Sara said because you did not allow her to enter on stage ... You have invented it all, Raúl, and now you believe that all you invented is true. If you had wanted to know what I thought, it was I whom you had to ask, without disregarding what I had told you other times already.

RAÚL: And how was I to know that you were not lying to me? Because it is as if we always wore a mask.

SARA: It is a risk that one must take. Or is it that you believe that one can go through life always shouting the truth?

RAÚL: Yes, we must go through life always shouting the truth. There you have *Your Better Half.*

SARA: *Your Better Half... Rules of Conduct ... Forbidden Games ...* Lies, you have told nothing but lies! Or is it that you believe that in that first act of ... of *Forbidden Games ...*

RAÚL: Of *Your Better Half ...*

SARA: ... Sam, Bob, Judy and you have told the truth at any time? ... Lies, they have done nothing but lie ... Only Sara has told the truth, because you left her behind the scenes ... (*Pause.*) But ... when you brought the libretto the first time, I thought that things were going to be different ...

RAÚL: But they have been.

SARA: All has returned to its place, as if it were the same. We have returned to the point of departure. A bit further back, when we did not know each other ... (*Pause.*) But ... When I opened the door for you the first time ... Do you remember?

RAÚL: Yes, I remember, goddammit. You looked so good, you did not seem real. (*Violently.*) When I saw you for the first time, I felt a desire to kick you, to kill you, to flay you with my teeth. I don't know how I contained myself because as soon as I saw you, I wanted to jump on you and bite you, to throw you on the sofa and to finish you off with my body. You remember, don't you?

SARA: I remember, yes, but I assure you that at any moment I would have forgotten all that. It would be as if it would have never happened. In reality I have already almost forgotten it.

RAÚL: And what did I seem like to you? Did I seem soft and milky like your husband? Did I remind you of Bob?

SARA: No, you did not remind me of him. At that time you had a beard and were badly dressed. The one that just called must be as you were.

RAÚL: Why do you say this?

SARA: Because since I opened the door for you, it seemed to me that I have been smelling you. Yes, it was your smell. It was as if you had kicked open the door and it was not a man who entered, but a foul-mouthed beast. Nor do I know how I contained myself, because since I saw you, the only thing I wanted to do was to throw myself on you and start biting you.

RAÚL: I must have had that special smell from the lower classes that drives many women crazy. That smell that is called

B. O. I was a "Latin Lover."

SARA: I assure you that if you had appeared to be a "Latin Lover" to me, I would not have gone to bed with you.

RAÚL: You looked so that you did not seem real. You were like an engraving, but like a movie. When I was a boy I went to see a Grace Kelly film. I don't remember which one, and when I saw you, it was she who came to my mind. She was so lovely that she did not seem real. So clean as if she had always just bathed and had left the water; at the same time she was made-up, dressed for me, but always natural, just born from water. It was she who came to my mind when I saw you, and I realized then that I had to finish you off, because you excited me all over, and I did not know how I could contain myself. You were so pretty that I believed that you were a fake, but your whole body and my whole body told me that you were real, and a half-hour later I already knew that you were more of a whore than any hen in a chicken house.

SARA: I bet that I didn't remind you of any of the Puerto Rican women that you laid in the Barrio.

RAÚL: But I must have reminded you of the delivery boy from the grocery, the one that was sent with your groceries; that "lunch" hour "Latin Lover" that's cheaper, the one that you take care of with a tip.

SARA: No, you didn't remind me of him.

RAÚL: I came close to killing you.

SARA: Yes, you almost killed me.

RAÚL: But afterwards you were bitchy, as if you had not been satisfied.

SARA: I had been satisfied.

RAÚL: As if you wanted more.

SARA: No, it was not that I wanted more. It was that I wanted you to finish me off.

RAÚL: You hated me, you detested me.

SARA: I wanted you to punish me, that in fact you finish me off, but not faking it, but really, not figuratively. I wanted you to execute me once and for all with that weapon that you had between your legs.

RAÚL: You hated me, you detested me, you abhorred what I was doing to you.

SARA: Yes, Raúl I hated you, I detested you, I abhorred you for all that you were doing to me.

RAÚL: But you wanted more, that I trample you, that I crush you for what you are, an American whore and bitch, just like those who go around seeking the males from the world of underdevelopment, sleeping with them at lunch time, taking advantage of the rise of the dollar and the fall of all the third world currency, of inflation and misery. Because that was what you were, right? And you knew, right? And you knew it as well as I. But I was not Bob, nor was I like any of the others you had known, in the corner bar, nor even like those "Latin Lovers," hungry beggars, who delivered the groceries for you, isn't that true? (RAÚL *throws* SARA *on the sofa. They struggle.*)

SARA: Yes, it is true.

RAÚL: And you were furious, furious with yourself and you were the one who wanted to be trampled, to trample yourself, because you thought that only I could satisfy you, that neither Bob nor any of those discolored Americans with whom you had deceived him time and again did you like, did satisfy you. You liked me more because I had that smell, that beastly flavor that came from some exotic place that not even you could imagine, that sweat that traveled over me and fell upon you and bathed you. I sweated as they did not sweat, that I did a conscientious job like a trucker, a worker, and that was what you wanted, a brute as in some Central Park fantasies where you saw yourself laid by Hispanics like me, mulattoes and Blacks from the barrio who fell upon you, because only you, who were a white American and blonde, and with money, could like them. (*They continue struggling in a brutal manner, in a scene of sexuality and violence.*)

SARA: Leave me alone! Leave me alone!

RAÚL: And it was then when you went to Bob with the story that I was a good for nothing, isn't that so? Because that's the truth, and I haven't made it up. Because that was what you thought of me while you had other reasons smuggled in the bed.

SARA: Yes, it is true. And it is for that reason Bob and I decided to finish you off, to castrate you once and for all.

RAÚL: What do you mean? (SARA *gains grounds and gets on her feet.*)

SARA: I decided it all. Bob and I decided to finish you off. To swallow you. To eat you whole. Or did you believe those words you repeated in my ear were caresses? "Whore,

whore, daughter of a whore." And you repeated it to me
in Spanish over and over, so that I might memorize it.
"Whore, whore, daughter of a whore" And that was what
I was for you. And I liked to hear it, yes, because you
insulted me, because you made me descend to what I am,
to what you were: "son of a whore, son of a whore, son of
a whore." (SARA *throws herself into a corner, toward the
front of the stage.*) And it was then that I felt the most,
when I would squeeze you tighter. And you repeated it to
me because you realized that was what I wanted to hear
too, those kicks of your voice that were a caress on my
body. And you repeated it to me. That sex that came out
of your throat hating and violating me as if all the blonde
American whores of the world were there, joined in the
sex that you had between your legs. (*After writhing upon
the stage,* SARA *begins getting up.*) I swear to you that I
have never desired so much ... loved so much ... I loved
you in a way that one cannot understand ... I waited for
that voice on the telephone ... An explosion that would
end everything ... a brutal discharge ... That the door
would be opened at any moment and you would enter in
a burst that would be the definitive ... The man, Raúl,
the man that you were ... that were indeed ... that you
were not going to give up ... That you would escape all
the laws of gravity that lead to an inevitable fall ... The
man, Raúl, that would not step back ... That you would
escape from me ... From Judy's glamor ... From Bob's
cunning ... From Sam's dollars ... the man, Raúl, the
man ... (SARA *is now standing.* RAÚL *is seated on the
sofa, stunned.*) Yes, you are right. You laid with me as
if you were involved in a class struggle. And I laid with
you for the same reason. We hated each other, didn't we?
It was beautiful, wasn't it? (*Pause.*) Until one day I realized that now it was different, that what happened had
to happen ... That now you were not here ... (*Pause.*)
I didn't know when it was exactly ... A gesture of yours
... (*Pause.*) Perhaps it was a word from Bob that gave me
the warning ... (*Pause.*) Good, I must confess to you, I
always have loved Bob also. In our way, we have loved
each other much. Also in a way that no one would understand. "*My better half.*" It is for that reason that Bob
and I always end up agreeing with each other. Or is it that
you believe that all this that you relate has caught us by

surprise? If you believe that you have given us a slap in the face, a humiliation, a blackmail, do not imagine that you are going to gain anything by it. In any case, Bob and I have always been in agreement. Or is it that you believe that all that you were doing you did behind my back? Or is it that you believe that Bob hasn't also called, the delivery boy taking care of him later with a tip? How naive you are! It was a war and we had to castrate you. I'm sorry, really, more than you could imagine, but we had no choice. A question of security, a preventive measure. For hygiene. As one does with dogs and cats, to keep them in the house so that they can lick the tips of our fingers. Understand. (*Pause.*) I fear ... I fear that you are going to have to write that first act again. (*The telephone rings.* RAÚL, *immobile on the sofa, raises his head, but he does not go to answer.* SARA, *determined, answers it.*) Hello ... Hello ... Hello ... (*Anxious.*) who is calling? What do you want? Who are you? (SARA *hangs up. The glass door that leads to the terrace is opened,* JUDY *enters, also very elegant, evening dress.*)

JUDY: Who was it?

SARA: I don't know.

JUDY: But what did he want?

SARA: Nothing, no one answered. It was ... as if he called in order to know ... to know if we were still here.

JUDY: Child, what ideas come to your mind. It must be some girlfriend of Raúl's ... or some friend, who knows of the many that he has.

SARA: What have they decided?

JUDY: Well, Bob and Sam can't agree. Of course, as Bob is a liberal Democrat and Sam a Neanderthal Republican, each one of them pulls for the opposite side. A different conclusion comes to each, although in the end they will agree. But honestly I don't know what will come of all this. Oh yes, they both want it to be a box-office success.

SARA: Then it will end in a happy ending.

JUDY: It's better that way, don't you think so? People come to the theater to have a good time and we'll not ruin it for them. Isn't that true, Raúl? (RAÚL *has remained mute and open-mouthed. Approaching* RAÚL, *affectionately, running her fingers through his hair.*) Poor Raúl, how puffed up he was at the end of the first act. (*Turning to* SARA.) What have you done to him?

SARA: Well, we had ...

JUDY: (*Caressing* RAÚL.) Oh, Sara, what a wicked person you are!

SARA: I only told the truth.

JUDY: And if that weren't enough?

SARA: The truth never hurts.

JUDY: Don't be foolish! (*To* RAÚL, *as if scolding him.*) Obviously you asked for it, doing things that you shouldn't. Who told you to get yourself in such a mess and to stick your foot in it? Because, let me see. Weren't you satisfied with Sara and me without having to make Bob and Sam do ugly things? Hah? Haven't I always been nice to you? Because, let's see, didn't I do all that you asked of me? Talk! Answer! (RAÚL *does not move.*) But don't get that way, Raúl! Don't take it so to heart! I don't know any play of Bob's that does not have a happy ending.

SARA: This is Raúl's play, Judy. Don't forget that he is responsible for all this.

JUDY: Yes, it's true. What a dunderhead I am! But after all, it's all the same. Since they wrote *Rules of Conduct* together, there is no difference between them and ... Poor Raúl! Don't you believe I'll always be eternally grateful for that end at the first act? It's so romantic! I hope that Bob and Sam don't get heavy handed ... Because if it had been between you and me, we would have already resolved it. We would have worked it out in some way. You know with that title of *Your Better Half,* I thought that it was much simpler.

SARA: Well, what happened was that Bob didn't want to collaborate in the play and he asked me to work with Raúl.

JUDY: Then you too have been writing it. No wonder that this has been such a mess.

SARA: No, I have not been writing it directly. Simply, Raúl and I have worked together planning the development of the plot, the characters, the situations, not to have to make so many changes later, when staging it. What happens is that later, upon writing it ...

JUDY: Then ... then you knew everything?

SARA: What's that?

JUDY: About Bob and Raúl.

SARA: Of course, Judy. It was my idea.

JUDY: And about Sam?

SARA: Well, that goes without saying. It's an economic law that can't miss.

JUDY: Then that's why Bob and Sam also were in agreement?

SARA: (*Surprised.*) How were Bob and Sam in agreement?

JUDY: Don't take it literally because with these mix-ups perhaps I am mistaken. (*With intent.*) But, Bob and Sam ...

SARA: Bob and Sam?

JUDY: As you hear it. They said something about that on the terrace, although they didn't go into details. But I thought that Bob didn't keep secrets from you.

SARA: Yes, but everything doesn't have to be explained. Going into unimportant details.

JUDY: Well, that must be it. I, really don't pay any attention to any of that. Definitely, I don't complain. Sam has his objections, but I have been coping. In any case, I was happy with Raúl. (*Looking at* RAÚL.) Poor Raúl! He is destroyed!

SARA: He asked for it. It was well deserved.

JUDY: Well, I have to confess to you that the thing with you two took me by surprise ... Well, I could not imagine that you ... with that type of yours, so well put together always ... I thought that you and Bob were happy.

SARA: Bob and I are happy.

JUDY: Yes I understand, because each one is happy in his or her manner. In any case, Sam told me that I should not trust you. That you were one of those who conquers them silently ... And Raúl ...

SARA: Raúl spoke to you about me?

JUDY: Well, not exactly.

SARA: What do you mean by that?

JUDY: They were epithets ... Well, better, insults.

SARA: But that was in bad taste, Judy.

JUDY: That's what I told him. But finally one must take into account that, after all, Raúl is a Latino. Perhaps Sam is right in what he says. That we are a superior race. We have fun but we think with our head. For that reason we are where we are. But they are so ignorant that they only think that way, and for that reason they are where they have remained. Finally, one must take into account that, after all, Raúl is also a Latino. What can you do? You liked for him to say bad words. He insisted that you ...

SARA: Say it, Judy, say it ...

JUDY: It is that, child ... I don't want to offend you.

SARA: No, no, say it once and for all.

JUDY: "Whore, American whore," "blonde, skinny whore," "degenerated whore." That you were a hypocritical whore. Well, what can I tell you! Suffice it to say that I believe that he was obsessed with you ... I warn you that he said the same to me, but as I am a brunette, saying "blonde whore" didn't apply to me, and he made me laugh. What madness! I don't expect to have offended you.

SARA: I'll have to castrate him! As if he were a cat or a dog!

JUDY: How barbaric, Sara! How can you say such a thing? As if this were the story of Judith and Holofernes! Where have you pulled that out of? (*Touching* RAÚL *affectionately.*) Look how you've got Raúl! You have him trembling from head to foot! I warn you that for that type of work don't count on me.

SARA: He is a bastard. A degenerate and an opportunistic Latino who detests all that women like us have. He's bitter, Judy, he has slept with us in order to humiliate our husbands.

JUDY: I don't know what to tell you, but as for me, I'm not going to get into that ... compete with you, fine; but with that beast of a Sam ... unthinkable. (*To* RAÚL.) Come on, speak, Raúl! Don't play mute! Did you or not, didn't you like going to bed with me? I warn you that with that muteness you're not going to get anywhere, because we have to make a decision and you will have to decide on someone. (*To* SARA *taking* RAÚL *by the chin.*) But do you believe that such a dark, handsome guy can like to be with a gorilla like my husband? Tell me about it, I have swallowed my bitter pills! And with Bob who must be such a boring man! (*Releasing* RAÚL, *a little like one who drops something.*) No, Sara he has his reasons. He may be a sinner, an opportunist, a bitter one, all that and much more. I'm not going to get into that, nor am I going to make him a paragon of virtues, but what is certain is that I spend my good moments with him and I'm sure that he spends them with me. You have stirred up a riot for nothing. I believed you more modern, more sophisticated. But never mind that, as I imagine that he isn't important to you, *I want you to leave him to me.*

SARA: Leave him to you? What do you mean?

JUDY: Nothing, to leave all this in a one act piece, and when Sam leaves the bathroom, I'll tell him that I stay with Raúl. If he wants to keep the apartment and all the mirrors, that, certainly at this point I have not been able to find out who had that idea ... In other words that I'll stay with him.

SARA: You will stay with a kitten, with a pussy cat, a little kitty.

JUDY: With a little kitty? Please, Sara, you know well that Raúl is not any pussy cat.

SARA: A kitty cat, a pussy cat, a small lap-dog that Bob and Sam will take out to walk along Park Avenue.

JUDY: Well, whatever you say, it doesn't matter a bit. I am staying with the kitty cat. Sam and I are finished, anyway. I can't bear him one more day. And I am sure that Bob will be able to find another small lap-dog from the thousands that roam around here ... Latinos, Italians, Greeks, Chinese also. Of all the types, sizes and colors. But you leave Raúl to me, he is my "Latin Lover!" (*To* RAÚL.) True, my love, that you want to stay with me? (*To* SARA.) Let him give me a kiss, let the curtain fall and let him stay with me.

SARA: (*Suddenly.*) Go to the kitchen and bring a knife.

JUDY: (*Without understanding.*) What?

SARA: Go to the kitchen and bring a knife.

JUDY: What are you saying? That I should go to the kitchen and bring a knife? Me? Dressed like this? You have gone utterly crazy, Sara. If you believe that I, who have interpreted the greatest plays that have been staged on Broadway, am going to go on stage dressed as I am and with a knife. It's evident that you are certifiably crazy and have lost all reason.

SARA: (*Threatening, quite unhinged, to* JUDY, *who recoils.*) Go to the kitchen and bring the knife. Go to the kitchen and bring the knife!

JUDY: Go yourself, you bitch! Go yourself, shitty whore! Enter through this door like a crazy woman. Be ridiculous like Anthony Perkins in *Psycho,* who forever was screwed and has never recovered. But as for me, do not count on me for that! (*The glass door is opened that leads to the terrace.* BOB *and* SAM *enter, both in tuxedoes, like* RAÚL. *At the same time, the telephone rings.* SARA, *distressed, looks at it.* RAÚL *raises his head and looks at it also, but he doesn't move.*)

SAM: What's happening here? What's all the shouting about? (SARA *takes two steps toward the telephone, but* BOB *hurries and answers it.*)

BOB: Hello! Hello! Hello! Hello! (*Hangs up.*)

JUDY: Nothing, Sam. Sara has gone crazy and wants me to go
      get a knife from the kitchen to ... (JUDY *puts her hand*
      to her mouth as if smothering a cry, without being able to
      end the sentence.)

SARA: (*To* BOB.) Who was it?

BOB: No one. Someone who dialed a wrong number, I suppose.

SARA: Are you sure?

BOB: No, of course not. How am I going to know?

SAM: Nobody said anything?

BOB: No, of course not.

SAM: Swear to me that you're not lying, Bob!

BOB: But why would I lie about such a stupid thing?

SARA: In order not to alarm me. I don't know! Or some other
      reason so that I wouldn't know the truth.

SAM: They have called before?

SARA: It's the third time. Perhaps Raúl has something going.
      Sam, God knows what he might have in mind. We're not
      going to have peace and quiet until we finish with him.

SAM: That's what I say. We're going to have to change the lock,
      since all the barrio has the key. At the least carelessness
      they'll be all over us. There are too many Latinos around
      here.

SARA: I'm afraid, Bob.

SAM: Sara is right. They're a bunch of delinquents.

SARA: Drug addicts ... degenerates ... prostitutes ...

BOB: Calm yourself, Sara. Use your head.

SARA: I can't, Bob. All of a sudden, I'm terrified ... It's as if
      they were going to attack us at any moment ... thieves
      ... assassins ... terrorists ... revolutionaries, perhaps ...

BOB: Come, come, don't get this way, you are a nervous wreck.
      (SARA *runs to the arms of* BOB, *who embraces her and*
      seems to protect her.)

JUDY: (*Desolate, in the middle of the stage.*) But who's going to
      want to harm us? What evil have we done, Sam?

BOB: (*To* SARA, *paternally.*) Your problem is that you want to
      take it all literally. You've frightened Judy with that story
      of the knife. It's not necessary to go to those extremes.
      Also, poor Raúl has wanted to carry things too far. Now
      he will be learning his lesson, as we have all learned at
      some time. (*To* RAÚL.) Because you wouldn't believe it,
      Raúl, that what has happened to you has happened to all
      of us. It happens to all of us, even though we might be

Anglo-Saxons. What happens is that it happens to us in English, and that's why people don't understand us.

JUDY: It's sad, Bob. Oh, I'll always be sentimental! Bob, don't make me cry.

SAM: Come on, Judy, don't be ridiculous.

SARA: Stop, Bob. Stop once and for all.

BOB: Look, Judy, hand me the libretto and give me the scissors. We have to make some cuts in the text. (SARA *moves away from* BOB, JUDY *goes to the small table where the telephone is. She takes a libretto and some scissors that are there. She takes them to* BOB. *He takes them and gives the scissors and the libretto to* SARA.) You do the cuts. (SARA *cuts the libretto and throws the pieces on the stage as she does her monolog. She reads on some occasions. There are no specific indications, but the text determines the violence and growing paroxysm of* SARA. *The stage begins darkening, although it never stays completely dark, but in a penumbra. A light follows* SARA, *and another falls upon* RAÚL *seated on the sofa with his head bowed.*)

SARA: (*Without speaking directly to* RAÚL, *as if it were a reaction to the text that she has in her hands.*) Since I read the first speech, I knew that we had to finish with you. To exterminate you, you and those of your breed, as if we sent them to the gas chambers. Swine! Degenerate! I didn't know who you thought were. (*Pause.*) The text was here on the night-table and its smell filled the room as if it were copulating ... That first act was a pitched battle, a war cry in order to finish us all off. The blue-eyed blondes like me. Cheap Judy's cheap life. Bob's bunglings. Sam's dollars. All the abuse that you have received, before and after, that you carried inside as if it had scarred you for life. It was a threat of destruction, a chaos that made me tremble at Bob's side. (*Pause.*) Bob snored blessedly ... (*Transition. Hysterical.*) Wake up, Bob! Wake up, Sam! Wake up, Judy! All of you wake up! (*Pause.*) The danger was there in each one of the words that were on the paper, with a past that dragged you backward, toward another idiom, toward another territory; a foreigner, after all ... Sam, thinking that his dollars were secure in the safe ... Judy, covered with furs ... always renewed once again ... just done ... And I with that text that was revolution and death and that made me tremble at Bob's side ... The words were there, in front of me, devouring me as he had

devoured me, threatening me. (*Transition.*) The cutting
had to begin! The sooner the better! To end once and for
all time with that language, with that body to body attack!
(*Violent.*) Yes, yes, chop away with the scissors! Cut them
one by one, Sara! Don't let them raise their heads! Dis-
member, murder, execute the text! That's it! That's it!
Cut them, chop them into small pieces! ... (*Long pause.*)
I was in danger of death, Bob. His language within mine,
possessing me, dragging me toward the base depth of his
origin ... One more Latino in the territory that was ours
... (*Pause.*) He, seducing me with that serpents's voice ...
And I, rising from the waters lovely and perfumed ... (*Reacting, violent.*) No, don't let yourself be deceived Sara.
Hurl those syllables, take them out of there! What does
it matter to you that he should be searching for a place
in the sun? He is being deceitful, see it? He only wants
to sleep with you, to exploit you, to humiliate you. Don't
heed the text, no. Use those scissors, ah? Let's go put
the scissor to it! Sentences full of hatred, paragraphs full
of rage, scenes full of filth, centuries full of misery, ran-
cor and desperation. (*Paroxysm.*) Tragedy! Melodrama!
Tragedy! Melodrama! A grotesque discourse that serves
nothing! (*Pause.*) Unable to raise your head? Fuck you!
Words, words nothing more! As if they said something!
(*Transition, erect.*) Not us! Clean, white, smiling coming
out of the waters! Prosperity, progress, well-being, luxury! (*Transition.*) And you there, naked on the paper ...
That smell ... That sweat ... Your body that carried everything with it ... Dragged erotically ... Through the
text ... Each letter ... each syllable ... each word ... A
lust ... an orgasm ... No! ... (*Transition.*) That's why
that time, when you appeared with that first act that I
had to cut ... (*Shows the scissors.*) with this blade, see?
(*Cutting.*) Like this and this ... in little pieces ... and I
alone in order to finish with you. (*Almost letting herself
go erotically.*) You ... who shook me from head to toe
... (*Transition.*) Bob! ... Bob! ... Wake up, Bob! Now!
At once! Finish with him ... Destroy him ... Digest him
... smoothly ... gently ... slowly ... Swallow him! One
must mould him, fabricate him anew, make him again ...
Made by me, for you, by us ... According to our interests
... Soft like you, Bob ... Let him think that he writes the
work, that he places the periods and commas. Let him

believe that, yes, indeed he is finally making it, that he's designing the plot, that he has his place in the sun ... That he might think that it's he who sets the trap ... Let him ... Work with him ... Take away a word here ... another there ... Asphyxiate it! (*Transition.*) Sam! ... Sam! ... Put the money between his legs ... Give him the key ... A place in the sun ... A place in the penthouse ... Buy him, Sam! Like the Italians ... the Greeks ... the Arabs ... Money! Money everywhere! Above ... below ... outside ... within ... in front ... behind ... Assimilate him! Swallow him! (*Transition.*) Fondle him, Judy! It is for sale, yes it for sale ... Pure merchandise! He gives it all! He surrenders it all! He is for sale like everything else! ... A bargain, Judy ... sale! Special offer! (*Pauses now in lower tone, almost "reasonable," gives up cutting.*) Soften it, Bob, soften it well as you know how to do so well ... Water it all down. Take the color from the words. Remove the fire from it. Teach him to write that language of success that all want to speak and all want to hear. Throw his words on the sewer. Prostitute his text. (*She raises her voice again, until reaching a paroxysm at the end of her monologue.*) Like that, like that, he cannot be a man! He can't say anything worth hearing, that is worth repeating! Let him say only what everyone wants to hear! Here, there, everywhere! (*She throws some pages into the air.*) Tricks ... techniques ... devices ... lies ... deceits ... synonyms... subtleties ... hypocrisies ... shadings! ... His place in the sun! Let success bury him! Let the words take him to his grave! To mould him ... reshape him ... to remake him! ... Let nothing remain from what he said nor from what he might say! Let him be silent forever! (*More cuts.*) Cut all his words at the root! Like this ... like this ... like this ... (SARA *reaches the paroxysm, destroying the libretto completely.* BOB *and* SAM *are next to* RAÚL, *almost on top of him. They take his face and slap it. The darkness increases, except for the light on the sofa.*)

BOB: He's dead, Sara. He's a pussy cat. A kitty cat.

SAM: Look at that scrap, Judy! He's a puppy dog! He's a small lap-dog! (RAÚL *jumps. He pushes* SAM *and* BOB, *who are unprepared.*)

RAÚL: (*With all the fury that has been accumulated during all the time in which he has not spoken a word.*) Fuck you!

Fuck you all! Fuck you, bastards! (SAM *and* BOB *react
immediately and jump on him. A struggle is started. The
sofa falls backward. All very rapidly.* JUDY *shouts.* SARA
with the scissors aloft, joins SAM *and* BOB. JUDY *runs
and turns out the light.* RAÚL *shouts again but without
being seen covered by the bodies of the rest: "Fuck you!" At
once, in unison, someone kicks the door, and it is opened
violently. Against the light is seen the silhouette of a man
in an aggressive pose with a submachine gun in his hand.
Curtain.*)

ACT III

*The stage is completely illuminated, as in the previous acts.
The street door is closed. All seems to be in order and in its place.*
RAÚL *enters, formally dressed, as in the previous act, very well put
together but somewhat nervous. He dials a number. He speaks, but
remains watchful of the door that leads to the terrace.*

RAÚL: María? ... Yes, it's me Raúl. Are you ready now? Yes,
now you can come, come ... Take a taxi and come here ...
Yes, they liked the first act very much ... A delight, a mar-
vel, a masterpiece. Things like these are not written anymore ... Well, that was what they said; what they think,
who knows. One cannot see below the surface ... Yes, I
believe that this time I have hit the bull's eye ... Imagine! It hasn't been easy. Sex, violence, homosexuality...
Whatever is in fashion, no? But superficially, so as not
to frighten anyone ... It's clear that the second act was
something else and they were dumbfounded ... Yes, yes,
I know that El Tiznado does nothing but screw things up
and a little bit at a time he gets them scared, dammit,
right up to that damned ending when he shows up and
wrecks it all. Well, you know how he is. I'm going to
have to strangle him, because the only thing he wants to
do is kick ass ... No, no, it's me, Raúl ... No, it's not El
Tiznado ... Yes, yes, I know that he wants to come out
again, but I've got him on a short leash because if those
people see him, they get scared and I'll never be able to
stage the play. I'll have to take measures for the third act,
don't be worried ... No, no, yes, I swear to you that I have

my mask on, and I have that jackass Jesus tied hand and
foot. (*Concealing the receiver.*) Tiznado, stop screwing
around! (*Continues speaking.*) Come at once, you're all
that is needed here to put on the finishing touches ... We
have to celebrate this! Nothing less than a Tony Award!
Well, I have to share it with Bob, but you already know
how it is. We are the Latino Stuff and they want us with
carnations behind our ears and castanets up our asses!
(*Covering the receiver.*) Jesus, Tiznado, shit, stop talking
rubbish! They are sure to cut that one! (*Removing his
hand.*) No, no, I swear to you that El Tiznado is not here
... This is between you and me ... Calm down! That was
a goof-up that won't happen again! I assure you that no
one is hearing us ... You know how they are ... No, I still
haven't told them yet. They're going to fall on their asses
when I tell them that we're going to get married ... I warn
you, El Tiznado is sweet on you! Well, I have to go, here
comes Doris Day ... Yes, yes, I'll put on my mask, she
is coming with hers ... Ciao ... See you later. (*RAÚL
hangs up. The glass door opens and SARA enters who, in
effect, now resembles Doris Day, because she has lost her
femme fatal look that she had in the previous act. It has to
be the dressy, beaded jacket, that she has on which makes
her less dramatic. RAÚL becomes tame as a pigeon. They
speak with naturalness and even with sincerity, but all that
they say is a lie.*)

SARA: What a lovely play, Raúl! I congratulate you!

RAÚL: Really?

SARA; Absolutely. It's a delicious play. As if you were now in
full control of your creative faculties. It's the best thing
you've written.

RAÚL: Do you think so?

SARA: I don't have the slightest doubt. It's come out really well,
Raúl.

RAÚL: Thanks, Sara. I appreciate that opinion much more coming
from you, as you're so demanding.

SARA: If I weren't true, I wouldn't say it. You know how I am.
My standards are very high.

RAÚL:You don't have to tell that to me.

SARA: I never tell lies, and much less in cases like this.

RAÚL: I know that very well, Sara.

SARA: It was such a great stroke of luck to know you! This is such
a lovely friendship, Raúl! So pure! For us, for Bob and

for me, you are like a brother.

RAÚL: You've both been so generous to me!

Sara Are you happy?

RAÚL: Happy doesn't say it. I am ecstatic.

SARA: I believe that we should go now. It's getting late and we
    should be there when they name the winners.

RAÚL: You believe that we're going to win the prize?

SARA: I'm sure. (*Pauses.*) Let me fix your tie.

RAÚL: Do you believe that Bob is happy too?

SARA: He is thrilled. (SARA *adjusts* RAÚL's *tie. The glass door
    opens and* BOB *enters dressed as in the previous act.*)

BOB: Great!

SARA: Speaking of the devil ... !

BOB: What a lovely play, Raúl! I congratulate you!

RAÚL: Thanks, Bob.

BOB: It's the best thing you've written.

SARA: (*To* RAÚL *smiling.*) Didn't I tell you?

BOB: Except the end, which of course has left us with our mouths
    open. Where did you get that hoodlum from?

RAÚL: I don't know. He just popped up. In the least expected of
    places.

BOB: But that can't be left that way, Raúl. You know it as well as
    I. Don't you think so, Sara?

SARA: Yes, of course, he'll have to...

RAÚL: What do you mean? Take it out?

SARA: To pull it out from where you've put it in. Because you're
    not going to have him shoot the machine gun.

RAÚL: But that is very common, Sara. Don't you read the newspa-
    pers? From time to time, someone shows up in a McDon-
    ald's or in a Jack in the Box, and he jumps from eating a
    hamburger and begins to shoot with a machine gun.

BOB: But that doesn't make sense.

RAÚL: I assure you that it must make some sense. Think about
    it.

BOB: Look, Raúl, stop with the nonsense. There are things in the
    theater that are simply not done. That character must be
    removed from the stage.

RAÚL: That isn't so easy, Bob. He is going to get furious. Later,
    no one will be able to put up with him.

BOB: That always happens, because I also have had my problems.
    But I assure you everything has a solution. He will be a
    bother to you for a while, but in the end he will die. Like
    everyone else.

RAÚL: He won't want to leave. He won't want to go away.

SARA: Stop your foolishness, Raúl. Don't forget that you're the playwright and he'll have to do whatever you want. You're definitely the one who has to say the final word.

RAÚL: I assure you that he doesn't understand reason. I'll have to blow his brains out.

BOB: Then do it once and for all.

SARA: But it's very important that he doesn't do it on stage, Bob. It would be in bad taste and in a play of this type good taste must never be lost.

BOB: That's taken for granted. You do it behind the scenes: a shot is heard, and that's it.

RAÚL: I am never sure about those deaths behind the scenes. It always seems to me that they are still alive.

BOB: Look, Raúl, I swear you were writing a masterpiece. A modern morality play. Light, fine, agreeable, where the public learns it's lesson without anxiety and without getting indigestion. It's for that reason that we were all also so pleased with that lovers triangle that you were handling so well. All said with shadings, without being strident. Very English, of course, that's the best I can tell you.

RAÚL: Shadings? Maybe we aren't speaking about the same play.

BOB: We're speaking about *Rules of Conduct*, aren't we?

SARA: But that is the charm that it has. You begin with rules of conduct and end with improper conduct. It's no more than a comedy of errors, delicious, amusing, pure entertainment.

RAÚL: I would never imagine that you were going to take it this way.

SARA: But how were we to take it, seriously? How foolish, Raúl! Life, like the theater, of course, is no more than a comedy of errors where all ends in its place. I'm not going to deny that yours doesn't have a message, but it's nothing more than a fashionable morality play, where things are not taken too seriously. I assure you that I thought that that was your intention.

BOB: It's for that reason that that exterminator, that assassin, has to be forgotten. You understand.

RAÚL: No, I understand what you're saying to me.

SARA: We are only saying it for your own good.

BOB: Those outbursts don't lead anywhere. Well, I've told you a thousand times and you know it.

RAÚL: "I have been taught by masters," as was said by Olivia de Havilland in Washington Square while she climbed the stairs.

BOB: Then learn the lesson. And let me repeat to you, that the rest is perfect. And if you allow me to tell you something else ...

RAÚL: Yes, of course ...

BOB: Well, that you Latinos don't write like that ... almost diplomatically ...

RAÚL: Diplomatically?

BOB: Well, most of the time, because I must confess to you that in the second act, the play was moving away from you in another direction, as if a different person were writing it. Isn't that true, Sara?

SARA: Yes, but those are minor things, Bob. It seems to me that, in any case, that situation can be fixed.

BOB: No, no, I don't have the slightest doubt of that. As always, some cutting and pruning would be in order.

SARA: Minor changes, I'd say.

BOB: But necessary, in order to give it unity with the first act, which is so well-crafted.

SARA: No, no. The first act has nothing missing and nothing extra in it. It's a delight, Raúl.

BOB: (*Persuasive.*) I'm sure that in the end we'll all agree. As always: This is a team effort, Raúl. What happens is, as you say, when you least expect it, you change how you speak and the unexpected pops up.

RAÚL: (*Sullen.*) Yes, that we like to say things suddenly. To slap you right in the face with it. As El Tiznado would say.

SARA: And who is El Tiznado?

RAÚL: That friend of mine who sticks his face in everything and doesn't follow rules of courtesy.

BOB: But do we know him?

RAÚL: On stage, Bob, on stage! El Tiznado is the one whose tongue you want to pull out and whose head you want to cut-off. (*With some violence.*) He is a bull who brutally attacks as if seeking the flow of blood.

SARA: What a barbarian!

RAÚL: Perhaps he has been writing the second act for me without my being aware of it.

BOB: In that case, you will have to remove all that he has written, because it doesn't make any sense.

SARA: I warn you, Raúl that that friendship doesn't suit you. El
　　　Tiznado must think he's a matador and I've never liked
　　　bullfights.

RAÚL: Me neither. It's for that reason that he and I are always at
　　　odds.

BOB: You see? That is precisely what I mean. It's the way one
　　　acts, the way one behaves. It's the way one does theater.

RAÚL: That is not doing theater, Bob. That is attacking and doing
　　　yourself in.

BOB: It's for that reason that you have to get rid of him and elim-
　　　inate him from the second act. If you're careless, he'll
　　　finish off the play and you'll be the one to pay.

RAÚL: So I should take him by the horns and lead him to the
　　　slaughterhouse.

BOB: I don't know if I expressed myself clearly, but that wasn't
　　　what I wanted to say. I've already told you that I am
　　　not in favor of violent measures. One must be able to
　　　manipulate. To get rid of him is not to order anyone to
　　　the slaughterhouse.

SARA: Put him to sleep?

BOB: (*Incisive.*) Do you understand?

RAÚL: Yes, yes, of course I understand. Don't think that because
　　　I am a Latino I can't understand those subtleties. "A good
　　　listener needs few words." Don't forget that we also have
　　　our own proverbs. (*Upset.*) Yes, I understand, yes! You
　　　and Sara always express yourselves clearly, although you
　　　speak with ambiguity. It's as if you used a more slender,
　　　more brilliant, more exact, and sharper stiletto that can
　　　penetrate more deeply, can cut with the skill of a surgeon,
　　　and the cunning of a serpent ... Because it's not a matter
　　　of writing a play with one's feet and attacking with a ma-
　　　chete, as if we were doing it out there in the Philippines
　　　... Isn't that what you want to say?

SARA: Please, Raúl, don't get upset that way.

BOB: What's wrong with you?

SARA: What's the matter? (SARA *and* BOB *look at each other.*
　　　There is a look of honest bewilderment between them.)

RAÚL: There's nothing wrong with me. Not in vain did Shake-
　　　speare manage intrigue so well. It is not by chance, don't
　　　you think? Shakespeare carried intrigue in his veins and
　　　that's why his characters buried the dagger with a mas-
　　　ter hand without the slightest tremor. And in the back,
　　　precisely. (*Transition.*) But one doesn't kill a bull with

treachery, Bob, nor with a scalpel. One kills it with a stab and face to face.

BOB: What exaggeration! What drama! You've taken a step backward, I assure you. Always that desire to fill your mouth with blood! I warn you that here, with those terms you won't get anywhere. On the contrary, if you remember the best scenes of *Rules of Conduct* and you tune in ...

RAÚL: (*Like one possessed*) Rules of Conduct! Rules of Conduct! El Tiznado, who speaks as if he were spitting, was right to tell me! That it would end up with you, writing rules of shit!

SARA: But Raúl! (*Great dismay. SARA and BOB look at one another, surprised.*)

RAÚL: (*Very disturbed.*) Pardon me, Sara. Pardon me, Bob. I don't know what's happened to me. I don't know what I'm saying.

BOB: Don't believe that I'm willing to suffer your insults, Raúl!

SARA: Do you feel bad? What's happening to you? Explain!

RAÚL: No, nothing is wrong with me. It was a bad moment. It was ... it was as if a wild animal had torn me from within ... (*Pauses.*) Then I saw red and I didn't know what I was saying. An attack, as El Tiznado would have said. I forgot my art of the stiletto, the precision of the scalpel. I am a boor, Bob.

BOB: I must have offended you somehow, but I assure you that it wasn't intentional.

SARA: Suddenly, you frightened us. As if it were another who spoke for you. As if it were El Tiznado who had put the words in your mouth.

RAÚL: I'm sorry. I'm really sorry. I hope that you'll be able to pardon me.

BOB: Let's go, let's go. Give me a hug and let the matter rest. (*There is a moment that seems sincere in which BOB and RAÚL embrace. Nevertheless, something remains in the air that makes it doubtful.*)

SARA: (*Pensively, SARA contemplates the scene. JUDY enters from the terrace, followed by SAM who is dressed as in the previous act. JUDY also is dressed as in the second act. But she is more lady-like, closer to Deborah Kerr than to Joan Collins. Make-up is reduced to a minimum; she wears no jewelry that would turn out to be showy and, possibly, the hairstyle has been arranged more discreetly. Anyway, she looks very elegant, wrapped in a mink stole.*)

Wrapping herself in the stole.) Oh! It's gotten chilly all
of a sudden! I feel like I'm going to freeze! (*Going to the
sofa, looking at* RAÚL.) Congratulations, Raúl! I assure
you that you've made me weep! It was so touching! So
moving!

JUDY: (JUDY *sits on the sofa and dries a tear with a theatrical
gesture, but then realizes that there is something odd in
the atmosphere.*) Something happened?

SARA: (*Evasive.*) No, no, nothing happened?

SAM: (*Embracing* RAÚL.) Great, brother! Congratulations, dear
boy!

JUDY: I was crying. Such sad and emotive scenes! Isn't it true,
Bob?

BOB: Stupendous.

JUDY: One doesn't know what to say ... One remains ...

SARA: Speechless.

JUDY: Yes ... With my mouth open.

RAÚL: You shower me with such praise.

BOB: Sara and I also think that it's a masterpiece.

JUDY: Of course, it is! The story of those four friends ...

SARA: Five friends ...

JUDY: Five friends ... united by a friendship so profound ...
that due to a misunderstanding, they are about to lose
their friendship ... I tell you, really, that it made me cry.

BOB: I hope that we are talking about the same play. I truthfully
find it excellent, Raúl, but I have to confess to you that
you didn't make me cry.

JUDY: But you are hardhearted, Bob! Look, you don't seem it.
Because even Sam, who at times is like a rock, was moved
... Isn't it true, Sam?

SARA: Yes, of course. It's that that theme, discrimination, hits
home.

BOB: Discrimination? But ... it seems that we are speaking about
a different play.

JUDY: What do you mean different? *Rules of Conduct,* isn't it?
Isn't it called that, Raúl?

SARA: I saw it as a comedy of errors, a little like Shakespeare ...
(*Somewhat disconcerted.*) And later we thought, Bob and
I, that it was a morality play, but a fashionable, modern
and entertaining one ... (*While she continues,* SARA *begins to approach* RAÚL *as if she were telling the story to
him.*) A lesson, a counsel, what the English call a "cautionary tale." My grandmother, who was very Victorian, a

little old lady from Philadelphia, always told me the story
of Rebecca, an intolerable and disobedient girl who did
nothing but slam doors, until one day she slammed the
door so hard that a bust fell down and killed her. Or the
one about Jaime, who ran away from school, went off to
the zoo, got into a cage, and was eaten by a lion ... I,
naturally, was frightened to death, and that's why I've always followed the rules of conduct ... I bet you anything,
Raúl, that you were told those stories too.

RAÚL: Yes, my mother told them to me, Sara, and the disobedient children always ended up in Hell. That's why I was
frightened to death too. (RAÚL *looks at her almost in a
prophetic way. For a moment the look is sustained, but
finally* SARA *diverts it and turns to the others.*)

SARA: Well, at this moment I don't know what to think. (RAÚL
*travels toward the glass door, opens it and exits to the ter-
race, the others follow him with their eyes.*)

SAM: It is probably that and much more, but I think that discrimination is the key to the play.

JUDY: For that reason, Sam wants to produce it immediately,
because that boy (*Referring to* RAÚL.) has suffered too
much. We must help him.

SARA: He doesn't look well. He has me very worried.

BOB: Perhaps that explains Raúl's state of mind.

SARA: And the ideas that El Tiznado has put in his head.

JUDY: El Tiznado?

SARA: That character with the submachine gun who appears at
the end of the act.

SAM: But that character has to go, because we can't have concessions on this. As for me, I don't negotiate with terrorists.
Not even on stage.

BOB: Then you think the same as us?

SAM: Yes, of course, that is understood.

BOB: We'll have to take radical measures.

SARA: With Raúl?

JUDY: With Raúl, no, that poor guy is incapable of harming anyone.

BOB: (*To* SARA.) With El Tiznado, he is the dangerous one. You
heard the coarse language he used.

SARA: Before you arrived ... But from Raúl's mouth. Raúl told
us later that he thought that he was eating him alive.

JUDY: Such an evil man!

SAM: Who?

JUDY: El Tiznado. Because to do that to anyone is a crime, but to do it to Raúl, who is such a fine, polite boy! And now, when success smiles at him. Fame.

SARA: Not to mention that El Tiznado has been writing part of the second act for him.

SAM: I already suspected something like that, because that second act seemed somewhat strange to me. That being the case, we'll have to change it. Raúl will have to do it over, without letting El Tiznado stick his nose in it.

JUDY: But that doesn't make sense.

SARA: We said that, Bob and I, but he doesn't agree. It is as if he had placed himself between each line in order to make him say all the opposite of what he thought. Even to make him say it to others. Because I have to confess to you that I suspected it from the moment I read that paragraph of Sara at the end of the second act, as if she were saying things that she didn't want to say. You understand? Well, I don't know if I have made myself clear.

JUDY: My God! What a mess! I thought that El Tiznado was an absent character who came alive at the end of the second act, but that he was not going to say what the others didn't want to have said.

BOB: It's evident that Raúl is going through a very serious crisis.

JUDY: (*To* BOB.) I thought that Raúl was writing the first act in collaboration with you because it seems a lot like what you write.

SAM: A little more "risqué," obviously.

JUDY: And that he was writing the second act in collaboration with Sara. And now it turns out that El Tiznado is the one who was writing the play.

SARA: Perhaps the simplest thing to do would be to eliminate everything that El Tiznado has said.

BOB: Raúl has been under a lot of pressure lately. He's not the first Hispanic who, after success, has shot himself in the head. (*Brief pause. They look at each other with heretofore unknown understanding.*)

JUDY: But that must be avoided.

BOB: At all cost.

SARA: Whatever it takes.

JUDY: (*To* SARA.) And you, what did you advise him?

SARA: Imagine! Get rid of El Tiznado. That he pull him out as if he were a thorn.

BOB: I wish to God that it were that, but I fear that it is much more serious. It's not going to be easy. Moreover, El Tiznado doesn't want to let go of him.

SAM: We'll have to send him a to shrink.

JUDY: I assure you, Sara, that I have an excellent one. He saved my life when I had those depressions and I got it into my head that I had to kill myself. Of course it costs an arm and a leg, but Sam will take care of the bill as long as Raúl doesn't remain twistcd. (*Laughs.*)

BOB: I don't believe that that will be necessary. Perhaps we can take charge of the matter, with a little of theatrical therapy. A couple of scenes, and that's it. What do you think, Sam?

SAM: I don't know, all of you know more than I about that.

BOB: But you are the one who puts up the cash.

SAM: Phooey! That scene will not cost a lot to produce, and if it is for Raúl's health, let's get going.

SARA: We will have to get rid of El Tiznado.

BOB: I warn you that he will resist.

JUDY: Who?

BOB: Both of them, Raúl and El Tiznado.

JUDY: I'm sure that Raúl will be willing to cooperate.

SAM: If it suits him. Because, truthfully, I don't know what he gets out of that damn, pathetic Tiznado.

BOB: The problem is that we don't know where he has him ... In his stomach ... In his heart ... In his brain ...

SAM: There are no problems in the stomach. The problems of digestion always are resolved with money. That is a laxative that always produces effect. (*Laughs.*)

BOB: The worst thing would be that the illness has extended throughout the body, because such resentment ... Or that it would have hidden inside the brain ... because ... in that case ... there would be no cure except to blow his brains out. (*Deadly silence.*)

JUDY: But, my God! How is it possible that Raúl has gotten this way? Haven't we been generous with him?

SARA: But we are Americans, Judy.

JUDY: So what? What else can we be?

SAM: Especially, I, with that name that you have given me.

JUDY: Life in the barrio must be terrible. Obviously, one is not informed of anything here. I, really ... Well, one knows what goes on from the newspapers, which is worse ... Or what we catch a glimpse of when we leave the theater ...

muggings ... robberies ... crimes ... rapes ... prostitu-
tion ... mariuana users ... cocaine users ... traffickers
... degenerates ... I don't even take the subway! Things
that one cannot even imagine, and others I don't even
want to find out! I, in short, prefer to remain ignorant.
And you, Sara?

SARA: That's it ... That's it ...

JUDY: And he is surrounded by such horrible people as El Tiznado, who doesn't do anything other than make it all
worse and frighten everybody.

SAM: Not to speak about discrimination. Because there are many
people who think they are better than everybody else, who
are up there and keep the better jobs, and, naturally, the
better salaries, which is the economic principle of discrimination, as if they, the Hispanics, were not as good as us.
Don't you believe that everyone thinks like us. Because,
although Bob and Sara might be a pair of liberals, and
Judy and I might be a pair of conservatives, when the
time comes, we believe that all men are equal.

JUDY: Well spoken, Sam!

SAM: I am not called Sam for nothing, isn't that true? Like that
uncle! (*Laughs.*)

BOB: What happens is that some men are more equal than others.

SARA: I am glad that we are not some cave-dwellers. Including
Sam, with all the money that he has, besides.

SAM: (*Festively.*) Sam's money had to come out at some point!
That couldn't fail, isn't it true? (*Cordial laughs.*)

BOB: Don't forget that there are many liberal millionaires in Mas-
sachusetts!

SAM: But I'm from New York, Bob!

BOB: There are also many liberal millionaires here, Sam!

SARA: I am glad that Sam has the guilt complex of the bourgeoisie!
Otherwise, he wouldn't give it away, nor would he tell you
where it was to find.

BOB: Someone has to put on the plays, Sara! (*Laughs. The glass
door opens and* RAÚL *appears.* SAM, *half-serious, half-
joking, points his finger at him, in a gesture that is nothing
but a tiresome joke.*)

SAM: "I want you," Raúl! As the uncle says! (*The laughter is frozen
when* SAM, BOB, SARA, *and* JUDY *focus upon* RAÚL's
*appearance, who seems to have gone to blows with someone
and whose clothes are all disheveled. In the sequence that
follows,* RAÚL *will speak to* EL TIZNADO *as if he were*

carrying him inside, and who, for his part, seems to strike him.)

RAÚL: But that can't be, Sam, because El Tiznado doesn't feel like it. (*To* EL TIZNADO.) Jesus, Tiznado, you've become such a bore! What a tanning you've given me! (*Doubles over, as if he had received a blow to the stomach.*) This is like carrying ... a bull ... to the slaughterhouse ... I'll have to kill him with a butcher knife! (*Receives blows as if connected to words from* EL TIZNADO.) What do you mean that I don't have courage, that I don't have the balls to do it! That to kill him one must be Tiznado like him, made of coal and fire, and that I'm a weakling and a coward because you've made me with a shitty paste! ... (*To* EL TIZNADO.) Pig, filthy, dirty mouth! You can't be among decent people, you can't speak like people speak, I can't even take you to the corner, do you realize? (*To the others.*) Nothing, he doesn't want to understand. I've told him a thousand times. To let me speak, that here one cannot go around spitting on everyone, that one has to say things backwards while thinking the opposite, in order to have them come out nicely and correctly. That people speak like that, and where they say "white," they mean "black," that one must follow instructions and obey the rules of conduct, the rules of the game ... Jesus, what more do you want? If this isn't a "cautionary tale," let God himself come and see it! (*Pauses.*) Nothing. Reasonable, logical, constructive! But he doesn't understand, damn it, he doesn't want to understand anything! That I am a puppet in your hands, a louse, I don't know! (*To* EL TIZNADO.) Fuck it, Tiznado, be reasonable! It would be better for all. For you, for me, for your brother, your cousin, and your pal, for the "mother" who gave birth to us! Little by little and one gets ahead. Do you understand? (*To the others.*) But no, he doesn't understand. Insults go! Insults come! Because he is stubborn and bitter with a tongue that corrodes as if it were acid. That I am a traitor, who abandoned my own people, went over to your side ... (*He too blows as if it were the voice of* EL TIZNADO *that insults him.*) "Traitor!" "Degenerate!" "Faggot!" (*He falls. Transition.*) That I have sold my mother and grandmother, that I have surrendered to the highest bidder as if I were a cheap whore, that when I say "Fuck you all, bastards!" it is nothing more than another shitty metaphor from the dung hill ... That all I want is silver, bank notes, dollars, money. I want you, Sam! I want you, Sam! (*To* EL TIZNADO, *firm.*) No, not that! I won't give you the machine gun! You won't come out again! You won't shoot! Get back, you bastard, get out of here! (*They struggle for the possession of the imaginary submachine gun.*) Give it to me, let it go! No, no! ... Give it to me, let it go! You're not going to create a massacre here! Give me the submachine gun! (RAÚL *wins, but* EL TIZNADO *hits him.*) Hit me, yes, hit me! Kick me harder! You beast! You beast! (*He falls. He gets up again.*) Don't think that you're going to win, Tiznado. You and I are lost. You fucked yourself, Tiznado! They fucked us! Use your head! Understand! But you can't reason it out! Because, throwing blind punches, what are we going to get? Don't you realize that first you must apply the chloroform, inject the anesthesia, so that they don't feel pain, and later stick the little knife in so that the enemy doesn't realize it until after the hemorrhage can't be contained? Are you so dense that you can't learn the technique of the perfect crime, of the murder whose murderer can't be discovered? I have been taught by masters, don't you realize? (*To the others.*) Isn't it so? Isn't that what you taught me? (*To* EL TIZNADO.) Fuck it, Tiznado, you bastard, I'm saying too much! It is you, you son of a bitch, who always makes me say what I shouldn't. Are you happy? Writing the word that I should have left out, that I should have stuck up my ass! Make me shut up, goddammit, make me shut up forever! So they can't fuck me! So they don't envy me! Hush! Hush! So that they don't cut me up like mincemeat! (*Seizing his throat, to* EL TIZNADO.) Take out the word for me, Tiznado! Eat it! Swallow it! Chew it with your teeth! Rip it with your fangs! (*To the others.*) Because I don't want to say what I shouldn't ... Because I don't want to say what I should keep to myself ... Because I should only say what you want to hear ... The words that you've dictated to me. Swine, degenerates! (*Transition.*) Do you see? I don't know what I say, because El Tiznado comes and twists himself around my tongue) like this! Like this! (*Like a crazy man, he makes grotesque contortions with his tongue.*) And he entangles it like a serpent, he bites it like a scorpion, and he twists it, and he messes it up!!!

He stings! He poisons! And I want to be quiet, but, shit, he comes to fuck me over, and he denounces me, he uncovers me, and gets me sent to the firing squad, to your firing squad, because it is you here who are the boss, because you could be sent to your death too, don't think you can't. (*Pauses, to* EL TIZNADO.) Jesus, Tiznado, isn't that what you wanted? To make me a villain in front of all these people, wasn't it? To give me the *coup de grace*! They shoot horses, don't they? To destroy me. Isn't it true? (*To them.*) And now what, the other beating, no? (*To* EL TIZNADO.) Look, Tiznado, look how they're enjoying this! The unexpected jumped up, I said what I had to say, I spit it out. So what? But do you think that this is going to be put on stage anywhere with all these fucks and shits? Stupid! Cretin! Product of bad seed! You've never learned the lesson. You're an ignoramus! Yes, you said it, so what? Now you are fucked. We are fucked! Do you think that people like to be insulted and kicked in the ass? Do you like it? Shit, look at yourself, Tiznado! Your ass is raw from so many kicks you've gotten in it! Fuck you, stupid! Spittle of shit! An outlet, no? A catharsis? They'll leave you at birth! (RAÚL *gets up. He turns. He looks at* SAM. *He extends his hand, palm up, as if he were asking for something.*)

RAÚL: I want you Sam! I want you, Sam! (SAM *takes out a pistol that he has hidden in his chest. He gives it to* RAÚL.)

ALL MINUS RAÚL: (*From this moment on* JUDY, SARA, BOB, *and* SAM *will form a choral group that will repeat the following in crescendo.*) "Kill him! Destroy him! Finish him off once and for all!" (*That is repeated several times, rhythmically while* RAÚL, *facing the audience, puts the pistol to his temple. The tension increases, until a point in which it appears such that it is prolonged too much, as when a character forgets to enter on stage and the actors are forced to repeat some lines. Finally the doorbell rings, they repeat the refrain as if to drown out the sound, but* RAÚL, *who was waiting for the bell to ring, removes the pistol from his temple, puts it on the table near the telephone and goes to open the door. It is* MARÍA, *she wears an evening gown but a short one, pretty vulgar. It is hard to say whether she is a decent but pretentious girl, or if she is a prostitute from 42nd street.*)

RAÚL: María!

MARÍA: Raúl! (MARÍA *and* RAÚL *kiss one another* SARA, JUDY, SAM, *and* BOB *"Stop acting," and they fall on the sofa, on the armchair, or on some chair, tired from the tension of the previous scene.*)

JUDY: Blessed God, I thought that that girl would never arrive. But that entrance is off. She'll have to do it again. For a moment, I started to think that Raúl was going to have to shoot himself, but as Bob had staged the scene and he doesn't like to kill anyone in front of the audience, that calmed me down.

BOB: I didn't stage the scene, Judy.

JUDY: And who staged it?

BOB: I thought Sam was staging it, because he was the one who had the gun.

SARA: I was shaking, because I got it into my head that El Tiznado was staging that scene.

JUDY: Please, Sara! I can't believe the things you come up with! That would have been too much. (*Looking at* RAÚL, *who continues hugging* MARÍA *at the entrance by the door.*) Poor Raúl ... They've made him like Spencer Tracy in *The Strange Case of Dr. Jekyl and Mr. Hyde.* I am glad we have a happy ending here ... I don't know how he manages to keep up his spirit!

SAM: The boy needs to relax.

JUDY: (*Looking at* RAÚL *and* MARÍA *who continue more or less the same.*) Yes, now I see it. (*Laughs.*)

SARA: (*Watching the time.*) But look what time it is! If we don't go, we'll miss the Tonys. (*They stand up and prepare to leave.* RAÚL *approaches with* MARÍA. *He leads her by the hand.*)

RAÚL: One moment, please. I want to introduce you to my fiance, Miss María Pérez. We're going to be married next month. (*The relevant introductions are made with ritual expressions and manifestations, kisses, embraces: "Charmed," "Very pleased," "The pleasure is mine," "Congratulations," etc. Here the director and the actors may take the liberties that they wish.*)

SARA: But how well you kept it to yourself, Raúl. What a surprise you've given us!

JUDY: María! Such a pretty name! It seems like a page taken from *West Side Story*!

BOB: And how long have you known each other?

RAÚL: Oh, for a long time! We've been engaged since high school.

SAM: The girl next door.
SARA: (*To* RAÚL.) But your mother must be delighted that you're
    marrying a girl from the barrio.
RAÚL: Yes, my mother is enchanted with María (*To* MARÍA.) Isn't
    it true, my darling?
MARÍA: Yes, it's true, Raúl's mother is very nice.
JUDY: (*To* MARÍA, *referring to* RAÚL.) I assure you that you're
    getting a jewel. Our Golden Boy! Our William Holden,
    as Barbara Stanwyck would say.
SARA: Our Robert Redford.
JUDY: I assure you, María, that if you delay one more minute,
    Raúl will have to blow his brains out.
SAM: You'll be a widow without having gotten to the altar! (*Laugh-
    ter due to Sam's new "joke."*)
MARÍA: It's difficult to get a taxi at this hour.
JUDY: (*To* RAÚL.) Honestly, for a moment there you had me
    worried as if really ...
RAÚL: And I was thinking the same thing. That Sam had taken
    it seriously and had given me the pistol so that I would
    really blow my brains out. I assure you that for an instant
    it came into my head and I thought that I had to do it.
    And what is worse, that you wanted me to do it.
BOB: But you knew that María had to arrive at any moment.
RAÚL: Yes, it's true. But I even began to think that María had
    been playing along with you so that I ... so that I would
    kill El Tiznado.
JUDY: Who, of course, probably is alive and well.
BOB: (*Brotherly.*) But I am sure that now you feel better, right?
RAÚL: Yes, I feel calmer. Thanks, Bob.
SAM: Come on, let's go, let's go, it's getting late!
SARA: (*Kissing* MARÍA, *saying goodbye.*) Congratulations, María!
    Until death do you part.
BOB: Ok, let's go!
RAÚL: You people go ahead. We won't all fit in Sam's car.
    And I have to clean up a little, because my clothes are
    a mess. We will take a taxi and see you at the award cer-
    emony. (*More goodbyes, everyone kisses* MARÍA. JUDY
    and SARA *kiss* RAÚL, *while* BOB *and* SAM *hug him. It
    is all a little exaggerated, especially as one realizes that
    they are going to be reunited again a few minutes later.
    They exit.* RAÚL *closes the door and with a gesture of
    exhaustion leans on it.*)
RAÚL: I thought that they'd never leave!

MARÍA: You must be exhausted.

RAÚL: Exhausted is the least of it. El Tiznado gave me a stomping that nearly killed me. Sometimes I don't know what I'm going to do with him. I believe that I'm not going to be able to continue. I am glad that since you arrived on the scene he has left me alone. He is quiet when I'm with you. But if he returns ... I don't know what I'm going to do. (*Referring to the others.*) What do they seem to you?

MARÍA: A bunch of swine ... A bunch of hypocrites ... a bunch of charlatans ... a bunch of degenerates ...

RAÚL: (*Embracing her.*) Didn't I tell you? I knew that you'd like them. (*They kiss.*) Why were you so late?

MARÍA: Why did you ask me if I was playing along with them?

RAÚL: I don't know. It occurred to me all of a sudden that that was also possible. All is possible in New York, isn't it?

MARÍA: Why didn't you blow their brains out?

RAÚL: El Tiznado?

MARÍA: No, them.

RAÚL: Imagine, what a blood bath. No, no that would have been in bad taste, very disagreeable. Besides, they would have put me in prison.

MARÍA: Then, shall we go? (RAÚL *bolts the door. Surprised.*) But I thought that we were going to leave ...

RAÚL: You're not going to tell me that at this point you believe all you hear and all you see.

MARÍA: But the Tony, Raúl. Think what that prize means to you.

RAÚL: Life is a dream, María. Don't make me laugh. I've invented all that so that they would go away and I could stay behind with you.

MARÍA: For a moment I believed that it was true. That we had known each other in high school, that I had been your girlfriend my whole life, and that next month I was going to marry you.

RAÚL: *Life Is a Dream.* (RAÚL *kisses her,* MARÍA *separates herself.*)

MARÍA: El Tiznado is going to become furious with all this. Why don't you let him go Raúl? Why don't you rest and blow his brains out? Why don't you give him the *coup de grace*? (RAÚL *kisses her with fury, as if he were trying to cover with his mouth what she is saying.*)

RAÚL: Be quiet, be quiet.

MARÍA: I'm afraid, Raúl. I'm very afraid. (*They kiss each other passionately.*)

RAÚL: I have a surprise for you. I've ordered the bedroom covered with mirrors as you asked me at one time. It will
seem to you the dream of *Las Meninas*. (RAÚL *drags*
MARÍA *toward the bedroom; the stage is slowly darkened,
until all is in shadows. One spotlight falls upon the table
where the telephone is, and where* RAÚL *has left the pistol.
The toilet is heard flushing on top of which the ringing of
the telephone is also heard. At two voices, they form a dialogue that is a grotesque counterpoint. The water stops being heard, but the buzz of the telephone continues ringing,
RAÚL leaves the bedroom, barefoot and with the bathrobe
he wore in the first act.* MARÍA's *voice is heard shouting
to him from the bedroom, it stops him in the center of the
stage.*)

MARÍA: (*Shouting from outside.*) Don't answer, Raúl! Don't answer! Perhaps it's El Tiznado! Let it ring! (RAÚL *goes
up to the telephone. He goes to take it, but he sees the pistol. He stops. He takes the pistol. Slowly he puts it to his
temple. He turns around to face the audience. He shoots.*)

The curtain falls while the telephone rings on.

Birds Without Wings

by

Renaldo Ferradas

Birds Without Wings

About the Author

Renaldo Eugenio Ferradas was born in Camagüey, Cuba in 1932. He grew-up in Oriente, Cuba and in New York City, where he arrived at age 15 in 1948. He had been acting in school productions since age six, giving him an early experience with the theater. Ferradas received his undergraduate education at Fordham University, obtaining his bachelors degree in 1979 with majors in Spanish and Comparative Literature. He went on to earn his Masters in Performance Studies from New York University in 1984. Ferradas's involvement with the theater as an adult dates from 1970 when he wrote the plays "Divine Madness" and "Beginnings and Ends." In 1972 he composed "The Burial of Jesus," followed by "Cuba" and "The Monkey's Garden" in 1973, "The Puzzle Game" in 1975. That year "A Crock of Daisies" was produced for the Fordham University Festival of the Arts at Lincoln Center. And in the same venue in 1977 he produced "Teatro." Diogenes Grassal directed in 1979 Ferradas's "Love Is Not for Sale" at La Mama Theater. In 1979–80 Ferradas received a Fellowship for playwriting for his play "La Visionaria." Also in 1979 a reading of "Betrayal in Havana" took place at the Puerto Rican Traveling Theater. In 1980 he presented two dramatic writing workshops, one at the East Orange Correction Facility and another at the Drew Hamilton Community Center. A year later Marcel Fidji directed a reading and a workshop of "The Visionary" at the Carter Theater in New York, and Henry Davis directed the Spanish version for New Dramatists in New York. In 1982 Ferradas had a brief acting interlude: he played the role of The Magician in Michael Kirby's off-Broadway production of "Incidents in Renaissance Venice," which was videotaped for South Korean Television. In 1984 his play "La Visionaria" was produced at the Anspacher Theater for the Public Theater's Festival Latino. In 1985 he wrote "Letter from America," followed by "The Cuban Lady" in 1986 and "A Million Dollar Whore" in 1987. That same year he wrote "Stone Flower," and in 1990, in addition to writing "In Search of an Empire, Hernán Cortés in Cuba," he conducted a series of creative writing and playwriting workshops at the New York Public Library. He has published *La puta del millón* (Madrid: Betania, 1989) and *La visionaria* (Madrid: Betania, 1990).

The mainstay of Ferradas is his teaching career at George Washington High School in Manhattan where he teaches Spanish.

But he has also distinguished himself as a songwriter of both music and lyrics. He is the author of over forty songs, five of which were published by Peer International Organization and they were also recorded; others were published by Reyno Music Publishing, Inc. in sheet music. With Carmen Montejo, the first lady of the Cuban stage (working in Mexico and New York), Ferradas founded in 1973 El Teatro de las Américas Unidas in New York. He is a member of Latin American Writers Institute, the Dramatist Guild, The Authors League of America, BMI and the UFT.

"Birds Without Wings" was written while Ferradas was staying in Caracas over the Christmas holidays in 1987. He attributes the creative ideas for the play to his early teaching experience in elementary school in the South Bronx. Ferradas was puzzled by the knowledge of suffering exhibited by his students at such a tender age. "Many times—he remarked in a letter to the editor of this anthology— ... they would share with me their visions of the world, their surroundings, their promiscuous family lines, and the hopeless future." Ferradas found a worse case in the secondary schools, where the adolescents had lost contact with their parents's cultural background and had disconnected themselves from their inherited identity, wanting little to do with them. For these reasons he was able to create a play which had great echo in his students's souls. At the Washingtonians, a socio-cultural club which he founded at George Washington High School in 1987 and for which he serves as faculty advisor, he presented Act II, scene IV in 1989. This followed a reading of the play at the City University of New York Graduate Center at the ALTA 11th Annual conference in 1988.

The play relates the story of Carlos who is 18 years old and Claudia who is 16, teenagers both with less than exemplary home situations. He, orphaned and exploited, comes together with her, instrumentalized by her parents to increase the family income by selling crack. Their first contact is typical of New York's underside: he tries to snatch her purse, which contains crack and the earnings from selling it to her peers at school. After the intervention of the police, her parents convince them that it was all a misunderstanding. The teenagers begin to feel attracted to each other and their roles take stage turns in the already absurd drama of their lives. The search for salvation lies in their mutual attraction, but it depends in great measure on the destruction of their parents or guardians, from whom they receive abuse. This is the major cause of their generational separation. "Birds Without Wings" is without doubt a drama for our times.

CHARACTERS

CLAUDIA, a sixteen year old girl. She is taller than Carlos.

CARLOS, a boy almost eighteen years old at the beginning of the play. At the end, he has already reached that age.

SERGEANT MEDINA, a man in his forties.

MAURICIO, a man in his forties.

ELENA, a woman in her mid-thirties.

FRANCES, a woman in her fifties.

None of the above characters in this play should appear to be a pure descendant of the Caucasian race.

ACT I

.... Scene I ....

At a subway station in Washington Heights. CARLOS hides behind a column, waiting for CLAUDIA. She enters the train's platform. The sound of an approaching train is heard. CARLOS runs toward the girl and tries to snatch her shoulder bag. The train stops at the station. CLAUDIA screams. CARLOS pushes her against the wall, covers her mouth with his hand and brings his face close to hers, giving the impression that they are kissing. The train leaves the station. Once again, CARLOS tries to snatch her shoulder bag.

CLAUDIA: What do you want?

CARLOS: You know what I want.

CLAUDIA: If you take my books, I'll have to pay for them at the end of the semester. You know how strict they are at school with these things.

CARLOS: Let me have the other thing.

CLAUDIA: I know who you are. I've seen you bothering the teachers in the hallways.

CARLOS: Get ready to die. (CARLOS *pulls* CLAUDIA *with all his strength. He pushes her next to the edge of the platform where the trains pass.*)

CLAUDIA: I lied. I've never seen you.

CARLOS: Son of a bitch, give me what you sell and I'll leave you alone.

CLAUDIA: Mother fucker! Shit thief.

CARLOS: Why don't you scream?

CLAUDIA: Because I don't want to hurt you.

CARLOS: Then, why did you scream a while ago?

CLAUDIA: I thought you wanted to kill me?

CARLOS: Don't be an idiot!

CLAUDIA: Common thief!

CARLOS: Scream and call the police so they'll find out what you're carrying in your bag. (*They struggle. A train approaches. CARLOS pushes CLAUDIA toward the rails. She holds*

onto him. A policeman enters. CARLOS *snatches* CLAU-
DIA's *bag and runs. The policeman opens his arms and
grabs* CARLOS *by the neck.* CLAUDIA *comes up to* CAR-
LOS *and takes her bag away from him. The policeman
pushes* CARLOS *toward the wall and searches the young-
ster. He speaks into his walkie-talkie.*)

SERGEANT MEDINA: This is Sergeant Medina. Send back-up
to the 181st Street IRT station. Only one of the elevators
is working. Hurry up.

CLAUDIA: Don't do that, Sergeant Medina. It was a lover's quarrel. (CLAUDIA *approaches* CARLOS *and pats him on
the back.*) I told you that, by force, I was not going to
kiss you. I'm free and you can't force me to give into
your whims. Anyway, let's make this clear, you and I are
through. Goodbye. (CLAUDIA *starts to walk away.*)

SERGEANT MEDINA: Where do you think you're going? The
two of you come with me to the precinct. I have to make
a statement about what happened.

CARLOS: Don't be so strict, Sergeant Medina. We love each other
very much and, because we're so madly in love, we're
always fighting.

SERGEANT MEDINA: (*To* CARLOS.) What is your name?

CARLOS: Legally, I don't have to answer any of your questions.
As soon as we arrive at the precinct, I want a lawyer.

SERGEANT MEDINA: Young lady, what's your boyfriend's name?

CLAUDIA: You're very curious, Sir.

CARLOS: Don't tell him my name.

CLAUDIA: Don't you either. Don't allow this sergeant to use you
in his search for rewards. How dare he want to know our
names!

SERGEANT MEDINA: Shut up. At the precinct, you'll tell me
everything (*Blackout.*)

.... Scene II ....

Two hours later. At the police station. CLAUDIA's *parents
talk to* SERGEANT MEDINA. *Both of them speak with a Spanish
accent.* CARLOS *sits with his back to the audience.* CLAUDIA
stands a few feet away.

MAURICIO: In our family, we never had any problems with the
law.

ELENA: Who could have thought of that, Mauricio?

MAURICIO: Elena, let me talk. Things have to be straightened out.

ELENA: Everybody knows that we are decent, hard-working people.

CLAUDIA: And next week for Easter vacation, the two of you are taking me to Disney World in Florida. Right, Papá?

MAURICIO: Why did yo get involved in this problem, dear?

CLAUDIA: (*Pointing to* CARLOS.) He started everything.

SERGEANT MEDINA: They were struggling over your daughter's shoulder bag.

CARLOS: That's not true.

CLAUDIA: Sergeant, you have no right to get involved in sweethearts' quarrels.

ELENA: How many times do I have to tell you not to get involved with the rabble.

CARLOS: Lady, I'd advise you to hold your tongue.

CLAUDIA: Mother, don't say anything more. You're always making mistakes.

SERGEANT MEDINA: Your daughter has a boyfriend and she doesn't even know his first name.

CLAUDIA: We take a class together. We've met recently.

MAURICIO: (*Jokingly.*) And because of jealousy, did you want to throw him in front of the train?

ELENA: Sergeant Medina, you know how young people are nowadays. We can't take them seriously.

MAURICIO: The boy carries a five-inch blade.

CARLOS: If I don't defend myself, who is going to do it, Sergeant?

SERGEANT MEDINA: If you had used that blade on the girl, she'd be in a hospital or at the morgue.

CARLOS: Some imagination, Sergeant!

CLAUDIA: How could he kill me, if we are in love?

SERGEANT MEDINA: Carlos Williams, come here, come closer.
        (CARLOS *stands up and walks towards* SERGEANT ME-DINA'*s desk.*)

CARLOS: What am I accused of?

MAURICIO: Of nothing, my son. Leave my angel in peace.

CLAUDIA: Father, stop talking silly. I'm old enough to know how to defend myself. Don't you see? I'm taller than he is.

ELENA: I don't know why, but you have always liked boys that are shorter than you.

CARLOS: Like Lord Nelson or the great Napoleon. I have the same high intelligence as both of them.

SERGEANT MEDINA: Stop being a clown, Carlos Williams. If these people place any charges against you, you'll go to jail until that grandmother of yours shows up with bail so you can put your legs out onto the streets again.

ELENA: Oh, my daughter! Why do you get involved with such trash?

CARLOS: I'm going to start singing.

CLAUDIA: Not yet, Carlitos, be patient. Mother, control yourself. You have no right to insult my fiancé.

CARLOS: Kiss me now, my pretty girl.

CLAUDIA: Show some respect for my parents.

CARLOS: Sergeant, Claudia and I will get married and you will be our best man. That I promise.

ELENA: My daughter is too young to get married, young man.

MAURICIO: Maybe later, but now she's only sixteen yours old.

CARLOS: Next month I'll be eighteen and I'll graduate from high school, and like a bird I will fly around the world with Claudia by my side.

CLAUDIA: He's delirious, Mother, don't listen to him.

SERGEANT MEDINA: In case you ever need me for anything, you'll know where to find me. Remember that, Carlitos. (*Blackout.*)

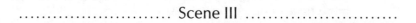 Scene III

Three days later at the same subway station as Scene I. CLAUDIA is waiting for a train. CARLOS enters. He carries a shoulder bag with his books. He approaches CLAUDIA. She pretends not to see him and seeks protection behind a column. A subway train approaches and stops. There is the sound of people getting in and out of the train. CLAUDIA as well as CARLOS stay on the platform. CARLOS whistles a tune and walks away. She looks at him with impatience. She follows him, steps in front of him, and looks him in the face.

CLAUDIA: Aren't you going to try to rob me today?

CARLOS: Do you believe me to be a common thief?

CLAUDIA: I'm carrying the same shoulder bag.

CARLOS: But you're no longer selling what you used to sell.

CLAUDIA: Only for Easter week.

CARLOS: Do you believe in that?

CLAUDIA: No, but my mother is very religious.

CARLOS: When are you planning to reopen your business?

CLAUDIA: Everything will go back to normal after Easter Sunday.

CARLOS: After that date, beware of me.

CLAUDIA: And now?

CARLOS: Leave me alone.

CLAUDIA: Why did you look at me with a snaky look in your eye?

CARLOS: The only snake I have is not in my eye. Do you want
     to see it?

CLAUDIA: I've never seen those things.

CARLOS: At your age, with those things?

CLAUDIA: How old do you think I am?

CARLOS: Old enough not to be so dumb.

CLAUDIA: Why do you insult me?

CARLOS: The truth is painful, isn't it?

CLAUDIA: Tell me anything you like. From you, I expect the
     worse.

CARLOS: Why did you approach me?

CLAUDIA: From a distance, I thought that Sergeant Medina was
     watching us.

CARLOS: Liar! He's not around. Why did you approach me?

CLAUDIA: I wanted to be sure that you were not going to mug
     me.

CARLOS: What I did was not against you. It bothered me to know
     that you are competing with me. As a pretty girl, you sell
     more than I do.

CLAUDIA: You have your clients. I have mine. There are enough
     for both of us.

CARLOS: My grandmother is sick. I need the money.

CLAUDIA: If I don't take enough money home, my parents punish
     me.

CARLOS: Great! That's wonderful news!

CLAUDIA: Why are you so happy?

CARLOS: Because it's not true that your parents love you as much
     as I thought they did there at the police station.

CLAUDIA: Love? They love me indeed! I'm sure.

CARLOS: What happened to your trip to Disney World?

CLAUDIA: That was my own invention to put off Sergeant Me-
     dina. But my parents love me very much, it's true!

CARLOS: That is a lie. What do they want for you? That you be
     taken to jail for selling drugs? That someone could mug
     or kill you for business competition?

CLAUDIA: I was born here.

CARLOS: Me, too.

CLAUDIA: We're Americans and we live in a free country; so all of us can do as we please here.

CARLOS: Laissez-faire?

CLAUDIA: I don't speak French.

CARLOS: If you want me to, I'll teach you.

CLAUDIA: What does that "laissez-faire" mean?

CARLOS: That here we can do any kind of business and nobody can do anything against us.

CLAUDIA: That's what I said.

CARLOS: That is a concern between the government and the people, but with me things are different.

CLAUDIA: Why?

CARLOS: Because I'm able to do anything.

CLAUDIA: Would you throw me in front of the train?

CARLOS: I would eliminate anybody who competes with me. It has nothing to do with you, that I swear!

CLAUDIA: If you swear, it's because you are a believer. Do you ever go the church?

CARLOS: When I was a child, I used to go with my mother. Now, I never go.

CLAUDIA: Why not?

CARLOS: Because my grandmother never goes to church.

CLAUDIA: Is she paralyzed?

CARLOS: Far from it, pretty girl. Instead of going to church, she goes to Atlantic City.

CLAUDIA: She switched religions, what a pity!

CARLOS: She switched the church for card games. (*A train approaches.*)

CARLOS: Will you come with me?

CLAUDIA: Where would you take me?

CARLOS: I'm going to the South Bronx.

CLAUDIA: I was born there.

CARLOS: I'm not asking where you were born, I'm inviting you to come with me.

CLAUDIA: Am I your hostage?

CARLOS: A hostage, of your own accord. (*The subway train stops. The two youngsters board it. Blackout.*)

.... Scene IV ....

4:00 P.M. CLAUDIA *and* CARLOS *climb what is left of what appear to be stairs of the skeleton of a burned-out building. When they reach the fourth floor,* CARLOS *waits for* CLAUDIA *who follows a few steps behind him. She is short of breath.*

CLAUDIA: How much further do we have to go?

CARLOS: We've arrived. It's here.

CLAUDIA: There?

CARLOS: Yes, it's here. Come up. With three steps or four stepping stones, you will arrive at what is my holy place. Come in. Make yourself at home.

CLAUDIA: Do you live here?

CARLOS: As a child, I grew up here.

CLAUDIA: Even though I can't see it, I can still smell the smoke and feel the fire.

CARLOS: I carry the fire inside my skin. That fire that spread out inside this house to destroy everything.

CLAUDIA: I'm afraid.

CARLOS: I'm sorry. I didn't mean to scare you. They were here.

CLAUDIA: Who are you talking about?

CARLOS: My parents.

CLAUDIA: Please, don't turn yourself into Frankenstein.

CARLOS: Don't you remember anything from your childhood?

CLAUDIA: The only thing I remember was the day that mother went to the market and left me alone in the house, and I tried to fry some eggs and I burned my right hand. Look, there's still a scar from the burn.

CARLOS: Your skin was destroyed and your body was able to recreate the cells that were needed to grow new skin over the burned skin. My parents were never recreated. They went away once and for all. The last I remember of them is in this room. (*By this time, they are already inside the shell of what once was an apartment. Through the window at a distance, we can see burned-out or abandoned buildings.*) Mother and father were sleeping in a king-size bed. I was sleeping in the other room next to my older brother. (*He walks toward the hallway and points out the door frame.*) Here.

CLAUDIA: How lucky you are to have a brother. I'm alone!

CARLOS: I'm alone, too.

CLAUDIA: Where is your brother?

CARLOS: When smoke filled the room, the flames turned the heavy bricks into an oven. My brother quickly took me out of the bed where I was sleeping. He carried me in his arms with such tenderness that, still to this day, I carry it inside myself. Never again have I felt so much love. That's the last I remember of them. Later on, I lived in a vague silence of a solitude marked by interviews of social workers, of unknown people, people who were unable to tell me if my name was Carlos or Charles. All of it was very strange.

CLAUDIA: Who do you live with?

CARLOS: With my grandmother.

CLAUDIA: Oh! Then you're not as lonely as you pretend to be.

CARLOS: I'm lonelier than what you might imagine

CLAUDIA: Do you come here often?

CARLOS: This is the first time that I have come here in ten years. I thought I had forgotten how to get here. But you gave me the incentive to do this.

CLAUDIA: I?

CARLOS: Yes, you. When I saw you at the subway station, inside of me I felt a very strong desire. Suddenly, I found that I needed ties that would bring us together. I realized that probably you had an awful image of me. I wanted to wipe out those bad thoughts.

CLAUDIA: Why did you try to mug me?

CARLOS: You never looked at me.

CLAUDIA: I never saw you.

CARLOS: That's why I did it. I had to show you that I was alive, that I was not a piece of stone or a floor one stands on, the one that keeps us from falling, and the one we rarely see. We walk without knowing the color or texture of what keeps us going.

CLAUDIA: I go to school to study. If yo had watched me, you would have realized that I never look at anyone in particular.

CARLOS: You stare at the teacher with the big moustache. You're always looking at him.

CLAUDIA: I like him.

CARLOS: Why? Because he knows more than you and I?

CLAUDIA: He's our teacher.

CARLOS: (*Touching his genitals.*) In the field of masturbation, I know more than he does.

CLAUDIA: Stop being fresh with me.

CARLOS: Do you want a little piece?

CLAUDIA: I'd give my virginity to the man, only to the man who would love me.

CARLOS: Why?

CLAUDIA: That teacher with the big moustache did. (*She hesitates.*) He told us in one of his classes. He told us that the body is something sacred, that we have to be aware of whom we share it with. That it could harm us if we gave ourselves to the first man who asked for it.

CARLOS: The son of a bitch was able to convince you.

CLAUDIA: I think he's right. Sex has a meaning when there is love. Without it, we'd stop being human.

CARLOS: (*Grabbing his genitals.*) What do I do with this?

CLAUDIA: Do what you've been doing until now. (CARLOS *approaches without control. He is possessed by desire. He embraces* CLAUDIA *and tries to kiss her. She pushes him away.*)

CLAUDIA: You're an animal, a donkey! That's what you are. Leave me alone. Don't fuck with my virginity, you son of a bitch.

CARLOS: If you insult me, I'll kill you.

CLAUDIA: Another death, Carlitos?

CARLOS: Yes, another. (CLAUDIA *begins to run like a gazelle followed by a tiger. At full speed, she runs down to the ground floor.* CARLOS *runs a few steps behind her. When they exit to the street,* CLAUDIA *keeps on running.* CARLOS *stops.*)

CARLOS: Claudia! Claudia, Claudia, don't leave. Claudia, I was only kidding. It was a joke. (CLAUDIA *stops in front of a street light. The noise of car motors and horns takes over the stage.* CARLOS *takes advantage of the occasion to get closer. From a short distance he talks to* CLAUDIA.) Forgive me, Claudia. I've brought you down to my parents old apartment because I love you.

CLAUDIA: Love me? What you want to do is to shake it, to masturbate it, son of a bitch, satyr!

CARLOS: Why don't you try to understand me? I'm alone, Claudia.

CLAUDIA: Get the love of your grandmother.

CARLOS: That old woman is not related to me. She gets paid for giving me shelter. For the last ten years she's been living off me. I'm her only subsistence. When I graduate next June, I'll be eighteen and I'll leave that apartment. That damn apartment! Claudia, listen, Claudia.

CLAUDIA: (CARLOS *still a few steps away.*) I don't believe you.

CARLOS: You'll have to believe me. She's already searching for a way to find another victim to take my place when I leave. In that house there is nothing to eat, there's nothing there. As a child, I went hungry and I was cold. She's into gambling and that's how she spends all the money she gets. Do you understand why I have to sell drugs?

CLAUDIA: I sell them to help my parents.

CARLOS: I do it for my own help.

CLAUDIA: I'm not as lucky as you. I have no one to trust.

CARLOS: Whom do I have to trust?

CLAUDIA: Your brother, talk to him.

CARLOS: He's dead.

CLAUDIA: Another of your inventions.

CARLOS: I swear that I'm not lying to you. When my brother, Julio, realized that the fire was engulfing us inside the apartment, he placed a blanket around my body and in his arms he brought me down by the fire escape stairs. He left me in the hands of some people who had gathered to watch the fire. With love, he looked me in the eyes and with tenderness he kissed my forehead and said, "Don't worry, I'm going into get our parents," and he never returned.

CLAUDIA: I don't understand why you have brought me here to this place so filled with unpleasant memories, with horrible things. I don't understand you.

CARLOS: If you could understand how much I like you, would you understand me?

CLAUDIA: Liking me? For sure, you are comparing me with a dummy in a window, one which you could use at will without any interest about what that dummy, if alive, would say.

CARLOS: Do you want me to punish myself because I wanted to give my body what I like? Claudia, I'm no masochist.

CLAUDIA: If we're to become friends, you must learn to control yourself. (CARLOS *realizes that there is an opportunity to regain* CLAUDIA's *friendship and to conquer her and he takes advantage of the situation, as they approach the grade school he attended, to change the conversation.*)

CARLOS: (*Pointing toward the distance.*) There, it's that school, I went to first and second grades. At that time, this neighborhood was populated by families, by workers like my father. We had many friends. Those were my best years. Father and mother were alive. I was going to school. My teachers were interested in me. They showed respect and love. At school there were monthly parties. We had balloon parties, funny hat parties, and sometimes famous people from the world of art. Musicians and singers came to entertain us. The teachers used to participate in the end of the school year like it was today. One time mother made a clown costume for the principal of the school. He jumped and jumped like a monkey. Life was so different from what it is today.

CLAUDIA: It must have been. Then, you didn't know how to masturbate.

CARLOS: I started doing it when I was four of five. When did you start?

CLAUDIA: I don't do those things.

CARLOS: Let me see your right hand.

CLAUDIA: I'm left-handed.

CARLOS: You're a devil.

CLAUDIA: Damn you!

CARLOS: Kiss me.

CLAUDIA: I will only kiss the man who offers me eternal fidelity.

CARLOS: Do you want to come with me?

CLAUDIA: Where do yo want to take me?

CARLOS: To Hunt's Point.

CLAUDIA: What is there?

CARLOS: A beautiful beach where my parents used to take me when I was a child. Today, I feel melancholic, I wish to share with you my innermost secrets. Come with me. (*The youngsters hold hands and walk. During their walk, they encounter burnt out and rundown buildings and vacant lots. By the entrance of some of the buildings, cardboard women, human size, appear. They are wearing overcoats. When* CLAUDIA *and* CARLOS *approach, these women open their coats and appear totally naked.*)

CLAUDIA: Your parents brought you here?

CARLOS: It wasn't like this then.

CLAUDIA: My parents are right when they say that everything has changed.

CARLOS: (*Pointing to the beach.*) There was never shit floating in the sea.

CLAUDIA: Don't be gross.

CARLOS: I don't disrespect you, Claudia. Look and tell me what you see. What do you see floating out there?

CLAUDIA: The sun is setting, but I swear that it's shit on the beach. Without any doubt, it is shit.

CARLOS: If you say so, I can't argue with you.

CLAUDIA: It's an ugly word.

CARLOS: It seems ugly to you because it reminds you of the beast inside you.

CARLOS: I think you're right.

CARLOS: Then why did you call me an animal a while ago? Why did you call me a donkey?

CLAUDIA: Because you don't know how to control your instincts.

CARLOS: Then for my next reincarnation, I'll ask the universe to send me back as a horse or a panther. they fuck whenever they feel like it.

CLAUDIA: You're so gross!

CARLOS: Hypocrite.

CLAUDIA: (*Looking at her watch.*) I have to go. It's later than I thought.

CARLOS: What are you going to do for Easter week?

CLAUDIA: Pray for your soul.

CARLOS: Liar!

CLAUDIA: I have the soul of a nun.

CARLOS: If that's true, then stop masturbating.

CLAUDIA: How did yo know?

CARLOS: (*Grabbing her left hand.*) Mother of God! You're growing a callous! (CARLOS *and* CLAUDIA *burst out laughing as they embrace. Blackout.*)

.... Scene V ....

At FRANCES WASHINGTON's *apartment. She is talking on the phone with* SERGEANT MEDINA. CARLOS, *wearing a baseball uniform, has a bat in his hands as he makes believe that he is playing ball.*

FRANCES: As I told you, Sergeant Medina, remember that the girl is innocent. She is a mere victim of her parents. The poor little one must be ashamed to be a witness to so much lack of respect for society, for everything that is part of our American traditions. I learned about it through a boy that lives in the same building that she does. Great! I'm grateful! Those five hundred dollars will suit me well. I'm proud to be conscious of honor, ethics, and responsibility to our country. To my name and address, you could add that I'm registered with the Department of Children's Welfare to assist those little ones who are abandoned or mistreated. I have a boy living here with me, under my care for more than ten years, but in two months he will graduate from high school and I will be by myself. I'd love to take care of that girl. For your information, I must tell you that Mrs. Thompson, whose telephone number I gave you before, has all my references. She has promised me that I'll be in charge of the teenager. Yes, of course. Call me any time. No, I'm not going out. I'll wait for your call. I want to be sure that the girl is in good hands. So long. (*She hangs up the telephone.*)

CARLOS: (*He lights a candle and brings it to* FRANCES.) You deserve an Oscar. Here is your award!

FRANCES: Carlos, when are you going to learn not to play with fire? (*She laughs and pours herself another drink.*) When I picked you up at the orphanage, they reminded me not to allow you to play with matches. How many times do I have to tell you, darling, don't play with fire!

CARLOS: Keep on playing with that goddamn fire. I don't remember anything about it. (*Blows out the candle.*) The least you could do is to thank me for the five hundred dollars you're getting for denouncing Claudia's parents. Aren't you grateful?

FRANCES: Thank you, sweetie pie, for everything I've done for you.

CARLOS: Grandma, Frances. (*Hesitates.*)

FRANCES: Yes, tell me what's on your mind. Speak up!

CARLOS: Were you ever in love?

FRANCES: What a silly question. Why?

CARLOS: Well, you've never had a child.

FRANCES: You never had a family.

CARLOS: Until I was seven, I had one.

FRANCES: Too bad. You still have memories.

CARLOS: Barren woman!

FRANCES: I had two lovers. Two who loved me. They left me with my memories. I didn't have time to have a child. My first love was in the Korean War. We were planning to get married. I never wore the veil. The second died suddenly. Do you remember him?

CARLOS: Before he came your way you never drank. That was before you started doing other things. That was before I started to sell for you. Do you think you are doing the right thing?

FRANCES: Those are the things that keep us going from day to day, from morning to evening, from winter to spring. Remember that I'm lucky to be alive. Don't accuse me of anything bad. I'm trying my best.

CARLOS: The other day I read in the newspaper that there is an organization of adopted children. They help members trace their families. I have their address somewhere in one of my notes. Would you like to have it?

FRANCES: What for?

CARLOS: Weren't you ever curious to find out who they were?

FRANCES: Was it worthwhile to hunt and search for the ones who abandoned me inside a shoe box at the steps of a church? And the falling snow almost covered me, but my lungs were strong, stronger than nature. I won over it. After a while the nuns came to pick me up when they heard my crying.

CARLOS: What would you have liked to have, a son or a daughter?

FRANCES: Three of each. Could you imagine the money I could make? Each child would go to a different school. I could have had six businesses going on at once all over the city. Carlos, you are not making enough money anymore.

CARLOS: I'm trying my best. Don't accuse me of failing you. You could have had a better life or been a better person.

FRANCES: Have I ever abused you?

CARLOS: I would never have allowed you to beat me.

FRANCES: What are you accusing me of?

CARLOS: Of exploiting me. For the last ten years you have lived off what the government pays for taking care of me.

FRANCES: Haven't I given you love?

CARLOS: Not enough for the thousand dollars I bring you every week. I'm the one who is taking a risk. You know that.

FRANCES: If you're taken in, I'll be taken in, too.

CARLOS: I'll get less time than you. I'm still a minor.

FRANCES: Until next month. then you'll be eighteen. Congratulations on arriving at adulthood.

CARLOS: I'll be the master of my own destiny.

FRANCES: I hope I have taught you what to do with it. Why did you give me information leading to information Claudia's parents.

CARLOS: I know you needed money. She was selling for her parents.

FRANCES: Now, she can sell for me. Thank you, Carlos.

CARLOS: I'm grateful to you.

FRANCES: I know you better than you know yourself. Tonight, you have behaved very different from any other night. Why?

CARLOS: What do you mean?

FRANCES: For the first time since you have been with me, you have asked me about my feelings, about my past. Why?

CARLOS: You're getting old. I want to help you.

FRANCES: Are you planning to leave me when you graduate from high school?

CARLOS: That's too far away yet. We have to wait another month and a half. I don't know what I'm going to do, grandmother spider.

FRANCES: Are you in love with this girl?

CARLOS: Stop that shit. I'm too young to be in love. I don't even know what love is. Why don't you explain it to me?

FRANCES: Believe me! The first time I realized what love was, was when I had to go to the morgue to identify Richard's corpse. There, I realized that I had loved him very much and that I had lost the only chance I ever had to tell him how I felt.

CARLOS: Is that why you started in the business?

FRANCES: You are asking too many questions. (*Blackout.*)

.... Scene VI ....

SERGEANT MEDINA *apprehends* MAURICIO *and* ELENA. *He puts handcuffs on their wrists.*

CLAUDIA: (*Sobs.*) What am I going to do without you, Father, Mother? What am I going to do? I have no one but you! I'm lost! Oh, God, what am I going to do?

MAURICIO: Pray to God. He will help.

ELENA: You are a big girl, darling. We'll be out soon. I didn't know that there was cocaine in our apartment. Who knows who brought it here. Someone wants to harm us.

CLAUDIA: I'm staying home until you return.

MAURICIO: Who is going to take care of the girl? She is a virgin. Who is responsible for her virginity?

SERGEANT MEDINA: Mrs. Thompson, a social worker, will be here promptly. She'll take care of your young girl. But the girl is responsible for her own virginity, mister. (*Blackout.*)

.... Scene VII ....

Later, at FRANCES' *apartment. The telephone rings.* FRAN-
CES *answers it.*

FRANCES: Yes, Mrs. Thompson. What wonderful news! How
     happy it makes me to know that, at last, that poor little
     one has been saved from living with such inhumane par-
     ents. Thank you. I'm grateful. Yes, yes, yes. (*Blackout.*)

.... Scene VIII ....

CLAUDIA: Did I offend you in anything?
FRANCES: It's okay. Remember that what there is in the kitchen
     and in the kitchen cabinet is to be divided between three
     people. Therefore, I hope that you are not a greed eater
     and show some consideration of others.
CLAUDIA: Is there anybody else living here?
FRANCES: My grandson. I think he studies with you in the same
     school.
CLAUDIA: Then I know him. At school I'm the most popular
     girl in all the classes, and in all the courses, ever since I
     started high school.
FRANCES: If you want to, you can call me grandmother.
CLAUDIA: I'd rather call you Mrs. Frances, for now.
FRANCES: You'll get used to it.
CLAUDIA: Soon my parents will come out and I'll return home.
FRANCES: Darling, that is going to take a long time. You ought
     to conform. The accusations are strong.
CLAUDIA: How do you know?
FRANCES: Starting today, you are under my guidance and respon-
     sibility. I must know everything, every step. If you don't
     follow the straight line which has been set for you by the
     authorities, the law will fall on your head as it has fallen
     on your parents'.
CLAUDIA: (*Trying to control herself.*) I'm sorry, but this con-
     junctivitis is making my eyes water. (FRANCES *exits the
     room.* CLAUDIA *closes the door in haste. She runs toward
     the suitcase and takes out her fathers's overcoat which she*

*puts on. The coat trails the floor. From a plastic bag, she
takes out a hat, also her fathers's and puts it on. She looks
at herself in a mirror and sobs.*)

CLAUDIA: Father! Father! Father! Help me, Father, help me!
(CLAUDIA *leans against the mirror and continues to cry.
Shy calls her father's name in a litany with funereal over-
tones. Suddenly, soft knocks are heard at the door. CLAU-
DIA composes herself. With long steps, she approaches the
basin. She washes her face. The knocks at the door become
stronger. CLAUDIA opens the door. To her surprise she
sees CARLOS. As if he were the last survivor on the face
of the earth, she embraces him as she pulls him inside the
room. She pushes the door closed with her foot.*)

CLAUDIA: Carlos, my parents were taken to jail. Carlos, Mother
and Father are in jail. The police came. The FBI came.
The Department of Drug Investigation came and looked
everywhere. They took a large quantity of cocaine. That
was going to be the last shipment that Mother and Father
agreed to receive. After that, they were planning to retire
in Florida.

CARLOS: When did this happen?

CLAUDIA: The day before yesterday. Carlos, I have been in a daze
like a flower waiting for the morning dew. I thought I was
going to wither. I had no one to confide in, the school
was closed for vacation, so I had no way to get in touch
with you. Carlos, I want you to help me to find the people
who reported my parents. I'll do anything you want, but
you have to promise me that if we find out which of our
neighbors is the son of a bitch who tipped off the police,
we will kill them. Do yo promise?

CARLOS: I do, Claudia. (*She embraces him crying. Curtain.*)

ACT II

.... Scene I ....

*At a men's detention facility. MAURICIO talks to his daughter.
He speaks loudly expecting to be heard by the guards.*

MAURICIO: My daughter, the biggest problem in my life was that I've run away from the word of God. You know that He observes us and that He writes everything in his private agenda. Your Mother and I sinned. We failed to follow the commandments. It's not our fault. The universe put us to a test. We let ourselves into the mirage of material wealth and we sinned. The first time was there in the mountains where we were born. I've never spoken to you about this. Your mother and I grew up together on the same farm. I can't go into details because it is so long ago that I don't remember. There was a civil war. There was a bloody civil war which tried to wipe out a dictator of equal dimensions. Beheading was the word, even of children. There, in our America, blood began to run as if Herod were resurrected. One day, the news arrived that the guerrillas wanted to let the world know that they were the force behind our town. Father, who was one of them, commanded us to mount two horses and he tied your mother and me to the saddles. That's how we started our descent from the mountains toward the sea. We arrived there almost dehydrated. After that, days passed filled with anguish in which we were taken from one place to another. We crossed country boundaries, everywhere they spoke our language. At an early age, we learned that ice and fire are temporary accidents. Your mother has not written to me. Neither she nor I have any idea of the time that we'll have to spend behind bars. But I want you to know and I would like you to reassure your mother about this when you see her, that from now on, I'll give myself to propagate the word of God. (MAURICIO *stands and vows.*) And besides this, giving all diligence, add to your faith, virtue; and to virtue, knowledge and godliness; and to godliness, brotherly kindness; and to brotherly kindness, charity. (MAURICIO *genuflects. Blackout.*)

.... Scene II ....

A week later at Fort Tyron Park. CLAUDIA *and* CARLOS *look at the Hudson River and plan what they want to do with their lives. At a distance we hear the final notes of a soprano singing "O Patria Mia," from the opera* Aida, *then the applause.*

CLAUDIA: I like salsa better.

CARLOS: I do too, but this crowd doesn't seem to be silly or stupid at all. Do you know who is sitting there next to that very attractive woman?

CLAUDIA: Who?

CARLOS: Your favorite teacher, the one with the big moustache. Do you see him? He's right there. (*He points with his finger.*) He's leaving.

CLAUDIA: (*Nodding.*) Then it must be a very important concert. If I had seen him before, I would have liked to say hello. By the way, Carlos, in yesterday's class he told the class that it was important to receive letters from the people we love. That way we can measure their spiritual and intellectual capacity. So, Carlos, what are you waiting for to write me a letter?

CARLOS: Why should I do that, when we sleep together?

CLAUDIA: Carlos, in two weeks you'll graduate from high school. I want to learn from you.

CARLOS: You still haven't learned to write a letter?

CLAUDIA: I want to learn from you. I want you to teach me everything you know.

CARLOS: Don't think that I know that much more than you.

CLAUDIA: The teacher with the big moustache, as you call him, is the only one who corrects the homework. Most of the time, I don't know if I answer the questions right or wrong.

CARLOS: You ought to spend more time at the library, like me. That's where I learned words like "laissez-faire."

CLAUDIA: What does it mean?

CARLOS: It means that government has no control or the right to interfere in any kind of business. Do you hear?

CLAUDIA: I feel guilty.

CARLOS: The police do it! Everyone we know does it. Why shouldn't we do it?

CLAUDIA: I never used it until you taught me.

CARLOS: Are you trying to pull the wool over my eyes?

CLAUDIA: I swear!

CARLOS: We have to set up our own nest far from grandmother spider. She's the one who's making the money.

CLAUDIA: But we are not learning because we're high all the time.

CARLOS: I still go to the library.

CLAUDIA: To sell.

CARLOS: And you go to the girls' lockers.

CLAUDIA: To sell for grandmother spider.

CARLOS: The first thing we have to do is to get away. To get away from it all. Do you accept my proposition?

CLAUDIA: Only if we celebrate our wedding in the garden of the Spanish cloister.

CARLOS: Why there and not in another place?

CLAUDIA: That place means a lot to me, Carlos. As a little girl, from my window in my bedroom there (*She points to the distance.*) I used to look toward this building and I felt like Prince Valiant's girlfriend waiting for him to honor me by coming down from his Middle Ages palace to ask for my hand.

CARLOS: Are you old enough to get married?

CLAUDIA: I'm only sixteen, but we don't have to tell them the truth. Why do you want to get married?

CARLOS: Because I'm planning to join the army and I want you to come with me to know the world. Somehow traveling has attracted me. Do you see that bird flying there in the distance? I envy it more than I envy any other animal. With its wings, it can transport itself to any place. When we get married, if you wish, you could join the army, too. Between the two of us, we could earn a good salary and we could save enough money to buy ourselves a small plane.

CLAUDIA: Carlos, I can't leave my parents abandoned in jail.

CARLOS: Do you love them that much?

CLAUDIA: Why should it surprise you? I've always told you that my parents were the best parents in the world.

CARLOS: How old were you when you started to sell crack?

CLAUDIA: Ten years old.

CARLOS: Who initiated you into this?

CLAUDIA: My parents never used any kind of drugs. I told you. They never started me in any wrong thing. You know very well that they used to sell it because they were trying to get away from this evil neighborhood. Everyone does it in this area.

CARLOS: Everyone?

CLAUDIA: Everyone we know. When we moved into that building there, Mother used to clean office buildings, Father used to work as a waiter. Slowly, they discover that their neighbors were earning three times as much as they did. Those neighbors convinced my parents to leave their jobs and dedicate themselves to an easy life. The police used to enter and exit from these people's house without any arrest. The first time that Mother witnessed that she was terrified until our neighbor told her that it was a routine. The police came and went to collect their tax. That's why I'm surprised that they are in jail. It must have been a report. If I ever find out who did that thing, I swear to you that I'll tear them apart with my bare hands.

CARLOS: Where is all the money that they earned?

CLAUDIA: I forgot to tell you. Mother confessed that it was in a safe deposit box at the bank. The police confiscated it.

CARLOS: Damn it!

CLAUDIA: Why in the world am I so goddamned lucky as to have a family so different from any other?

CARLOS: My family was great.

CLAUDIA: That's why you are so wonderful.

CARLOS: Do you really think so?

CLAUDIA: I really do, Carlos.

CARLOS: I don't know how in the world I have given you that impression. My life has been filled with mosaics, with fragments of remembrances, with impossibilities of achievements, I feel like a bird without wings. I want to fly and I can't. Everything is denied to me.

CLAUDIA: Everything is possible if we only try.

CARLOS: Maybe you're right. Maybe we still have a chance.

CLAUDIA: Yes, we can still make something out of our lives. I hardly can write well, Carlos. You know, at times I think that we are different. You and I are not white with blue eyes and light skin. I think that to the teachers of another culture, we are worthless.

CARLOS: In the army, everything will be different. I used to want to be a baseball player, but I was too short for that. When I went to the medical center to visit their endocrinologist clinic, the doctor told me that my bones had already grown enough. He assured me that I had no problem of dwarfism and that my pituitary gland was working all right. Does it bother you that I'm shorter than you?

CLAUDIA: You're my Adam.

CARLOS: You're my Eve.

CARLOS/CLAUDIA: What should we do with paradise?

CARLOS: Let's destroy everything.

CLAUDIA: Why?

CARLOS: Because we are too far from paradise, Claudia. Let's go.

CLAUDIA: I don't want to leave this sunset. Look at it, isn't it marvelous? (*The sun is setting and the light changes the illumination of the afternoon.*)

CARLOS: That is an illusion of life, Claudia. Is the sun what we believe to be the sun, and the one in which we place our hopes for the future. For the rich it's a promise of luxury and greediness. For the poor like you and me, it is a promise of deprivations. For the fools who believe in heaven and hell, it is a promise of a better life. What has man done? We have traveled to the moon. We have built telescopes that can see nebulae that ceased to exist long ago. Meanwhile, here on earth we can't even eat a chicken. Everything is poisoned, cattle and fish, fruits and vegetables. And the last thing which we have left, the warmth of a body next to ours, it's also a putrefying thought. With all this thing about AIDS, I waited until I found a woman like you so I could give myself to life. Do you understand? I chose you because I knew you were not a prostitute. I never saw you whoring with anybody in school. If your parents get out, would you leave me for them?

CLAUDIA: I love them, but I wouldn't leave you.

CARLOS: (*Embracing* CLAUDIA.) Your parents were strange trunks. By their own effort they never got anywhere. Their branches only gave a single flower. You.

CLAUDIA: Father told me recently that he and Mama grew up together in the mountains. Since then, I ask myself, are they brother and sister? Are they my real parents?

CARLOS: Let's destroy the flowers and the trees, let's destroy the stinking air smelling of gasoline. Let's destroy earth. Let's destroy the fish and the sea. Let's destroy the heavens and the faraway galaxies. Let's destroy the sun and the moon. How about a suicide pact?

CLAUDIA: You kill yourself. I don't want to die.

CARLOS: Don't you realize that it is not worth it to keep on living if we don't even know where we came from or where we're going. Don't you realize how sad it is to know so little about the ones who brought us into the world?

CLAUDIA: You're crazy. A while ago you asked me to marry you. Later we planned to travel to visit faraway worlds and suddenly you want to destroy everything. What the fuck is happening to you.

CARLOS: Claudia, tell me the truth, does it bother you that I'm shorter than you?

CLAUDIA: Until now, I had not realized it.

CARLOS: If you never wear high heels, and I wear them, and if you tie your hair up close to your scalp, you'll only be a little taller than me. (*They kiss. Blackout.*)

.... Scene III ....

That same day in the evening. At FRANCES' *apartment.* CAR-LOS *and* CLAUDIA *search for his identification papers in the closet and in the drawers. The TV is on as well as the cassette player.*

CARLOS: Like every Friday evening, with her friends from the neighborhood, she goes to Atlantic City to play seven and a half and roulette.

CLAUDIA: She's due any moment now, it's eleven.

CARLOS: Where the hell has she hidden my papers? We can't get married without them.

CLAUDIA: Did you look on all the shelves?

CARLOS: You were next to me. Didn't you see the way I looked and looked everywhere? Look after me. You'll find nothing.

CLAUDIA: I wish she had a lover, so she would stop depending on us.

CARLOS: When I came to live with her, she had an old crazy man who soon left her. According to her, that poor devil died in the Bower, drunk, lying on the sidewalk. But she's not to be trusted in anything she says. She lies for the pleasure of lying. (FRANCES *enters. She is drunk.*)

FRANCES: What are you looking for?

CARLOS: For my papers!

FRANCES: Stop that noise. I don't like to bother my neighbors. Stop this fucking around that has been going on for a while. I don't want to be responsible for a pregnancy. I'm too young to become a great-grandmother.

CARLOS: Don't worry about it. Claudia and I are getting married.

CLAUDIA: You are right, grandmother spider. I think I'm pregnant.

CARLOS: And the baby is going to be as tall as his mother. Maybe even taller.

FRANCES: How old is the girl.

CARLOS: Old enough to do what pleases her.

FRANCES: We will talk about that later. Carlos, fix me a drink. I'm depressed. I lost ten thousand dollars, my baby.

CARLOS: Where did you get so much money?

FRANCES: Family savings. What makes you think that I'm a helpless orphan like your?

CARLOS: The orphan has grown up and wised up.

FRANCES: Still, you are under my command. I'm in full control of your lives. When are you going to get those five thousand dollars that we owe Morales?

CLAUDIA: Carlos, say something.

FRANCES: Morales has given me until tomorrow to pay him back. If I don't pay him, we are out of the business. "No money, no cocaine." That's what he said. That's why I went to Atlantic City to try to win that money. At first, good fortune brightened my path with five hundred dollar. I won ten thousand lovely looking greenbacks in one hundred dollars bills. I must have lost my mind. I put everything on number 13, forgetting that today is Friday! Carlos, you must get that money for tomorrow. Claudia, you are responsible, too. Tomorrow you have to go out and look for those who are always a reliable source of income.

CLAUDIA: Tomorrow I'm going to see Mother. I'll talk to her about this.

FRANCES: Talk to her about whatever your asshole wants to talk about, my child. But for now, give me a massage on the neck, please.

CLAUDIA: Aren't you afraid of what I might do?

FRANCES: You have a good sense of humor. That I like. I love having you here with me. Listen, use condoms if you don't want to get pregnant or get AIDS.

CLAUDIA: My ass is cleaner than your tongue, grandmother spider.

FRANCES: Stop fucking around. Let me alone. Go ahead and fuck, but don't make too much noise. I'll see you in the morning.

CARLOS: Sleep well, Mrs. Bat.

FRANCES: Dignity, homeless angels.

CARLOS: I pray for the devil to take your soul before morning.

FRANCES: I'm sorry to leave you alone, children of Lucifer.

CARLOS: Old rat, I wish you the worst nightmares of the universe.

FRANCES: Even though you might not believe this, I love you so much that one of these days, I'm planning to poison you. Believe me, the boat is sinking. By tomorrow, we need five thousand dollars. If you don't get it, I'll find a way ... but you're going to be sorry.

CLAUDIA: We're not afraid of you, grandmother spider. We're young and strong and you're old and decrepit.

CARLOS: Tomorrow, when you're sober, we'll talk about my papers. Don't die before that, son of a bitch old witch! (FRANCES *exits. The youngsters put the cassette back on.*)

CLAUDIA: Where is the money?

CARLOS: She'll never find it.

CLAUDIA: We have to get away. If she finds out that we took that money, she'll kill us.

CARLOS: I'm small but strong and I have a very clear thinking brain!

CLAUDIA: That I know, baby. (*He caresses her belly.*)

CARLOS: I'm so happy to know that it was true what we suspected. Still, I can't believe it.

CLAUDIA: Remember what the doctor said, no drugs or alcohol.

CARLOS: We'll get married and join the army.

CLAUDIA: I believe that the army will save us.

CARLOS: The army will provide us with the medical insurance to bring into the world a healthy baby.

CLAUDIA: (*Dancing.*) Another day, two days, three days ... Soon we'll be free to do what we wish.

CARLOS: (*Dancing.*) I'll have a diploma and we'll get married.

CLAUDIA: While you train, I'll get a diploma.

CARLOS: You'll be my wife ... you'll be my woman ... you'll be mine alone.

CLAUDIA: I can't wait to see Mother's face when I tell her that she's going to be a grandmother ... that I'm having your child! I had a very strange dream last night. I dreamt that Mother was telling me something that I didn't want to hear. While she was talking to me, I had my hands covering my ears. What could that mean?

CARLOS: Maybe you shouldn't go to visit her in that horrible jail. You'll be depressed. Don't go!

CLAUDIA: I have to see Mama. I miss her very much. I have the premonition that she will tell me who informed on her and Papa.

CARLOS: How could she know?

CLAUDIA: Mama is a very smart woman. She knows everything, and I believe in dreams.

CARLOS: Don't go. Forget about them. Your parents are worthless.

CLAUDIA: I have to go.

CARLOS: Would you still go if I ask you not to?

CLAUDIA: Don't ask me not to see my own mother. I have to see her. She gave me life. Do you understand? (*Blackout.*)

.... Scene IV ....

Next day. In a women's detention center. CLAUDIA *is talking to her mother.* ELENA *appears to be tormented by thoughts.*

ELENA: Daughter, you ought to take care of yourself as if you were an emerald. I had to talk. The police promised me that if I supplied them with the names of the ones who provided us with that thing, you know, they would pardon five years of the possible ten that I will be condemned to serve.

CLAUDIA: That's too many years, Mother.

ELENA: You have to take care of yourself. You'll know where to find me. I will have no way to communicate with you. (*Sobs.*)

CLAUDIA: Mother, you'll always know where to find me, I promise.

ELENA: Child, move away from the house where you're living now as soon as possible.

CLAUDIA: Where can I go, Mother?

ELENA: Anywhere, far away, far away from where we used to live. Nobody ought to know where you are. From now on, deny that you are my daughter. Deny that your father is that man who is my husband. Change your name. If you want to survive the revenge of those I have informed on, you have to deny everything. You know nothing of your past. You ought to start a new life.

CLAUDIA: Why did you report them?

ELENA: Don't accuse me of being a coward. I shouldn't have said those things. I wish I had the power to wipe out those things, that confession. I only thought of myself. I thought of the years I would save from being behind these bars. Don't blame me. As an independent being from us, which you are, you ought to save yourself.

CLAUDIA: Mother, Mother, what am I to do?

ELENA: I'm sure that you will survive. I survived horrible things and in order to not lose my mind. I hid them under a turtle shell which I set off to sea, the one which, in my mind, is waiting for me far away in the Galapagos, sunning itself on a pristine beach next to a spring of magical powers, which will eventually give me back my youth.

CLAUDIA: Why do you talk that way, Mother?

ELENA: Don't worry about me. I know how to defend myself. I'm capable of everything. You are the one who needs protection. My enemies are waiting to eliminate you. They don't forgive.

CLAUDIA: There is a boy who wants to marry me. What should I do?

ELENA: Do you love him?

CLAUDIA: Very much.

ELENA: What is the problem?

CLAUDIA: The woman who owns the apartment where we live opposes our marriage.

ELENA: What right does she have over you?

CLAUDIA: All. By law she takes care of me.

ELENA: Who is the boy?

CLAUDIA: The one who tried to rob me at the train station.

ELENA: I smell a rat.

CLAUDIA: What do you think?

ELENA: There might be a conspiracy between him and that woman to fuck us up. They might be some of our enemies.

CLAUDIA: He loves me.

ELENA: Watch out for him, watch out for all of the. Get away!

CLAUDIA: Where do I get the money to leave, Mother?

ELENA: Life is more important than money.

CLAUDIA: Mother, I have wanted to ask you this question for a long time. Are you and Father brother and sister?

ELENA: What makes you think that?

CLAUDIA: When I saw Father last, he talked about a trip that you two made a long time ago, when you were children. He told me that you had grown up together and that one day, his father had tied the two of you to the saddles of two horses and that was the way that you had come down from the mountains to the sea.

ELENA: Your father remembers more things than I. My first memories are of growing up with the nuns in Arizona. The other past is hidden under a turtle's shell.

LOUDSPEAKER: All visitors should be out of the building in five minutes.

CLAUDIA: Mother, how do I communicate with you?

ELENA: Write to me, but never give me your address. God bless you!

CLAUDIA: Mother, I'm going to have a child.

ELENA: Have an abortion.

CLAUDIA: I want to have the baby.

ELENA: Even if I never see you again, God bless you! (*Curtain.*)

.... Scene V ....

Later that same day. At FRANCES' *apartment. She enters all dressed up, carrying a bridal bouquet.* CARLOS *watches television. He suddenly sees* FRANCES. *He stands up and turns off the TV.*

CARLOS: Where is the groom?

FRANCES: Not far.

CARLOS: Do I know him?

FRANCES: Quite well. Did you get me the money?

CARLOS: I didn't even try.

FRANCES: The five thousand dollars?

CARLOS: I was waiting for you.

FRANCES: Let me have the money that you and Claudia made today.

CARLOS: This morning you sneaked out on me.

FRANCES: Where is Claudia?

CARLOS: She went to visit her mother.

FRANCES: Carlos, if you don't give me that money, I'll send you to a reformatory.

CARLOS: If you don't give me my birth certificate, I'll turn you in to the police.

FRANCES: You're an ungrateful ill-bred boy. What the fuck do you want those papers for?

CARLOS: I'm going to join the Army.

FRANCES: So, you'll have to wait. I don't know where the hell I've put them.

CARLOS: Search for them, son of a bitch, or I'll break you in two.

FRANCES: If you raise your hand against me, I'll kill you. (CAR-LOS *approaches aggressively.* FRANCES *grabs the bat, the one with which* CARLOS *had been playing and threatens to hit him. He retreats.*)

FRANCES: For your information, I must tell you that legally you're married to Morales' sister.

CARLOS: Me, married?

FRANCES: Yes, Carlos. Morales wanted his money. I'm not a magician. I couldn't even try if I wanted to. His sister, who is only nineteen, had to legalize her situation the U.S. A friend of Morales impersonated you. We went to court and without being present, you got married. (CARLOS *bursts out laughing. At that moment* CLAUDIA *enters. She gets scared to see* CARLOS *and* FRANCES *laughing. She remembers her mother's warnings.*)

FRANCES: Don't be frightened, baby. Nothing is going on here. The only thing is that your boyfriend is no longer single. He has a very sexy looking wife and as soon as he meets her, he's going to be crazy about her.

CARLOS: This son of a bitch used my papers to marry me to Morales' younger sister.

FRANCES: Now, you don't have to worry about the five thousand dollars that you stole from me. He'll leave you, because this wild pony has suddenly changed into a wingless bird. (*She laughs.*) I have him and you under my power.

CARLOS: (CARLOS *strikes* FRANCES *in the face.*) Old witch, you're going to pay for this. (FRANCES *hits* CARLOS *with the bat on the right arm.*)

FRANCES: Never again will you be able to hit a woman. You're going to have a crippled right arm, son of a bitch!

CLAUDIA: (CLAUDIA *picks up a chair and fights* FRANCES.) Let him go, old witch. Let him go! (CARLOS *loses control of his right arm and falls to the ground. His body twists in pain.* CLAUDIA *dials the phone.*) Sergeant Medina, well Captain Medina, the address is 987 Audubon Avenue, apartment 16. Bring an ambulance. Carlos is badly hurt.

FRANCES: This was an accident. He fell in the bathroom.

CLAUDIA: You'll go to jail, I promise you.

FRANCES: Don't take his side before you know who this armless bird is. He was the one who talked to me about you and about your parents, illicit business. We turned them in to make money. (*She bursts out laughing, realizing the pain that she has brought upon* CLAUDIA.)

CARLOS: I swear that she never gave me one cent of that money.

FRANCES: I couldn't give it to you, even if I wanted to. That money and what I collected for your wedding was lost playing roulette. This business is over.

CLAUDIA: Why did you do it, Carlos?

CARLOS: Because I'm madly in love with you.

CLAUDIA: Don't you realize the tragedy that you've brought on my family? My parents are in jail. They're behind bars for a long time. You destroyed my family.

CARLOS: You never had a family, Claudia. They used you at their will to make money.

FRANCES: Baby, nobody has a family. That's an old myth. When the police arrive, don't say a thing. I'm the owner of the apartment. I'll take care of everything. A thief tried to steal our valuables and Carlos fought him. The rascal broke Carlos' arm with a bat. (*The police siren is heard approaching. The door bell buzzes.* FRANCES *opens the door.* CAPTAIN MEDINA *enters.*)

CAPTAIN MEDINA: The stretcher bearers are coming up the stairs. What happened.

FRANCES: A robbery. My dear grandson tried to defend us and the thief attacked him with a bat.

CLAUDIA: (*To* CARLOS.) You're not a man.

CAPTAIN MEDINA: The same familiar faces. Who owns the lease to this apartment?

FRANCES: This is my pigeonhole. I'm the big mother pigeon, the one who gives shelter to the homeless birds without nests.

CARLOS: To exploit and to bleed us.

CAPTAIN MEDINA: (*Taking notes.*) Describe the thief.

FRANCES: He was a tall, dark and strong man. It seems that he entered through the window. We were out and when my grandson and I came in he attacked us. My grandson is a hero. He saved my life.

CARLOS: There was no such thief. This old witch attacked me. This old woman is a liar and a hypocrite. She is also a thief. She has been abusing me for ten years. Now I want to report her and to take her to court so the weight of the law will strike her. We have to set an example. Please give me something for the pain. She broke my arm.

CLAUDIA: I'm a witness that everything he said is true.

FRANCES: Don't listen to them, they're lying and they hate me. (*The policeman wraps the bat up in a plastic bag.*)

CAPTAIN MEDINA: The experts will know whose fingerprints are on the bat. (FRANCES *falls into a chair.*)

CARLOS: Do you forgive me, Claudia?

CLAUDIA: Today, I forgive you. We have a lot to talk about. But first you must get well.

CARLOS: I hope to be able to play baseball again. I didn't tell you before because I saved it to tell you after dinner, as a present. Regardless of my height, I've been accepted in the United States Army. (*Blackout.*)

With All and for the Good of All
(Cuban farce in two acts)

by

Uva A. Clavijo

Translated into English by David Miller

With All and for the Good of All

About the Author

Uva A. Clavijo was born in Havana in 1944. She completed her elementary education in Cuba, but her secondary schooling was divided between the Ruston Academy in Havana and Stone Ridge, Convent of the Sacred Heart in Washington, D.C. She obtained an Associate in Arts from Mercy College in Miami in 1980 and by 1981 had graduated Summa Cum Laude from Biscayne College (now St. Thomas University) with a B.A. in Spanish. In 1984 Clavijo received her M.A. in Spanish literature form the University of Miami, where again she graduated Summa Cum Laude. At Miami she is a doctoral candidate.

Her writing dates to the late fifties when she was a contributor to *Diario La Marina* and *Información*. After arriving in the U.S. she also published in the following periodicals, magazines and journals: *Diario Las Américas* (where she has been a regular since 1961), *El Nuevo Herald* (previously *El Miami Herald*), *Revista Réplica*, *West Kendall Gazette*, all in Miami; *Crítica* and *Américas* (OAS magazine) in Washington, D.C.; *La Opinión*, *20 de Mayo* and *La Prensa* of Los Angeles; *Círculo*, *Círculo Poético*, *Cubanacán* and *El Tiempo* in New York; *Letras Femeninas* in Houston; *El Puente* in Madrid; and *Vista*, *Nuestro* and *Hispanic*, all of national circulation in the U.S. She has also had her articles distributed by ALA, Agencia Latinoamericana de Prensa, to several newspapers in Latin America. She has written for *Hombre de Mundo*, *Opiniones Latinoamericanas* and *Vanidades Continental*, which are Miami based publications for distribution in Latin America, as well.

Her political activism, so evident in her journalism, has also become manifest in her speeches, her work in several organizations and her leadership in others. As an example of some of her activities in this regard, it is useful to mention that she has participated in numerous radio programs, such as *La universidad del aire* and *Mesa revuelta* in Miami, in several television programs on panel discussions, such as *Actualidad Semanal* (Spanish International Network) and *Ante la Prensa* (for Channel 51, the Telemundo affiliate in Miami). She is a director and an officer in the Instituto Jacques Maritain de Cuba, and an *Of Human Rights* member and a member of the Committee of Intellectuals for a Free Cuba, among others. One of her speeches in commemoration of the birth of Cuban poet and patriot, José Martí, was later reproduced in the February 15, 1979 issue of the *Congressional Record*.

Uva Clavijo's creative writing, however, is equally of major importance in her life. Also from an early age she has been writing poems and stories for periodical publications. It is in 1972 that she published a book of vignettes entitled *Eternidad*. This book, with a prologue by Eugenio Florit, saw the light in Madrid in 1972 under the care of Plaza Mayor. In 1976 she offered *Versos de exilio* in Miami, a collection of poems. Her first book of short stories, *Ni verdad ni mentira y otros cuentos*, appeared in 1977 (Miami: Editorial Universal). Her book *Entresemáforos (poemas escritos en ruta)* (Miami: Editorial Universal, 1981) was sponsored by the Cintas Foundation and was a result of a prestigious Cintas Fellowship. It also carried another honor, an introduction by José Antonio Rasco. *Tus ojos y yo*, another poetry collection followed in 1985 as a title in Universal. Her book, *No puedo más y otros cuentos* (Miami: Editorial Universal, 1989), brought her back to the world of the short story. As it happens, Clavijo had begun garnering literary awards when, as early as 1956, she received the first prize in the Ruston Academy's Short Story Contest. They have not stopped since. To name but a few, here is a sample: "Premio Alfonso Hernández Catá" Short Story Contest sponsored by the Asociación the Críticos y Comentaristas (ACCA) Miami, 19776. Cintas Fellowships (mentioned above) granted by the International Institute of Higher Education from 1980-1981; the Simón Bolívar Award, a joint award by the University of Miami and the Venezuelan Consulate in 1983; The "Premio Juan J. Remos" by the Cruzada Educativa Cubana in 1983, and the "Premio de Poesía Federico García Lorca" by the Casa de España in Hollywood, California.

"With All and for the Good of All" was written in 1986 in Spanish with the title "Con todos y para el bien de todos," a celebrated and often repeated maxim of José Martí. Clavijo subtitles the play as "A Cuban Farce in Two Acts." Perhaps because it is her only play, she has not fallen prey to the typical schizophrenia of Cuban and Cuban American playwrights who tend to divide their work between serious theater and "teatro bufo" or low comedic farce. Clavijo avails herself of the model utilized by Pío Baroja in *Paradox, Rey*, a dialogue novel, where Baroja seeks to explore the problems faced by his country upon the European discovery of the New World. What to do there in that utopia? Baroja, though centering his work in Africa, and following the pastoral utopic tradition that harks back to Plato, Vives, More, Bacon, Defoe and others, nevertheless is addressing the issue of Spain in America. For Clavijo the technique proves equally irresistible when confronting the anticipated problem of the Cuban exile community and post-Castro Cuba. It attempts to answer the questions everyone wonders about. Who will really return and stay? What help will they provide? What role will the past play in this new future? In order to further her aims, she deftly uses the typical characters of the Miami Cuban community. The language, the pace of the dialogue and the situations are the elements which help to carry the play forward, lightening a heavy topic. These techniques make it possible for Clavijo to use humor to demythify and debunk the rigid monoliths of prevailing thought five or six years ago in Miami. Clavijo is a keen observer of the Miami scene, and has the talent that allows us to see with her eyes.

CHARACTERS

SIR PRETERIT PERFECT, 77
MADAME PAINS CROSS PERFECT, 68
CHEO CALLEOCHO, 50
JOHNNY KNOW-IT-ALL, 36
WITNESS ALL-KNOWING, 42
HOPE STILL, 25
DON'T-HAVE-A-CHOICE, 27
PHILLIP BIGMOUTH, 60
MR. BLOND, 45

PLACE

The first scene takes place in Miami, the rest of the play on the island of Cutopia.

TIME

The present. (1986)

Original text in Spanish.

ACT I

The setting—very simple and schematic—will show a hangar and, toward stage left, the interior of a small airplane, with six seats plus that of the pilot. CHEO CALLEOCHO, *dressed in camouflage fatigues, with his shirt open in such a way that an undershirt is seen, with several gold chains around his neck, among them one with a large medallion, an identification bracelet on his right wrist and a large watch on his left wrist, is seen inspecting some boxes and bundles that are in the back of the plane. He might hum a song.* PHILLIP BIGMOUTH, *dressed in a polyester suit, with a tape recorder hanging from his shoulder and a microphone in his hand, enters from stage right while interviewing* MR. BLOND, *who carries several files in his hands.*

MR. BLOND: (*With pursed lips in a prissy attitude.*) I don't know how you were allowed in here. I gave strict orders that the press should not find out. It is a secret mission.

BIGMOUTH: Don't get mad, friend. I'm just doing my job. Besides, people have a right to know. Aren't you always talking about human rights in this country? Don't you believe in the rights of a radio reporter?

MR. BLOND: Of course, but some things have to be secret. (*Eyeing his watch.*) Also I believe in being on time ...

BIGMOUTH: While we wait, I would like for you to make some exclusive statements to The Voice of Exile.

MR. BLOND: I've already told you. This is a secret mission. I can't speak on the radio. Don't bother me any more, please ...

BIGMOUTH: Look here, bud, let's make a deal. You give me the interview now, and I give you my word that I won't broadcast it until you return from your mission.

MR. BLOND: I don't know ... Phillip ... I don't know ... (*He buries his head in the files.*)

CHEO: (*Approaching* BIGMOUTH.) Hey, big boy! Any problems?

BIGMOUTH: Oh boy! Am I glad to see you here! Can you give me something on this mission for the seven-o'clock-news? That dumb gringo is full of ... mystery.

CHEO: (*Puffing-up his chest.*) Well, old man, this is very serious business. You know, we do have to be careful, the infiltrations ... all have to avoid a repetition of 1961.

BIGMOUTH: (*Speaking to the mike.*) Bulletin, bulletin. This is an exclusive news bulletin for Radio Shout. A secret mission on exile Cubans leaves for Nicaragua. We are here in an unidentified place in Florida as the plane is about to take off on a mission of assistance and combat. We are going to interview Cheo Calleocho, a most distinguished member of our glorious brigade. Tell me, Cheo, what is the purpose of this mission?

CHEO: I am unable to explain it to you as it is a secret mission. You know, we Cubans have to lend a hand to our Nicaraguan brothers who are fighting freedom and democracy. They need arms and medicine. We know a lot about this stuff ... you know ...

BIGMOUTH: Then you are taking arms and medicine to the Contras?

CHEO: Man, are you something! Of what? You got it! Well, yeah, that's what we are going for. You know, with my experience ...

BIGMOUTH: Let's ask Cheo Calleocho, in this exclusive interview for Radio Shout, what is your responsibility in this transcendental mission?

CHEO: I'm the pilot, my man. (*He signals* BIGMOUTH *to turn off the tape-recorder. Enter* HOPE STILL *and* WITNESS ALL-KNOWING. HOPE *is wearing jeans, sneakers, and a bandanna, looking a little unkempt.* WITNESS *will smoke a pipe, and he'll carry a shorthand-dictation-type notebook and a pen. He will dress simply. Perhaps chinos, a sports shirt and a windbreaker.*)

BIGMOUTH: (*Approaches them with the microphone..*) Friends, all of Miami is aware of this important secret mission and we wish to know how you feel in these moments that could be transcendental for the history of the New World! And of ... why not say it? Of the whole world!

HOPE: I am very excited. We have lived under a communist regime and I know that without help it is impossible to overthow. I believe it is the duty of Cuban youth to think about all the young people in other countries who need our help.

WITNESS: (BIGMOUTH *sticks the mike under* WITNESS' *nose, and as he is about to speak,* WITNESS *waves him off with a brusque motion.*) You all are always equally irresponsible. You are going to spoil this before it begins.

BIGMOUTH: Are gou yoing to behave like the dumb gringo and

tell me that this is a secret mission when everybody knows about it?

WITNESS: Well, in any case, I have no comment. I am going as a reporter, and as a responsible journalist, I will not interject my opinion. Rather, I shall transmit objectively what others think. And that, after the fact, and not before. (HOPE *meanwhile has approached* MR. BLOND *who is sitting down with some papers and speaks with him in low tones.* CHEO *has returned to his inspection of the plane.* BIGMOUTH *doesn't pay much attention to* WITNESS' *comments and begins to look over the new arrivals. Indeed,* SIR PRETERIT PERFECT *and* MADAME PAINS CROSS PERFECT *arrive.* SIR PRETERIT *will be dressed with a three-piece suit, tie-clip, with a Cuban flag or preferably a pin with the Cuban Bar Association insignia in his lapel.* MADAME *will dress elegantly, with heels, a patterned dress, leather bag; she is made-up, but not too much.*)

BIGMOUTH: Sir Preterit, would you grant me a few words, exclusively for Radio Shout, The Voice of Exile.

SIR PRETERIT: Most happy to oblige, Bigmouth, of course I would.

BIGMOUTH: (*Speaking to the mike.*) We have before our microphones the illustrious Republican Sir Preterit Perfect, who has devoted himself so for the Cuban cause of freedom, in the very moment that he is about to board the airplane for Nicaragua. Could you tell us, Sir Preterit, what is the historical significance of this mission?

SIR PRETERIT: (*As if to give a speech, in a formal oratorical attitude.*) Our Apostle Martí taught us that the peoples of Our America ought to help each other. And even though the governments of Latin America have behaved very badly toward us—not in vain did Bolívar say, who knew the cloth from which he was cut, that he had plowed the sea—Cuban freedom flows through Managua, and we are to hold an encounter with the Nicaraguan leadership, because it is unavoidably imperative that they sign this manifesto which I carry, so that it may be published, and the whole world will have notice of the renowned race of patriotic freedom fighters of Central America.

BIGMOUTH: Madame, Lady Pains Cross of Perfect, you who are the very symbol of Cuban womanhood and who always accompanies your husband, would you say a few words for us?

MADAME PAINS: Preterit always wants me to accompany him. I must remind him when it is time to take his pills.

BIGMOUTH: Good, good, we see that behind every great man there is a woman who cares for him. But, tell me, Madame, I understand that the Cuban Ladies Association has contributed toward this enterprise.

MADAME PAINS: Indeed. We held a great banquet and dance ... there was the cream of Cuban society ... (*In a confidential tone to* BIGMOUTH.) Because you know that nowadays ...

BIGMOUTH: Well, Madame, Mrs. Perfect, but what has been the result of the fundraising?

MADAME PAINS: (*Very pompously.*) I am very proud because I have been chosen as the one to take to the rebel fighters a Martí basket because it is the way in which we Cuban women honor Martí.

BIGMOUTH: You have heard, an exclusive for Radio Shout, Madame Pains Cross of Perfect in representation of the Cuban Ladies Association, who have generously, and without fear of sacrifice, been able to collect, and see what a beautiful gesture, a Martí basket to hand over to the Nicaraguan freedom fighters. (JOHNNY KNOW-IT-ALL, *dressed in a contemporary suit with a designer tie, an attaché case, approaches, a little breathless, looking at his watch.* BIGMOUTH *sides-up to him immediately.*) Ladies and gentlemen, the well-known business man, Johnny Know-It-All, candidate for city council of Little Guanabacoa, who has just arrived to this secret place where a mission of Cubans is ready to leave for combat zones where the brave Nicaraguans fight to overthrown the bloody communist dictatorship, is going to make a statement, in exclusive, for Radio Shout. Tell us, Mr. Know-It-All, what has made you join this historic mission?

KNOW-IT-ALL: Well, Bigmouth, you know that I came here when I was very young, but I always carry Cuba in my heart, and that is precisely why I am running as a councilman por Little Guanabacoa, because Cubans have to have more power in order to fight communism. I am very happy to be a part of this mission with people that I admire so much, like Sir Preterit, because I have promised that if they vote for me in order for us to get respect, I'll fly to

Washington and go to see Reagan to find a solution to this topic. (*The others have been occupying their seats in the plane.* CHEO *in front as a pilot.* SIR PRETERIT *next to his wife.* HOPE *and* WITNESS *each alone in their row.* MR. BLOND *walks, clipboard in hand, among them, checking to make sure everything is in order. Finally, he approaches* KNOW-IT-ALL.)

MR. BLOND: You must leave now. You are one hour late.

KNOW-IT-ALL: Boy, and here I thought we were using Cuban time. (KNOW-IT-ALL *gets on and sits next to* HOPE. BIGMOUTH *goes to the far end of stage right.* MR. BLOND *stands in front of the passengers and pilot.*)

MR. BLOND: First of all, I will make an important announcement. Everyone pay attention. According to federal regulation 1723x52 it is necessary for you to fasten your safety harness, you know ... seat belts. (*A sound travels throughout the plane mixing laughter and protest, while they fasten their belts.*)

MR. BLOND: Number 2. You all must sign a document which is at your seats which exempts the government from all responsibility. (*Again they search for the papers and pens and they sign.*)

SIR PRETERIT: (*To his wife.*) These Americans don't change. They always want paperwork, forms, signatures. They want to jump in the water without wetting their clothes. (HOPE *picks-up the papers and hands them to* MR. BLOND.)

MR. BLOND: Number 3. Everything is in order. Cheo and I checked the boxes with medications, equipment, and confidential material. When you land in Honduras ...

SR. PRETERIT: Excuse me, Mr. Blond, but I thought we were going to Nicaragua.

MR. BLOND: That is imposible because of security reasons. You go to the border and hand over the materials. (*General murmur of protests.*) Those are orders from above. I had nothing to do with them.

CHEO: Well, but once we are there, if the opportunity presents itself ... we can cross the border.

MR. BLOND: (*Looking at his papers.*) That is not in the book. I think you are better off not doing it. (CHEO *and* SIR PRETERIT *exchange winks.*) Does somebody have a question?

KNOW-IT-ALL: Will there be any problems in returning by the
     date of return? I have a very important meeting to attend.
MR. BLOND: No, no problem. Time to leave. You all have your
     instructions. Lots of luck! (*The sound of motors fills the
     stage as* CHEO *is pushing buttons on the dash, talking on
     the radio, turning the wheel, etc.*)
BIGMOUTH: Ladies and gentlemen, let us get this plane off the
     ground with these brave and self-sacrificing Cubans that
     are about to enter Nicaraguan combat zones to help their
     brothers in this ferocious battle to return Cuba and Nica-
     ragua to the company of free nations of the world ...

     *The lights begin to dim and the sound of a plane flying can
be heard. Suddenly the motors start missing. And the sound of a
crash landing accompanied by all sounds appropriate to an aviation
mishap. Meanwhile, the lights come up slowly, and little by little
the plane and the characters, as in slow motion, will fall, dropping
or turning packages, paper, etc. In the final seconds of this pan-
tomime of the accident's impact, there will be absolute silence. Or
the accident could be simulated with slides very guidely. Lights.
Everyone is semiconscious. They awake slowly. They have their
faces and clothes stained and appear disheveled. Things are scattered throughout the stage. Pieces of the aircraft are in the floor,
etc. The backdrop that looked like a hangar is gone and now there
is one simulating lush vegetation as from a Caribbean island.*

HOPE: What a whack! It's everyone Okay?
MADAME PAINS: What happened, Holy Sacrament?
SIR PRETERIT: Don't you worry, woman ...
KNOW-IT-ALL: Lucky we had our belts on.
CHEO: This plane is for shit ...
SIR PRETERIT: We must remain calm ...
MADAME PAINS: What a rough landing ... !
WITNESS: I hope my camera didn't break ...
MADAME PAINS: Oh, don't you dare photograph me, I'm a mis-
          ery ... I have ruined my dress and I must have my hair
          a mess ...
HOPE: Madame, and what does that matter? What matters is the
     historical evidence ...
MADAME PAINS: Well, my girl, you're very young and will come
          out looking great in any photo you're in, but not me. If
          I am not combed and made-up, I look like a scarecrow.
          And then, imagine what people will say ...

WITNESS: Madame, I do not believe it is a matter of looks, but of values ...

CHEO: We have to get in touch with Mr. Blond immediately so that we may be rescued.

KNOW-IT-ALL: First of all it will be better if we check to see if the plane is working and where we are.

SIR PRETERIT: Cheo, you should try to start the air ship.

CHEO: You know, when I was in the army they tought us all that: What to do in case o emergency. No problem, old man, leave it to me.

KNOW-IT-ALL: Then, let's get going. Let's try it.

MADAME PAINS: Soon it will be night ...

CHEO: (*With a confident attitude, checks the buttons, makes adjustments, etc. and, while everyone holds their breath, he tries to start the engine. The motor sputters and dies.*) I think it died.

MADAME PAINS: And isn't it possible to call the AAA?

SIR PRETERIT: Why don't you check to see if the emergency motor will start?

HOPE: (*To* WITNESS.) And this old man knows it all?

CHEO: The back-up motor ... ? Oh, yes, yes, let's see ...

MADAME PAINS: Isn't there a telephone nearby?

WITNESS: Madame, we don't even know where we are!

KNOW-IT-ALL: I imagine that the plane has a computerized compass.

CHEO: (*Bringing in his hand a large compass.*) This is what there is, brother.

KNOW-IT-ALL: That's appalling! When I return I'll write a letter to my senator. Can you imagine sending us on this mission with twenty-year old equipment and this pilot who doesn't even know where the back-up motor is ... And to bring out that compass!

CHEO: (*Ready to fight.*) Listen to me, I won't take that. I was in the Bay of Pigs and when I have to fight I fight!

SIR PRETERIT: Calm down, easy, gentlemen. What we Cubans cannot do now is to fight among ourselves when we have ... when we are shipwrecked!

WITNESS: I believe we should find out where we are.

ALL: Yes! Yes!

HOPE: And if we landed in Cuba?

MADAME PAINS: What an idea! It's the last thing we need ...

SIR PRETERIT: Well, the place looks like it ... could be ...

KNOW-IT-ALL: I don't remember ...

HOPE: I do, because I left only six years ago, and I don't think this is Cuba.

CHEO: I have a navigation chart ...

SIR PRETERIT: Can you read it?

CHEO: Please, Sir Preterit, listen, your question offends me! (CHEO *takes out the chart. Looks at the compass, then the map.*)

CHEO: This compass is like the little pilgrim ...

MADAME PAINS: Whatever do you mean?

CHEO: You don't know the story of the little pilgrim?

SIR PRETERIT: Cheo!

HOPE: Nothing, Madame, that compass is pure shit.

SIR PRETERIT: These young people of today, they don't respect anyone ...

HOPE: But you knew the story ...

SIR PRETERIT: Yes, but I don't repeat it in front of ladies.

HOPE: That is hypocritical.

MADAME PAINS: My God!

WITNESS: Well, Cheo. Do you or do you not know where we are?

CHEO: I don't think so, because according to this, we are in the Philipines.

KNOW-IT-ALL: According to the maximun speed that is possible in this plane and the time we were flying, that is absolutely impossible.

SIR PRETERIT: Let me see. Give it to me. (*He studies the compass and the chart carefully..*) Well I would dare say with almost total certainty and without fear of having erred, that we are in the Island of Cutopia.

ALL BUT WITNESS: Cutopia?

SIR PRETERIT: It is an uninhabited island?

WITNESS: Well, there have been times when there has been some inhabitant or another, almost always shipwrecked people ... Many times they have tried to civilize it, but for some reason or another it always returns to its original virginal state.

SIR PRETERIT: And that is so, even when it is an island with a great many natural resources and a strategic geographical location.

HOPE: And how do you know that we are in Cutopia?

SIR PRETERIT: Because in Cuba we studied geography, and not like the young people here who think that Córdoba is a type of auto.

KNOW-IT-ALL: It's Córdova and Chrysler makes it.

MADAME PAINS: My husband is right. Education in Cuba was far superior to that of the U.S.

KNOW-IT-ALL: Madame, at the University of Havana they may have taught fine, but there was no academic rigor. I've been told that ...

SIR PRETERIT: Young man, you cannot hold an opinion about something you know nothing about. I can assure you that next to ours, Harvard is nothing.

KNOW-IT-ALL: Don't you pick on my alma mater.

HOPE: And do you know American universities? Because, as you said old man, "you cannot hold an opinion about something you know nothing about."

SIR PRETERIT: You are nothing but an insolent ... !

WITNESS: Allow me to interrupt. You are comparing apples and oranges. Each system has its faults and its merits.

CHEO: I don't care in what university you learned it, but let's see who knows how the radio works so that we can call Mr. Blond, otherwise we're up the creek ...

HOPE: But don't you know how to work the radio?

CHEO: Of course, sister, but this radio is different.

KNOW-IT-ALL: Let's see. (CHEO *hands him the radio.*) It works like the RX7.

SIR PRETERIT: Young man, all radios work through codes.

KNOW-IT-ALL: No, I mean that like the car it works by means of a computer.

MADAME PAINS: Oh, my God! Computers are taking over everything.

WITNESS: Madame, we already know that progress and civilization are not synonymous.

HOPE: Yes, there are lots of advances, but still a lot of children to to bed hungry.

MADAME PAINS: Don't you believe that, girl, that's Communist propaganda. In today's world no one goes hungry, much less children!

HOPE: Madame, are you going to tell me that in Haiti and in Ethiopia children don't go to bed hungry?

MADAME PAINS: Well, but they are ...

HOPE: What are you going to say, that they are Black? For you, of course, they are inferior ...

SIR PRETERIT: My wife did not say that. And you are somewhat right, Miss, because we know that in Cuba and in Nicaragua, for instance, there is a lot of hunger and misery.

HOPE: Well, let me tell you, Sir, I suffered a lot of in Cuba, so nobody can tell me stories, about hunger, real hunger, no.

SIR PRETERIT: Perhaps your family was ...

HOPE: Perhaps my family was Communist? Is that what you were going to say? Is the world for you a neat division of black and white? Of Communism and Anti-Communism? Do children feel hunger only under Communism and the rest of them can go to bed hungry, and as long as they have freedom, that word so used and abused, they will not feel hunger?

SIR PRETERIT: Miss, you are very confused. Forgive me, but ...

MADAME PAINS: Over there they brainwash them, and how ... All in all, each day that goes by I am very happy that I was able to raise my children in the U.S.

WITNESS: I understand it Madame, but if you think a little bit, in a certain way, American youth also receive a little bit of a brainwashing ever day ... although for different reasons ... it's the consumer society ... the culture of the image ... They have to eat a certain cereal to grow, brush with a certain toothpaste to have a successful love life, drive such and such a car to achieve status ... Since early childhood they also have a value confusion ...

KNOW-IT-ALL: No confusion whatsoever! Advertisements are nothing but a simple mechanism of a market economy, which in the last analysis, is the only one that works.

HOPE: Witness, you cannot really compare them! Capitalism may have a host of problems, but ...

MADAME PAINS: What I have to say is that the family is not as it used to be. Not here, not there, not anywhere.

CHEO: Hello, hello, can you hear me? Mission 3502 speaking. Can you hear me? This is Cheo ...

VOICE: Please repeat.

CHEO: They are speaking English.

KNOW-IT-ALL: Of course! What did you expect, that they had an interpreter waiting for you?

SIR PRETERIT: Young man, this is the time to be cooperative. Why don't you try to see if they can understand you?

KNOW-IT-ALL: Hello? Hello? This is Johnny Know-It-All, President of Mistrust Bank, talking for Mission 3502.

VOICE: We read you. What seems to be the problem?

MADAME PAINS: What is he saying? What is he saying?

SIR PRETERIT: Quiet, woman!

HOPE: He wants to know what is the problem.

KNOW-IT-ALL: Our plane has crashed. We are lost.

VOICE: What plane? We have no record ...

CHEO: Do they think that we want them to play a record for us?

KNOW-IT-ALL: Mission 3502 ... over ...

VOICE: That is a secret mission. You are not supposed to know about it.

HOPE: (*Interpreting.*) He says that we should not know about our mission.

KNOW-IT-ALL: We need your help, we need you to rescue us ...

CHEO: Taken for a ride! Again!

KNOW-IT-ALL: Please, answer ... hello ... hello ... hello ...

CHEO: The radio has died.

MADAME PAINS: Do we have to spend the night here? We have no beds, we have nothing!

WITNESS: Madame, don't worry about one night. Perhaps we have to spend the rest of our lives here.

KNOW-IT-ALL: Don't worry, Madame. Even though we have had a breakdown in communications, they know what is happening and they will come to rescue us.

CHEO: This guy is really naive! This is just like the Bay of Pigs ... Another ride ... I don't know why the hell I got involved in this mess ...

SIR PRETERIT: Cheo, Cheo ... don't use those curse words: There are ladies present.

HOPE: Don't worry about me, Cheo, because words are not good or bad ... nor do they possess morality.

MADAME PAINS: I can see how young people have lost all sense of shame.

HOPE: Madame, when one has to spend a year in agriculture, as I had to when I was twelve, not only does one lose one's shame, no ... and not only does one lose that which you are now imagining, one also loses all sensitivity in one's body because of the pain in one's hands and back ... and because of the unforgiving sun ...

MADAME PAINS: Do you see what I mean? All in all, television cannot do as much harm as that inhuman system.

HOPE: Well, at least on that point, we agree.

SIR PRETERIT: Well, well, if we have to spend the night here, we best get organized.

KNOW-IT-ALL: We have to make a list of things to do and then we must establish priorities. (*They all look at each other in surprise.*)

CHEO: Here you don't have a secretary ... Hey, buddy, do you really think you are still at the bank?

KNOW-IT-ALL: Witness, you and I will explore around to see if we find out anything ... Cheo can stay behind in case they call on the radio. Hope, can you stay and help him with English? (*She nods.*) You four can prepare a fire so that it is easier for the helicopters to find us ... and perhaps prepare some food.

CHEO: Do you think the helicopters will come, Sir Preterit?

SIR PRETERIT: Cheo, I don't know ... don't know ... what to tell you ... I would like to believe that they will ... (*Looking at his wife.*) ... yes, of course, they will come. (*Aside to* CHEO.) I have my doubts ... with these gringos one never knows ... How often have they not withdrawn from their allies?

MADAME PAINS: Look what they did to the Shah of Iraq.

SIR PRETERIT: Pains, The Shah of Iran.

MADAME PAINS: Oh, yes, I get all those countries confused one with the other. (*Meanwhile,* WITNESS *and* KNOW-IT-ALL *prepare to leave.*)

KNOW-IT-ALL: (*To* WITNESS.) Are you armed?

WITNESS: Armed, me? No. And you?

KNOW-IT-ALL: Of course, I was not going to come to this party without my pistol. You'd better get a gun from one of those boxes.

WITNESS: No, I'd better not. Anyway I don't know how to use them. (*They exit, from whatever side of the stage lies toward the South.*)

MADAME PAINS: Don't delay ...

HOPE: What do you want, Madame, that they call on the phone if they are going to be late?

MADAME PAINS: It wouldn't be a bad idea ... if you knew ...

HOPE: I was being sarcastic!

SIR PRETERIT: We know, my little girl, we know ...

HOPE: I'm not your little girl.

SIR PRETERIT: You could be my grandaughter.

HOPE: So?

CHEO: That the devil's wisdom is a product of his age, not his nature.

HOPE: So now Cheo is going to come out with proverbial philosophy, just like Sancho Panza.

CHEO: Philosophy? Let's see ... let's see ... that is not my strong suit, but I had an uncle in Cuba who had read even the

old ones ... those ancient ones ... classics ... What do
you call them?

SIR PRETERIT: The Greeks?

CHEO: Yes ... and one in particular that he quoted from a lot ...
Arisocrates?

SIR PRETERIT: Socrates?

CHEO: No, no, a really famous one ...

SIR PRETERIT: Plato?

CHEO: No, no, a serious guy, truly.

SIR PRETERIT: Cheo, Plato was serious. Aristotle?

CHEO: Yes, that's the one, the very one. And my poor old uncle
would say, and I say poor because he died, not because
he didn't have any money, and I didn't know why he said
this: "Poor Cubans, they will never understand Aris ...
totle!" Did I pronounce it right?

HOPE: I don't know why he said it, because there are Cubans
educated enough to understand Greek philosophers.

CHEO: Not me, Miss, ... philosophers I don't know except for
Hyacinth the neighborhood butcher where I used to live.
They called him Hyacinth-the-Philosopher because he was
always explaining why there was no meat for sale.

MADAME PAINS: Cubans have a wit that can take advantage of
everything.

HOPE: It would be better more for them not to make fun of everything.

CHEO: Well, gentlemen, let's see if philosophy helps us to make
fire.

HOPE: Cheo, we are not boy scouts! We have matches, don't we?

MADAME PAINS: I think this is a good place. (*They assemble
leaves, small tree trunks, etc. and place them in the middle
and light it. There will be some type of artificial fire on
stage. A red lamp or something like it.*)

SIR PRETERIT: Cheo, do you believe that we could use something
from the provisions that we were taking on the mission?

CHEO: Of course. Isn't it for the needy? And who is more in need
than we are now?

HOPE: (*Aside.*) Now Sancho is also the comic of the work. (CHEO
begins to take out some cans of provisions.)

MADAME PAINS: Do we have an opener, Cheo?

CHEO: Madame, there I believe that we are in bad shape. But I
have a penknife ...

MADAME PAINS: And place-settings?

HOPE: (*Sarcastically.*) And candelabras, Cheo?

SIR PRETERIT: Young lady, you are very hostile. Perhaps you are tired.

HOPE: Listen, I'd better not answer that ... (WITNESS *and* KNOW-IT-ALL *return.*)

KNOW-IT-ALL: Have you called on the radio?

CHEO: No, son, that is kaput.

MADAME PAINS: But what have you seen?

KNOW-IT-ALL: We have not wanted to go far away. The island seems deserted ...

WITNESS: But there are some signs ...

HOPE: Like what?

WITNESS: I thought I saw human tracks on the beach ...

SIR PRETERITO: Footprints?

WITNESS: No ... some initials ... a drawing ... perhaps I am mistaken ...

KNOW-IT-ALL: It's his idea ...

WITNESS: In the morning we'll be able to explore more. Now, as it already got dark ...

MADAME PAINS: We were trying to prepare something to eat ...

WITNESS: The island is very beautiful ... you know? (*To* HOPE.)

CHEO: (*He has been searching the boxes.*) Look what I've found! (*Removes a box that says "In case of emergency."*)

ALL: What is it?

MADAME PAINS: Open it!

CHEO: Here's my penknife.

KNOW-IT-ALL: Wait, Cheo, you must read the instructions carefully.

WITNESS: Perhaps it refers to another type of emergency.

CHEO: What's all the fuss ... I'll open it ... Give it to me here ... (*Struggles with the penknife—which is small—but the carton does not yield.*)

SIR PRETERIT: Allow me, Cheo? Watch, if you cut it here, it is easier ... (*The box is opened.*)

CHEO: These blondes are incredible.

KNOW-IT-ALL: They'are very organized.

MADAME PAINS: They think of everything ...

SIR PRETERIT: (*Aside.*) This gives me a bad feeling ...

MADAME PAINS: Well, it'll come in handy ...

HOPE: Always the same, they think they can solve it all with food.

CHEO: Oh, girl, don't tell me, I was traded for jars of stewed fruit.

WITNESS: Primum vivere deinde philosophari. (CHEO *takes out some boxes of Kentucky Fried Chicken, or something similar, and some soft drinks.*)

MADAME PAINS: I don't know how it is possible, the food is hot and the soft drinks cold ...

HOPE: How the Russians invent! ...

MADAME PAINS: Young lady, the Russians are incapable of these advances ...

HOPE: (*Aside.*) It's useless! They don't understand ... (*They have been sitting down and begin to eat. For a moment, all are silent. The scene gets dark, until it becomes night and stars are seen.*)

CHEO: What silence ... you all ...

KNOW-IT-ALL: We were hungry.

HOPE: In my house, they said that an angel had passed ...

WITNESS: And in mine, that a soul had risen to heaven ...

HOPE: It is pretty, after all, isn't it? Those legends that are transmitted from generation to generation ...

SIR PRETERIT: I did not believe her to be interested in learning about her elders ...

HOPE: So you see ... one never knows ...

MADAME PAINS: The truth is that a moment ago, I don't know, it seemed to me that I was in Cuba again.

CHEO: You know, Madame, it happened to me also.

MADAME PAINS: Yes, it seemed that I was in Cuba, on the estate of my uncle Pancho, and nothing had happened.

HOPE: Nothing had happened, Madame? But do you believe that one can erase a quarter of a century of history from a country, thus, with a blink of your eyes in order to return to your uncle's estate?

SIR PRETERIT: Young lady, I understand that at your age, one takes everything seriously. My wife did not say it with political intentions.

HOPE: And how do you know with what intention she said it? Why do you have to respond to everything your wife says?

MADAME PAINS: Every woman is represented by her husband ...

HOPE: Look, Madame, I don't know what intentions you said it with, but I want to tell you two that the Cuba you left, and you live constantly longing for, you're never going to return to, because it doesn't exist.

SIR PRETERIT: It is true that there have been many deaths ...

HOPE: The corpses, although it may seem very cynical, are the ones that count. It is the living ...

WITNESS: The people think differently ... they have had other experiences ... it was easy to see with those who came through Mariel, and nevertheless, they have been well integrated to the society.

HOPE: Yes, but in the first place, in spite of the "undesirables," it was a matter of people with initiative. The proof is that they made a decision in a specific moment. They risked it all. They had to have courage to enter the Peruvian Embassy and even more to go away via Mariel ...

MADAME PAINS: Besides, they received a lot of help ... you're not going to deny that?

WITNESS: Yes ... and no ... but the important thing is than we were in a country with many resources. And Cuba, the day that one could return, is going to be a country without resources.

CHEO: The blondies will put up the bread.

WITNESS: Or they'll say, as with our missions Cheo, that they don't know about us.

MADAME PAINS: But do you believe that they really will abandon us?

WITNESS: It's possible. All is possible.

KNOW-IT-ALL: No, don't worry. They will come.

CHEO: After all, it's our fault. By falling into the same trap.

WITNESS: It's that Platt Amendment-type mentality with which the flawed republic and each one of us was born.

SIR PRETERIT: Young man, our republic was an example ... You youngsters have come to believe that Marxist propaganda that the American "liberals" have helped to spread, that Cuba was the whorehouse of America, an underdeveloped country ...

WITNESS: (*With irony.*) No ... indeed, what I have come to believe is that it was the Paradise Lost.

MADAME PAINS: And indeed, son, one does not know what he has until he loses it, but in Cuba one lived very well.

HOPE: And from what one sees in the society news, there are still many people who live very well.

SIR PRETERIT: Don't be ironic, young woman. There will always be all kinds ... And that's how it has to be. The equality of classes is a Communist myth. The important thing is equality before the law. And in Cuba we not only had a constitution that was an example, but also social legislation that still the Americans nowadays would want ... One worked 11 months and got payed for 13 ... The law of the paid vacations ... and the sugar coordination law ...

MADAME PAINS: And the maternity benefits ...

WITNESS: Then you also believe that the Revolution was a fluke because all was perfect there?

SIR PRETERIT: No, not perfect, but economically the country was taking off. We were the third American country in per capita ...

WITNESS: Look, Sir Preterit, I do not wish to argue with you. But in Cuba, as is true everywhere, there were inequalities, injustices, racial prejudices.

HOPE: When I arrived here, after living up to the age of fourteen in Cuba, it seemed to me that Communism was living, but upside down.

MADAME PAINS: How can you say that?

HOPE: Very simple, Madame. There, they spend all the time speaking ill of the Americans, exalting the Revolution, and if perhaps one feels some desire to know about the years before the Revolution, he manages to find out only that everything was bad. Here, it is the same, but upside down. They spend time speaking ill of the Communists, exalting one another and the glories of the republic. Now I understand why Cheo's uncle said that the Cubans will never be Aristotelians. We are people of extremes.

CHEO: The truth is that it's certain that in Cuba one lived well, but there also were problems ...

MADAME PAINS: Well, there are problems everywhere ...

SIR PRETERIT: What happens is that you, young people, are not interested in finding out about Cuba. Some neither know nor speak Spanish correctly, and they use Cuba like demagogues for their political aspirations in the United States.

KNOW-IT-ALL: Look, Sir Preterit, if that description fits me, it's certain that my Spanish is bad, but you don't have the right to tell me that I don't love or feel for Cuba.

WITNESS: Can you truthfully tell me that the rulers in Cuba were honest? That there was no government corruption? That Machado was not a dreadful dictator? You yourself participated in the Revolution of '33 ... And what happened with that Revolution? They gained nothing ... It remained stopped-up. Castro's Revolution had its reasons ...

SIR PRETERIT: Then you are one of those who sustain the thesis of the Revolution betrayed?

WITNESS: No, Sir Preterit. What I want to say is that things have a historical process.

SIR PRETERIT: What is historical is that Herbert Matthews made
　　　　Castro the Robin Hood of the Americas, and the Ameri-
　　　　cans withdrew their support of Batista.

KNOW-IT-ALL: At times it seems that the only two men in Cuba
　　　　were Batista and Castro.

HOPE: What I have never understood is that if Cuba was the mar-
　　　　vel that it was, why was Castro able to triumph, and why
　　　　did so many Cubans go away fleeing instead of defending
　　　　that country that they love so much?

MADAME PAINS: Oh, young woman, you do not remember be-
　　　　cause you were young, but the people who helped Castro
　　　　were of a breed ... you had to see those who descended
　　　　from the Sierra ... what types ... on January first, people
　　　　that one had never seen went out to the street.

WITNESS: Of course, Madame, as they did not frequent the Yacht
　　　　Club ...

CHEO: The truth is that I left because I never thought that the
　　　　Americans would tolerate Communism in its own face.

WITNESS: And you tell me that there was no Platt Amendment-
　　　　type mentality? Everyone leave and then let the gringos
　　　　solve the problem ... Isn't that so?

SIR PRETERIT: Not so either, Witness. You are also too young to
　　　　remember, but one must recognize that Castro did things
　　　　very well. He deceived many people. We left little by
　　　　little. And when we realized what was happening, it was
　　　　too late. By then he controlled it all.

KNOW-IT-ALL: And later? What do you say ... ?

SIR PRETERIT: We have always struggled for Cuba's freedom.
　　　　And we continue doing it. You, the youth, are the ones
　　　　who live indifferent to the tragedy of Cuba.

KNOW-IT-ALL: You're always speaking about the youth, criticiz-
　　　　ing us, as if we were, I don't know, extra-terrestrials! And
　　　　as if the old ones had the monopoly of the exile's pain.

WITNESS: Our lives have been truncated from the beginning. You
　　　　at least occupied positions in your countries, participated
　　　　in the political process.

SIR PRETERIT: Yes, that's right, but you have been able to study
　　　　your careers here, it goes well for you, you make money,
　　　　you have success, you forget Cuba. You don't know what
　　　　it is to have dedicated all your life to create a republic
　　　　and see it trampled. When I went into exile, I was already
　　　　fifty years old. I did not know English. My life had been
　　　　politics and Cuba. It was as if my whole world had died.

MADAME PAINS: We thought that the first years had been the hardest. A man of the prestige of Sir Preterit ... who had been a Senator ... and had to sell automobiles, insurance, even was a cab driver. Do you remember, Preterit, that time they tried to rob you?

CHEO: Tell us, Sir Preterit.

SIR PRETERIT: It was nothing ... nothing ... I was working the night shift in the airport because by day I sold insurance. I had just left a couple in the Hotel Columbus and a young man got into the back seat, he put a pistol to my temple and demanded all my money. The only thing that I had was the eight dollars I had just collected.

CHEO: And what did you do?

SIR PRETERIT: In my poor English, I told him that I would give him the money, but that he was making a mistake for which he would en up in prison or dead, that he should work, study ... and we ended up drinking coffee at the Little Tavern.

WITNESS: If it's a matter of speaking, you don't lack for words.

CHEO: In those times, everyone has his story. Once I took a correspondence course to fix TV sets. And I had my share of trouble! If I was able to carry the TV set to my house, it was smoother, because I followed the instructions until I succeeded, but the bad thing was to have to fix it in the client's house. I would say that I had to look for a part in the truck in order to consult the manual. But at times I couldn't find the problem. And when the mistress of the house would not move from my side ... I had to be asking her for a glass of water so that I might have a few minutes to myself. The worst day was when I managed to have the TV set work, and when I went to arm the apparatus and put it back together again, there were extra parts! I ended up by carrying them secretly in my pocket ... (*Laughs.*)

MADAME PAINS: What stories those are. But at least we had the illusion of the return ...

SIR PRETERIT: Now we are tired. We can live, we live, dedicated to Cuba. And it is so little what one can do! No one helps. No one cooperates.

CHEO: Sir Preterit, you know how life is here. Now you say that, and I feel guilty. I send my small check from time to time, and I cooperate in what I can, but I understand that it is not enough. And you know me well ... you know that I understand that it is not enough. And you know me well

... you know that when I had to risk my life ... that I am willing to die for Cuba ...

WITNESS: We are all willing to die for Cuba. The difficult thing is to live for her.

CHEO: It's true. When I left prison, I still had the illusion that we would yet do something ... Later I got married, the children came, the job ... one becomes estranged. And now what good am I? I am not an intellectual. I cannot write a manifesto. I could only go to fight. And I am so fat ... and so out of shape ... that not even that ...

SIR PRETERIT: I understand all that, Cheo. One cannot make revolution part-time. For that reason, the Communists win the game from us. They do not refrain from sacrifices. They live dedicated to their cause. In any case, you are an educated man, who knows the problem. We can always count on you when the time comes. What pains me most is the indifference of the youth. You do not see young faces at any act or event. Many know nothing about Martí, nor what May 20 signifies ...

MADAME PAINS: Our own grandchildren ... for all that we have tried ... and that infernal music that they listen to!

KNOW-IT-ALL: And who could be to blame? We have not made the present world. We have inherited it.

WITNESS: Not all the past is negative, Johnny. I have felt so many times the weight of the great responsibility that my generation has ... it is the bridge generation ... the one that must pick up a heritage and transmit it to the younger ones ... at times I think that we are the last generation of Cubans ...

SIR PRETERIT: We have lived with the word "Cuba" in our mouth, trying to teach them ...

KNOW-IT-ALL: To teach them? And what can you teach us if for each one of you the clock stopped the day you left Cuba? We are not at fault for what happened. You lost Cuba and have not known even how to make yourself agree on how to recover her.

SIR PRETERIT: You are insulting me. And moreover, you do not know what you're speaking of. Those old people that you disparage so much are also responsible for all the good that the Republic had. With what right ... ?

KNOW-IT-ALL: ... With what right ... ? Then I'm going to tell you ... With the right that I came to this country at the age of only ten, that I lived with an American family in

Kansas, where no one spoke Spanish. And I didn't even know how to say "yes." I have always been thankful to them, but it was the saddest year of my life. I missed my parents, my high school, my brothers. At school, they made fun of me ... because I had a Latin name. With what right do I speak? When my mother came the next year, we moved to New Jersey ... Mom worked in a factory ... I arrived alone from high school. I made myself the brave man. As Papa wasn't there, I was the man of the house. But when I arrived home from school and had to walk by those dark halls and open the door of the apartment ... I always thought that I was going to meet someone inside. Everyone made me afraid from my earliest memories of muggings. And already in Cuba, we always lived with fear ... All my childhood, I remember feeling only fear ...

MADAME PAINS: And your father, was he able to come later?

KNOW-IT-ALL: No, Madame, my father was a prisoner for fifteen years. He died in prison.

MADAME PAINS: I am sorry, I did not know ...

KNOW-IT-ALL: Never mind. I have never said it in any political campaign ... My mother has never recovered ... nor has she stopped blaming herself for having left him there. But imagine, she had the children on the other side.

CHEO: There is no love like that of a mother.

HOPE: And when you moved to Miami?

KNOW-IT-ALL: It's been ten years ... When the old man died ... I had just graduated from college ... I had opportunities there, but my mother was very depressed, as if all the struggle had not made any sense. I thought that she was going crazy. It has gone well for us, although I didn't find all that I expected.

HOPE: In what sense?

KNOW-IT-ALL: I came fiercely anti-Castro. I wanted to avenge the death of my father ... to inquire about Cuba ... the roots of our drama ...

WITNESS: And?

KNOW-IT-ALL: That's what makes me furious, Sir Preterit. I approached all the exile organizations. It was always the same. The old ones spent their time speaking of the Paradise that was Cuba. Each time that I had an idea, they said that I didn't have experience, that I didn't know anything about that. They were the ones who spoke at the meetings, always quoting Martí.

WITNESS: But in that Cuba of all and for the good of all, it seems as if the youth are not included. Nor those who would think differently from the elders.

HOPE: How can you not get mad? It is still that way, and one sees so many things. I have not seen women more frivolous than the Cubans. They all die to get their picture in the newspaper, and spend so much on the dresses for those balls supposedly for the benefit of charity ... If they'd give only half to the poor ... They are moved by the death of the son of Franco's niece, whose picture appears in *Hola*, or by the death of Grace Kelly ... but they are incapable of shedding a tear for the victims of Armero, or Mexico ...

MADAME PAINS: My child, as my husband always says ...

HOPE: And besides, they don't even know how to think. They are the shadow of their husbands ...

MADAME PAINS: And what do you want me to do? It is a matter of education. They raised me in the old-fashioned way, the mission of the woman was to get married. I grew up in a house full of servants. When I came here, I never had made my bed. At the age of forty, I was totally useless. My children were still small when we arrived. At that age, I confronted life for the first time. Even learning to make rice was an odyssey. I depended on Preterit for everything. Well, it has always been like that. Later I had no choice but to go out to work. I have never been able to learn English ... Now the children are grown. We have grandchildren. At times I do not understand what they say ... About the computers and those things ... It is true that at times I go to those lunches and I read *Hola*. What do you want me to do? It is the little bit that I enjoy. I have two or three old friends like myself. We watch television, soap operas. We knit. On the other hand, I have always had a dress ready so as to follow my husband, and I have encouraged my husband in the matter of Cuba ... Isn't it true, Preterit?

CHEO: I know it, Madame, because I have always seen you at all the functions with him.

HOPE: When one hears you, it seems as if the only ones that have suffered have been the ones who left. You speak of Cuba all the time and you do not know what Cuba is today. You do not know what it is to have learned to read with "C" for Castro, "R" for Raúl ... You do not know what it is to see yourself forced to be a pioneer ... to be nine years old and not have a gift for Christmas ... To have never chewed gum ... to work picking tomatoes ... to have to go to the public square in a bus ... to do volunteer work in order for a popular assembly to decide if they give or don't give a fan to one ... and that departure via Mariel ... when they threw us to the dogs ... when I saw the woman whom they took away with the child in her arms ... when ... (HOPE *begins to cry and all surround her.*) I don't like to talk about this ...

WITNESS: Do you remember the case of the little girl who arrived alone at Key West because all her family had died at sea ... ? It is Hope.

HOPE: I do not know if I will ever be able to love again ... I do not know if I can forgive ...

CHEO: Oh, girl, one forgives but does not forget.

ACT II

The following morning. Setting: the same. All sleep. Toward the right side, SIR PRETERIT *and* MADAME PAINS, *totally clothed, semi-reclining upon some baggage and covered up to the waist. Toward the middle,* CHEO, *on his back, uncovered, with the T-shirt that allows one to see the belly. Toward the left,* WITNESS *and* HOPE, *in sleeping bags and in fetal positions.* KNOW-IT-ALL *is not seen. Dawn. The scene will remain in silence some seconds, with the exception of the breathing of the sleeping characters, and the snoring of* CHEO. DON'T-HAVE-A-CHOICE *enters, dressed like a militiaman. He inspects with astonishment the sleeping characters. At once,* SIR PRETERIT *opens his eyes, and they are seen face to face.* DON'T-HAVE-A-CHOICE *clutches his rifle.*

DON'T-HAVE-A-CHOICE: Put your hands up! Nobody moves! (*All awake in great confusion.*) Nobody moves! Nobody moves! (*Behind* DON'T-HAVE-A-CHOICE, *a movement is heard. He turns quickly and shoots at* KNOW-IT-ALL, *but the weapon does not work. This gives* KNOW-IT-ALL *time to draw his pistol, then* DON'T-HAVE-A-CHOICE *runs away.*)

MADAME PAINS: Has anything happened, young man?

KNOW-IT-ALL: Don't be worried, Madame. Nothing.

CHEO: Then the island is not as abandoned as we thought ...

HOPE: He seemed frightened ...

SIR PRETERIT: I do not think ...

MADAME PAINS: Will he return ... ?

WITNESS: He'll probably return, and with reinforcements.

KNOW-IT-ALL: He gave us no time to explain ...

SIR PRETERIT: Nor is he going to. We better prepare to defend
    ourselves.

WITNESS: Come on, Sir Preterit, don't be ridiculous ... (*Sounds
    as of horses are heard.* CHEO *takes some binoculars and
    looks toward where* DON'T-HAVE-A-CHOICE *went away.
    The noise is heard closer.*)

CHEO: They're going to attack us! Battalions are coming ... and
    battalions ...

SIR PRETERIT: Then we must defend ourselves. Distribute the
    weapons. There is no time to lose. (*Tremendous confusion
    ensues. They open the boxes with weapons and distribute
    them, including* HOPE, *but not* MADAME PAINS, *who
    cries out and puts her hands on her head. They take po-
    sitions, backs to the public and facing the invaders, who
    come from the background. Shots begin to be heard. They
    fire. They go from one side to the other. They seek more
    munitions. Noise. Shouting.*)

CHEO: They seem to be stubborn ants.

KNOW-IT-ALL: Where the hell are they coming from?

WITNESS: Come on, come on.

SIR PRETERIT: Careful, careful ... on that flank.

HOPE: I don't like this at all ... (*Finally, a great explosion is heard,
    and a great silence ... All look at one another.*)

SIR PRETERIT: We beat them.

ALL: We won, we won. (*They take one another by the hand and
    move away, making a ring and singing, "We won, we
    won!"*)

CHEO: (CHEO *observes with the binoculars.*) They've put up a
    white flag.

KNOW-IT-ALL: (*From one of the flanks, a stone covered with a
    cloth falls.*) It's a bomb!

HOPE: I'm sure it's a message.

CHEO: We'd better see.

SIR PRETERIT: Wait. It could be an ambush.

MADAME PAINS: Oh, my God, be very careful.

WITNESS: (WITNESS *approaches, unties the rope that fastens the cloth to the stone.*) It's a message.

ALL THE REST: What does it say? What does it say?

WITNESS: They want to send an emissary.

SIR PRETERIT: Of course! If Maceo and Martínez Campos had a meeting after the protest of Baragua ...

MADAME PAINS: It won't be a trick?

KNOW-IT-ALL: There are too many of us for them to deceive us.

HOPE: We don't know how many they are ...

MADAME PAINS: Nor what they want. Will there be coffee to offer them?

KNOW-IT-ALL: We must answer them.

SIR PRETERIT: We must submit it to a vote. I present the assemblage a proposition to be accepted, but with the condition that I would be a lone delegate. Does anyone second the motion?

WITNESS: Such formality isn't necessary ...

CHEO: I second it ...

SIR PRETERIT: All in favor, raise your hand. (*All raise a hand, resigned.*) A delegate now has to draw up the reply and submit it to the aproval of the assembly. (*The young people look at one another, and they laugh.*)

WITNESS: We shall finish ... (*Takes the white cloth, a pen, and writes.*) There it is. "We agree to receive a lone emissary and who is not armed."

SIR PRETERIT: Good, very good. Now we must seek the best way of sending it. (WITNESS *looks at him somewhat impatient and in jest, but with a certain tenderness. He throws the rock in the direction from which it came.*)

MADAME PAINS: Now we must wait ...

HOPE: Will the same one who came before come now ... ?

SIR PRETERIT: You should have fixed the hour and day.

WITNESS: And also the place?

CHEO: There he comes, there he comes! Yes, Hope, he's the same one.

DON'T-HAVE-A-CHOICE: (*Enters and becomes solemn.*) Lieutenant Don't-Have-a-Choice from the Army of Cutopia ...

SIR PRETERIT: Cutopia. I told them.

KNOW-IT-ALL: At ease.

DON'T-HAVE-A-CHOICE: What?

SIR PRETERIT: Relax. (DON'T-HAVE-A-CHOICE *obeys.*)

SIR PRETERIT: Good, young man ... We would desire to explain
  that we have not come to harm them. Our plane has
  fallen, and we are awaiting rescue.
DON'T-HAVE-A-CHOICE: And where do you come from? The
  United States?
ALL: Yes ...
HOPE: But we are not Americans ...
DON'T-HAVE-A-CHOICE: What are you, then?
ALL: Cubans.
KNOW-IT-ALL: And you?
DON'T-HAVE-A-CHOICE: Cutopians, of course.
MADAME PAINS: We know nothing about your country ...
DON'T-HAVE-A-CHOICE: No, Madame, no one knows anything
  real about our country. Nothing more than lies have been
  published.
SIR PRETERIT: We ... we are interested in knowing ...
HOPE: (*Timidly.*) About you ... about the inhabitants ... about
  the customs ...
DON'T-HAVE-A-CHOICE: It is a large island. It has ten million
  inhabitants. It is very beautiful.
WITNESS: How is it possible that one could know so little about
  this island? When was it discovered?
DON'T-HAVE-A-CHOICE: In 1959. Previously, there had been
  a colony here, and later a manipulated republic, but in
  1959 King Nicastro ascended to the throne and began the
  First Republic of Cutopia.
WITNESS: You could not remember that ...
DON'T-HAVE-A-CHOICE: No, I was born that same year. I belong to the generation of the new man.
HOPE: And how is that new man?
DON'T-HAVE-A-CHOICE: He was supposed to be a man dedicated to the Revolution, who would have no more god
  than King Nicastro, who would work voluntarily sixty
  hours a week, who would hate the imperialists, who would
  live from the air, and who would conform with construct-
  ing a better society for his great-grandchildren. Ah, of
  course, and he would know how to applaud.
HOPE: And isn't the new man like that?
DON'T-HAVE-A-CHOICE: No way! ... To begin with, not everybody is equal. But I can tell you a little about me. Many
  of the things that I do are because I have no choice.
WITNESS: Like what?

DON'T-HAVE-A-CHOICE: Well, like having gone to Angola to fight ... like applauding five-hour speeches ... like imprisoning a comrade for having bought provisions on the black market ... like my having spent my life preparing for an invasion from the north that will never come ... like proclaiming hatred, vengeance ...

WITNESS: And are there many who think like you?

DON'T-HAVE-A-CHOICE: Many ... there is much confusion ... to begin, we like pitusas ...

MADAME PAINS: Pitusas?

DON'T-HAVE-A-CHOICE: Blue jeans ...

MADAME PAINS: Ah!

SIR PRETERIT: But King Nicastro has a powerful army, doesn't he?

DON'T-HAVE-A-CHOICE: King Nicastro has just died.

ALL: Are you sure?

DON'T-HAVE-A-CHOICE: Very sure. I have seen him.

SIR PRETERIT: And what is happening in the country?

WITNESS: The inevitable, don't you think?

CHEO: Is everybody fighting?

DON'T-HAVE-A-CHOICE: We are at the edge of a civil war ...

HOPE: What horror ...

DON'T-HAVE-A-CHOICE: You alone are our hope ...

ALL: We ... ?

DON'T-HAVE-A-CHOICE: Yes ... we have arranged for King Nicastro's foreign guard to leave the country. We do not want more foreigners, but you are like us. We speak the same language. We see that you not only have weapons, but have superior equipment. Other knowledge, modern techniques. We need your help.

SIR PRETERIT: How?

DON'T-HAVE-A-CHOICE: You make the choice. We want one of you to be our king. To guide us, to lead us out of this bog ... Finally, to govern us.

WITNESS: It seems to me that I'm living in a novel by Baroja. Is this dream or reality?

DON'T-HAVE-A-CHOICE: Look ... what there is on this island is a nightmare. And we are all anxious for peace. The spilling of blood has to end. What do you say to my proposal? (*All look at one another.*)

SIR PRETERIT: I think ...

WITNESS: That you have to give us some time to think about it.

DON'T-HAVE-A-CHOICE: How much time do you need?

SIR PRETERIT: Imagine ... it is a difficult decision ...

WITNESS: One week?

MADAME PAINS: One week? But Mr. Blond will come looking for us before ...

DON'T-HAVE-A-CHOICE: The people are very impatient. No, one week is too much. We need a reply in twenty-four hours.

WITNESS: Do we accept? Can we make a decision in twenty-four hours?

SIR PRETERIT: It is a complicated matter ... and complex.

CHEO: But urgent ...

KNOW-IT-ALL: The quicker, the better.

WITNESS: Hope?

HOPE: I believe that we must help them.

SIR PRETERIT: We cannot act hastily ...

WITNESS: If all are in agreement, young man, you'll have our reply in twenty-four hours.

DON'T-HAVE-A-CHOICE: It's a deal. (*Extends his hand.*)

HOPE: But do you have to go already?

DON'T-HAVE-A-CHOICE: Yes ... I must inform ...

HOPE: But we know so little of Cutopia. How can we govern it?

DON'T-HAVE-A-CHOICE: I do not know. But I beg you to seek a solution. (DON'T-HAVE-A-CHOICE *marches off, looking at* HOPE. *Throughout the scene, their glances have reflected the attraction of the young people for each the other.*)

SIR PRETERIT: We have come to put ourselves in a fine mess!

WITNESS: Well, I believe we must accept.

KNOW-IT-ALL: I need to return to the United States at once.

WITNESS: Why?

KNOW-IT-ALL: My whole life is there ... my plans ... my aspirations ... my security.

WITNESS: But didn't you speak a moment ago about your difficulties in adapting, your love for Cuba?

KNOW-IT-ALL: Yes, but this is not Cuba.

WITNESS: No, but it could be ... Don't you realize the opportunity that it offers?

CHEO: We can bring our family later on ...

SIR PRETERIT: We have nothing to lose. Isn't that so, Madame Pains? Yes, I am willing ... we shall help them ...

HOPE: Hooray, hooray! (*Embraces* SIR PRETERIT, *who is surprised but smiles.*)

MADAME PAINS: But, Preterit, what about your health? You
　　　　have to be careful ... (SIR PRETERIT *makes a loving
　　　　gesture which, however, signals that she should not disturb
　　　　him.*)
CHEO: (*To* WITNESS.) And you? What do you say?
WITNESS: Well yes, of course.
SIR PRETERIT: Then only Mister Know-It-All wants to return ...
WITNESS: We need you. You are the only one in the group who
　　　　knows of economic matters ... and you know business
　　　　administration very well ...
KNOW-IT-ALL: It's impossible for me. I have many things to do.
　　　　My bank. My campaign. My family. My taxes. (*They all
　　　　look at him entreatingly.*)
KNOW-IT-ALL: Good, I accept temporarily ... but only until they
　　　　find a replacement.
SIR PRETERIT: Then, all that's missing is to designate the king!
WITNESS: Not so fast ... not so fast. Why a king? Monarchies
　　　　are in decadence.
KNOW-IT-ALL: It is what they have requested ...
WITNESS: They don't know anything else ...
CHEO: A king? A president? It's the same thing. A matter of
　　　　words. A few who rule, and many who obey.
SIR PRETERIT: No, don't say that, Cheo. There is no system
　　　　like democracy. At least up to now. What happens is
　　　　that there are moments in which the people need a strong
　　　　hand.
WITNESS: For me, there is nothing that could justify a dictator-
　　　　ship, neither of the left nor of the right.
CHEO: Listen, you're not going to compare Pinochet with Castro
　　　　to me!
WITNESS: But don't they realize that one thing brings the other?
　　　　That Somoza is the most direct cause of Sandinista-ism?
SIR PRETERIT: And Batista is the culprit of Communism in
　　　　Cuba, right? (*In an ironic tone.*)
WITNESS: One of them. Although in the case of Cuba, if we
　　　　had to point out culprits, I believe that one would have to
　　　　condemn ninety percent of the Cubans. It was a collective
　　　　fever ...
SIR PRETERIT: Witness, I understand that democracy is best, but
　　　　what happens is that it is a matter of a system that is not
　　　　prepared to defend itself from Communism.
CHEO: But, old man, that is the fight between the lion and the
　　　　tied-up monkey. And still, as with the joke, they tell you

to fight cleanly ...

WITNESS: In my opinion, the ills of democracy can only be cured with more democracy.

SIR PRETERIT: Well, well, if we are in agreement that democracy is the ideal ... let us go on ...

CHEO: All of us believe in freedom.

KNOW-IT-ALL: And free enterprise ...

HOPE: And social justice ...

WITNESS: And national sovereignty ...

MADAME PAINS: And respect for private property ...

KNOW-IT-ALL: And for the law ...

SIR PRETERIT: I have the solution.

CHEO: What solution?

SIR PRETERIT: We shall set ourselves up in Constituent Assembly and give Cutopia a constitution, a Fundamental Law.

ALL: Bravo, bravo!

CHEO: Old man, now you hit the nail on the head.

KNOW-IT-ALL: It will be fast, because we are in agreement.

HOPE: Then let's get on with it.

WITNESS: I'll take it down ... let's see ... (*Takes out a pad and a pen.*)

MADAME PAINS: What name shall we give it?

KNOW-IT-ALL: Constitutions don't have a name.

SIR PRETERIT: Of course they do. It will be called the Constitution of Cutopia of 1986.

HOPE: And if they already have a constitution?

SIR PRETERIT: It will be no good.

HOPE: How can we know? Don't-Have-a-Choice should not have gone away.

WITNESS: (*Looking at her.*) He will return soon enough ... soon enough ...

SIR PRETERIT: Good, let us begin ... I believe that an important topic is the one of private property.

WITNESS: Do we all believe in private property?

HOPE: Yes, but ...

WITNESS: But what?

HOPE: But we must offer alternatives to lead to the logical common good, within a perfectly sympathetic declaration.

SIR PRETERIT: Man is born with the instinct of possession. The first thing he learns to say as a baby is "mine."

WITNESS: That's true. But there have to be controls, otherwise the large estates which have been the great evil of our countries get amassed ... some public services, like the

telephone, electricity, transport, must be kept national-
ized.

CHEO: But if there is no competition, then each time they want
to raise the price, the one who is injured is the client. In
Miami ...

MADAME PAINS: Oh, yes, no one could understand those bills
from the telephone company ... and one has no choice
but to pay.

KNOW-IT-ALL: You know? I believe that the economic model of
the United States ...

WITNESS: You're comparing apples with oranges. You can't think
of the economy of a country so advanced ...

HOPE: It's just that we know nothing of Cutopia.

KNOW-IT-ALL: By its geographical position, its natural ally is the
United States.

SIR PRETERIT: It seems to me, young man, that you are an annexationist.

KNOW-IT-ALL: Annexationist? And what are you trying to say?

WITNESS: The best that we can hope for is to outline the model
that we think best and later adapt it to the realities of the
place.

SIR PRETERIT: But if all is changed later, of what use will it be
...

WITNESS: It's necessary to be flexible.

SIR PRETERIT: I believe that it is best to be conservative with
regard to the economic system. We need laws to guarantee
respect for property and investment, national as well as
foreign.

HOPE: Well, well, not so fast with the matter of foreign invest-
ments. We don't want the island to be seized by foreign
capital ...

KNOW-IT-ALL: The dollar brings nothing but prosperity.

MADAME PAINS: In Cuba, everyone wanted to work for American firms. They paid better.

WITNESS: And in Latin America? Can anyone deny the abuses
that have taken place, and deny that they still exist?

SIR PRETERIT: And who is more at fault, the one who buys or
the one who sells himself?

KNOW-IT-ALL: That's why we cannot sell this island to foreign
capital, no matter where it comes from.

KNOW-IT-ALL: Today's economy does not allow economically independent countries to exist. Without injections of foreign capital, the country will not be able to take-off.

HOPE: One must also take into consideration how these people feel. Don't-Have-a-Choice has said that they have expelled some foreigners and do not want more.

CHEO: They will have to submit.

WITNESS: If what we will do is to impose ourselves upon them
...

SIR PRETERIT: Haven't they asked us to govern them?

KNOW-IT-ALL: It will be best to vote on the issue of private property.

SIR PRETERIT: I maintain that the central ideal of the nation must be a robust economy, based upon private property and free enterprise, with an advanced social legislation framed by the Fundamental Law.

WITNESS: It seems to me that a country in transition needs a mixed economy.

CHEO: My old man, who was a peasant from the mountains, told me that the most important thing, the only sure thing, was the land.

HOPE: It will be necesary to draw up a plan of agrarian reform.

MADAME PAINS: Agrarian reform? Do not frighten me ... please!

WITNESS: It's necessary to avoid the large estates ...

KNOW-IT-ALL: Better to seek new markets, industrialize the country.

SIR PRETERIT: In Cuba, it was enough for us with sugar. Look at all the experiments that they have now made, even planting eucalyptus trees along the central highway in order to make furniture ... and nothing! All failure. Cuba depends upon sugar ... and maybe, also tobacco and coffee.

WITNESS: And it survives only by the gigantic subsidy that it receives from the Soviet Union. If not, now that caffeine and tobacco cause cancer, and everyone takes Sweet'n Low so as not to get fat, Cuba is going to "do" very well!

KNOW-IT-ALL: But is it necessary that everybody must measure everything by the Cuban standard? There are other examples. Some Caribbean islands have made a great industry of tourism.

SIR PRETERIT: We come back to the same thing. Without foreign capital ...

HOPE: The major capital of the people is their human resources.

WITNESS: That's another factor that is an unknown quantity. In what mood is this people after more than twenty-five years of a totalitarian government? Because all the dictatorships castrate the people.

CHEO: Or make them wake up.

WITNESS: That is no more than Calleocho's rhetoric.

SIR PRETERIT: You are very skeptical.

WITNESS: It's just that I've seen many things ...

CHEO: It may be rhetoric or whatever you say, but definitely when things get tough, people search for a way to cope.

SIR PRETERIT: The blood shed in the revolutions demands that all the frustrations be overcome.

KNOW-IT-ALL: It's necessary to develop an effective strategy.

MADAME PAINS: I believe that an important problem is education. These days, the youth does not have good manners.

SIR PRETERIT: Woman, those are external manifestations ... the youth of today has been confronted by a very difficult world ... it has other worries ...

HOPE: Of course ... (*Smiles at* SIR PRETERIT *between amazed and thankful.*)

KNOW-IT-ALL: The most important thing in education will be citizen participation in the democratic process ...

CHEO: The vote should be obligatory.

WITNESS: Watch out! Democracy cannot convert itself into a strait jacket. One must guarantee ideological pluralism, include participation of the adversaries in the political process.

SIR PRETERIT: Adversaries, yes, but enemies, no. The Communist Party must be prohibited.

WITNESS: I don't agree ...

KNOW-IT-ALL: Neither do I.

MADAME PAINS: Well, I do.

CHEO: So do I.

HOPE: Not me.

SIR PRETERIT: But have you not learned from the Cuban example?

WITNESS: And are you going to tell me that it happened in Cuba because the Communist Party was legalized?

SIR PRETERIT: No, but ...

WITNESS: But nothing ... look at the example of Spain ...

SIR PRETERIT: Spain! It will be a disaster. Felipe González is a Communist dupe.

WITNESS: All he is, is a watered-down Socialist ... !

MADAME PAINS: And is he a friend of Fidel ... ?

WITNESS: He has to make concessions to the Part ...

KNOW-IT-ALL: You see Communists even in the soup ...

CHEO: One cannot trust anyone. There is an international conspiracy. How else do you explain ... all these phenomena?

HOPE: It is no mystery. The Communists are persons of flesh and
bone. Some good. Others bad. They are fanatics. The
believe in it. They live dedicated to a cause.

WITNESS: For that reason where they have most difficulties is in
the countries where they have religious fanatics. Look at
the beating that they're taking in Afghanistan.

HOPE: Perhaps if the people in Cuba had been more truly Catholic
and not giving lip service ...

SIR PRETERIT: But the Church ... Now, co-existing with Castro
...

WITNESS: The mission of the Church is to survive. To carry the
sacraments to the faithful.

SIR PRETERIT: It is an ignominy.

CHEO: They are going to be fooled, dummies.

WITNESS: It's a game. The thing is who has better cards.

KNOW-IT-ALL: But as the dealer is Fidel ...

HOPE: Some day it will be his turn to lose.

WITNESS: People, we can't stop talking about Cuba. We are obsessed. Don't you realize what this opportunity means for
us? We have to prove that we are capable ... of seeking
a thesis of agreement, to see if we can play the complete
symphony.

CHEO: Very pretty! (*Applauds.*) ... You intellectuals always have
an apt phrase. Do you know what is lacking? A lot of
beatings so that the people will walk straight. Work and
food. The rest comes by itself.

MADAME PAINS: There is nothing that exalts more than work
...

HOPE: Do you say it from experience?

KNOW-IT-ALL: I believe that the most important thing is to create
a democratic conscience.

HOPE: You are like the Americans, who believe that what is good
for them is good for everybody else.

WITNESS: Socialism at times ...

MADAME PAINS: For God's sake ...

SIR PRETERIT: Young man, you must be one of those repentant
Fidelistas, imbued with the Marxist virus, who no matter
how much they call themselves "dissidents," they cannot
be cured ... they carry it in the blood.

WITNESS: You're always the same, Sir Preterit, putting labels on
people. This one you classify as "annexationist," that one

"confused insolent one," me "repentant Fidelista." And you, where are you situated ... ? Tell me ... Where do you fit?

SIR PRETERIT: My only commitment is to Cuba.

WITNESS: And what do you want, a medal?

HOPE: Don't fight any more ... with the need to construct the civilization of love in the world ...

WITNESS: That is very beautiful, Hope... but man... will always be the wolf of man.

CHEO: Yes, with all the good that the Cubans are, because the truth is that they are good men and hard workers, do you know what gets them lost? Envy. Always that blessed envy.

HOPE: And ego.

CHEO: Yes, egotism.

HOPE: That also, but I want to say the "I" is always the most important being to each one. Will the Cutopians be the same?

WITNESS: All people are the same.

KNOW-IT-ALL: I don't agree ... the Anglo-Saxon tradition ...

WITNESS: Well, now, other elements come into play there, history, circumstances, as Ortega y Gasset would say.

HOPE: If the Cutopians have asked us to govern them, it is a sign of modesty.

WITNESS: Or incapacity.

CHEO: Or desperation.

HOPE: We cannot fail. The clock is ticking, and we are not in agreement.

CHEO: But down inside we all think the same, don't we?

SIR PRETERIT: I cannot sign a document where the Communist Party is legalized.

WITNESS: Nor I one where obstacles to freedom are placed.

KNOW-IT-ALL: First, one must hold some elections.

SIR PRETERIT: Before, it will have to have a constituent ...

HOPE: We must take these people into account.

CHEO: The ones here are not in agreement.

MADAME PAINS: Because the Constitution ...

CHEO: Because when the Bay of Pigs ...

SIR PRETERIT: Because one must found the Authentic Party ...

HOPE: Love is the basis of the society.

WITNESS: Democracy is a responsibility. (*All speak at once in a violent manner, without reaching any agreement.*)

SIR PRETERIT: One must give back the properties ...

WITNESS: The mixed economy ...

HOPE: The democratic institutions ...

SIR PRETERIT: Human dignity ... (*Puts his hand on his breast as if aching.*)

MADAME PAINS: Do you feel bad, viejo? (SIR PRETERIT *dries his sweat, and with much calm, extracts a small box from his pocket and puts a small pill in his mouth.*) When he is excited ... Now you see how he becomes.

HOPE: Do you want a little bit of water? (CHEO *helps* SIR PRETERIT *sit down and gives him a drink from a canteen ... He wants to open his shirt but is denied.*)

MADAME PAINS: Do you want some paregoric elixir?

SIR PRETERIT: No, no ... it's nothing. It will soon pass.

KNOW-IT-ALL: We'd better take a break. (*Steps are heard. All listen toward the side from which they originate.* DON'T-HAVE-A-CHOICE *enters.*)

DON'T-HAVE-A-CHOICE: May I?

SIR PRETERIT: Young man, two hours have not even gone by ...

DON'T-HAVE-A-CHOICE: Yes, I know ... but things are happening fast, every minute ... the people are very disturbed ... we need a solution ...

SIR PRETERIT: Our session had been interrupted for several minutes. We shall soon return to our meeting. Meanwhile, perhaps you could give the young man some basic information about Cutopia that we need in order to continue ...

DON'T-HAVE-A-CHOICE: With much pleasure. (HOPE *and* DON'T-HAVE-A-CHOICE *sit at one side.*) What do you want to know?

HOPE: If there are many stubborn old men ...

DON'T-HAVE-A-CHOICE: What are you saying?

HOPE: I was joking ... it's just that these old men of ours are something ... one ends up by paying them respect ... and even affection, but they are so obstinate ...

DON'T-HAVE-A-CHOICE: If you knew that one of our problems is that we don't have old men ... we don't have a past. It's very difficult living without memories.

HOPE: But at times memories are so sad.

DON'T-HAVE-A-CHOICE: Even so ... they are as important as illusions. Don't you think?

HOPE: I had never thought about it ... but you are right. Perhaps these old men are eternal because they do not lose the hope of returning.

DON'T-HAVE-A-CHOICE: I believe that one never returns to any place.

HOPE: Why do you say that?

DON'T-HAVE-A-CHOICE: Those who go away from here never return ... perhaps, as tourists, and so changed that they would seem to be others.

HOPE: I don't know how the others will decide ... but ...

DON'T-HAVE-A-CHOICE: It would please me for you to stay.

HOPE: I am a teacher ... perhaps I could help in something.

DON'T-HAVE-A-CHOICE: We need it all ... technicians, economists, teachers, lawyers ... journalists ... doctors ... engineers ... and ...

HOPE: And what else?

DON'T-HAVE-A-CHOICE: I don't know. I was going to say "much love," but perhaps you would have laughed.

HOPE: No ... I'm not laughing ... on the contrary, nowadays everybody lives with a mask put on. It is lovely that someone would say what he feels ...

DON'T-HAVE-A-CHOICE: You know, perhaps it is the first time that I have been totally sincere with anyone. (*The rest have stayed,* MADAME PAINS *attending to* SIR PRETERIT, CHEO *looking over the equipment,* KNOW-IT-ALL *and* WITNESS *conversing in a low voice, and the latter taking notes.*)

WITNESS: (*Approaching* SIR PRETERIT.) Do you feel better?

SIR PRETERIT: Yes, yes, it has been nothing. If you wish, let's continue.

CHEO: (*At that point,* CHEO, *who has been fooling around with the radio, makes contact.*) Hello, hello.

VOICE: This is control base Q.

KNOW-IT-ALL: This is mission 3509 on the island of Cutopia.

VOICE: We have spotted your location. Rescue mission on its way. Should be there in less than an hour.

MADAME PAINS: What do they say?

KNOW-IT-ALL: They'll be looking for us in an hour.

MADAME PAINS: Thank God!

HOPE: But are you going to leave?

SIR PRETERIT: With Sir Preterit feeling this way ... there he has his doctors ... his clinic and his children and grandchildren are there.

KNOW-IT-ALL: I always said that I had to return ...

CHEO: Well, it's very difficult to leave one's things behind.

WITNESS: I thought that over there was not home.

CHEO: Well, old man, but one has struggled much to save a few
    pennies to now begin again ... without guaranties, nor
    knowing what is going to happen ...

SIR PRETERIT: If we were younger ...

DON'T-HAVE-A-CHOICE: We need you.

HOPE: I'll stay.

WITNESS: Me, too.

MADAME PAINS: Think it over carefully.

SIR PRETERIT: These things have to be considered in a coherent
    manner, to make decisions with relative objectivity and
    with a certain empirical and realistic spirit. You know
    the old saying, "If at the age of twenty one isn't a revolu-
    tionary, he doesn't have a heart, and if at the age of sixty
    he is one, he doesn't have a head." But you want a rev-
    olution! What we need is to prohibit revolutions forever.
    (*Noise as of helicopters is heard.*)

MADAME PAINS: There they are. We'd better gather our stuff
    together.

KNOW-IT-ALL: I believe that, after all, I'll make it in time for my
    meeting ... (MR. BLOND *and* PHILLIP BIGMOUTH
    appear, the latter with the microphone.)

MR. BLOND: Is everybody okay? The helicopter is waiting. Come
    fast.

BIGMOUTH: We find ourselves in the dangerous marshes in the
    middle of the rescue operation to the valiant Cubans who
    have been wounded by the Sandinista airplanes ...

WITNESS: Don't tell lies. (*To* SIR PRETERIT.) Do you want to
    return to that? To those exaggerations? To that smoke-
    screen? To that falsehood? Stay with us.

HOPE: Yes, we need you. You have an unmatched experience. We
    have to count on you.

MADAME PAINS: It's his health ...

SIR PRETERIT: I wish ...

MADAME PAINS: It is too much responsibility for me alone ...
    What will the children say if something happens to him?
    Look at the pain that he has already suffered ...

SIR PRETERIT: It is too late for me ...

BIGMOUTH: Listen ladies and gentlemen, the airplanes of the res-
    cue mission to these grave combatants for the principles
    of democracy ...

MR. BLOND: Hurry up. (*Movement of gathering of things.*)

DON'T-HAVE-A-CHOICE: It would have pleased us if you had
    stayed ...

MADAME PAINS: Writ ...

HOPE: And you also ...

SIR PRETERIT: Perhaps I could return ... if you need some counsel ...

WITNESS: Sir Preterit, all your life is a counsel. We shall always have it present ... (WITNESS *and* SIR PRETERIT *embrace.* MADAME PAINS *approaches* HOPE *and delivers a box to him.*)

MADAME PAINS: It is the small Martí wicker basket. Perhaps some day, when you have your children, you might be able to use it and remember me.

HOPE: Madame, I did not want to offend you ... it's just that there are moments ...

KNOW-IT-ALL: It's getting late.

CHEO: Christ, these boxes weigh a lot! Listen, Rubio, couldn't we leave these people the food and the medical equipment? They need it all.

MR. BLOND: I don't know. Regulations ...

HOPE: Do you see, Cheo, we are not like that, with so many regulations? There are times that the heart ...

MR. BLOND: Let's go. (*They all march off, among embraces, goodbyes, tears, baggage, confusion, etc.* DON'T-HAVE-A-CHOICE, HOPE, *and* WITNESS *remain for a moment in silence.*)

HOPE: It is a pity. They are all people who have something to contribute.

DON'T-HAVE-A-CHOICE: And this country needs so much help to reconstruct it.

WITNESS: But it was impossible to reach an agreement.

DON'T-HAVE-A-CHOICE: Perhaps as things progressed ...

HOPE: You know, that they are all partly right ...

WITNESS: Sir Preterit exasperates me ... and Johnny the same, but they are people who are worth a great deal.

HOPE: And Cheo is a good soul.

WITNESS: Perhaps this moment has arrived too late for many.

DON'T-HAVE-A-CHOICE: There is no time for lamentations. We have much to do to construct the new Republic.

WITNESS: I believe that Sir Preterit was right in that we must begin with the Fundamental Law.

HOPE: So let's get to work!

WITNESS: Where is the pen? (*They start to work.*)

CURTAIN

A Little Something
to Ease the Pain

by

Réne R. Alomá

A Little Something to Ease the Pain

About the Author

René R. Alomá was born in Santiago de Cuba in 1947. There he received his elementary education from the Jesuit Fathers at the Colegio de Dolores. After leaving Cuba he enrolled in 1962 at Assumption College School in Windsor, Canada where he spent his high school years. There he became the literary editor for the school paper *The Lancer* and joined the drama club.

Alomá graduated in 1966 and went across the U.S.-Canada border to college at Wayne State University in Detroit, Michigan. He attended Monteith College, majoring in Fine Arts and Languages. He was awarded the Woodward Scholarship in 1967–68 and the Sara Leopold Scholarship a year later. During that period Alomá was accepted as a Theater Apprentice at Bonstelle Theatre where he trained as assistant director, stage manager and director. In 1968 he married Canadian actress Zoey Adams (nee Marie Romain), and taught theater arts at Holy Trinity School in Detroit, Michigan. In 1969 he received his bachelor of arts degree from Wayne State and toured Ohio, Indiana and Michigan as actor/director of the Migrant Theatre Force.

After that, entered the Masters program in Modern Languages at the University of Windsor where he was appointed as Teaching Fellow. But by the next year he was in England studying theater design at Central School and at St. Michael's College of Art in London. He directed some courses at the London City Literary Institute, and became the Road Manager for the Argyle Theatre Company in Birkenhead, England, touring northern England. The 1971–72 school year found Alomá back at the University of Windsor completing his masters and writing a master's essay on "Contemporary Theatre in Spain and Latin America" with Professor Ron Pazik. That year he served as a Teaching Assistant in the Hispanic Department while freelancing as a costume designer for the University of Windsor's School of Drama and for the Theatre Centre Windsor.

For the next two years Alomá taught at De La Salle College in Toronto while also directing two original musical plays, "Sunnyside" and "You're a Good Man, Charlie Brown." In 1974 he wrote "Once, a Family," a two act Gothic drama. This play he was able to workshop at the Tarragon Theatre in Toronto where he had been accepted as Playwright in Residence from 1974–75. Later in 1975 he went to New York to study improvisation and scene study with Bernard Hiatt of Neighborhood Playhouse. Back in Toronto he directed "Fiddler on the Roof" at the Hart House Theatre and "Blithe Spirit" and "Dracula," both at Theatre Five.

In 1977 under the direction of Muriel Spark and starring Rosemary Prinz, the Memphis Repertory Company produced "Once, a Family" giving at once great joy and a heartbreak to Alomá. The play later won the Clifford E. Lee Award, but the Memphis production invalidated the award and it was retracted with a letter of honorable mention. Tireless, he directed "The Diary of Anne Frank" for On stage Productions in Toronto and "Gigi" and "Kennedy's Children" also in that venue.

Alomá in 1978 perfected his knowledge of the theater by continuing to learn the craft of directing with "West End Story" for Toronto's Tarragon Theatre, "Our Town" for Seneca College's Octagon Theatre, "Applause" for the University of Toronto's MacMillan Theatre and "Picnic" for the Lexington Avenue Playhouse. He studied directing, as well, with Alan Arkin and Edgar Ross of the Yale Drama School at the Lexington Avenue Playhouse in New York. While there he audited acting classes with Uta Hagen. He also taught acting classes for On Stage Productions in Toronto. The renewal marked by the year 1978 was completed by the birth of his daughter, Miranda.

A year later he would draft the first version of the play in this anthology. "The Exile" received the first prize from the Smile Company Playwriting Award from Southhampton University in Long Island. That year the Toronto Youth Festival presented his direction of "David and Lisa" at the Harborfront Theatre.

And finally in 1980 "The Exile," now entitled "A Little Something to Ease the Pain," was produced by Toronto Arts Productions and directed by Edward Gilbert at Toronto's St. Lawrence Centre for the Arts. In 1981 Alomá wrote a radio adaptation of the play for the Canadian Broadcasting Corporation. He also received a Canada Council grant for work on "End of Year," a two-act drama, unfinished at the time of his death. That year he directed "Skin Deep" with Rosemary Radcliffe and Nika Rylsky at the Ports in Toronto, and once again in 1982 for the Charlotte town festival in Prince Edward Island. Thereafter he joined the Playwright's Workshop at INTAR in New York, run by Obie Award-winner María Irene Fornés. There, in 1983, he wrote and directed "A Flight of Angels" with Zoey Adams and Philip Galbraith. Meanwhile, the play "A Little Something to Ease the Pain" was produced in Spanish in Caracas, Venezuela. Still at INTAR in 1984, he wrote and directed his one act play "Mountain Road." Back in Toronto he directed "Mass Appeal" and "Pyjama Game," as well as his friend Milcha Sánchez's "A Cuban Swimmer" and his own "Mountain Road" for Theatre Autumn Leaf.

In 1985 he began working on a new two-act play in English entitled "Secretos de Amor." In 1986 during the final weeks of his life, he completed the final draft of the existing version of "A Little Something to Ease the Pain" and completed work on "Secretos de Amor" in the hospital with the able assistance of his wife, Zoey Adams. He died of cancer that year. In 1986 Teatro Avante produced the play in translation as "Alguna cosita que alivie el sufrir" under the direction of Mario Ernesto Sánchez. This production is invited by Joseph Papp to be featured in the Festival Latino at New York's Public Theater in August of 1986. The next year both English and Spanish versions are presented by the New York Puerto Rican Traveling Theater under the direction of Mario Ernesto Sánchez. In 1988 the Coral Gables Theater presented the Teatro Avante production of "Alguna Cosita que Alivie el Sufrir" again under Mario Ernesto Sánchez's direction. Currently León Ichaso is developing an adaptation for the screen.

In addition to these gifts, he left a number of musical plays for children which were a joint effort with his wife Zoey Adams. He authored the dramas and she wrote the music. The list includes "A Friend is a Friend," "Pinocchio," "The Magic Box," "Red" and "Fit for a King." The productions of these children's musicals in the U.S. and Canada are numerous.

"A Little Something to Ease the Pain" is a semi-autobiographical account which follows the double movement of exile and return which is mirrored in the relationship between two cousins. The vagaries of freedom and the certainty of conscience on the one hand, and the certainty of freedom and the uncertainty of conscience on the other, are the twin forces that bring about the moment of recognition between the two men. One, an apparently committed revolutionary in Cuba, the other, a seemingly smug playwright, come to terms with the tantalizing secret fantasy that each hold dear: to become the other. The potentially dangerous cliché of a dramatic switch is aborted because of a rare combination of authenticity and talent. Alomá eases by small steps to a place where the pain of miscommunication and lack of communication yields to the raw pain of total communion. Both forces, both people finally bare their souls to each other and the play is done.

CHARACTERS

CARLOS RABEL (PAYE), a visiting exile
NELSON RABEL (TATÍN)
DOÑA CACHA (ABUELA), their grandmother
DILIA (TÍA), their aunt
CLARA (TÍA), their grand-aunt
ANA, Tatín's wife
AMELIA, a student
JULIO RABEL, a cousin
FR. EPHRAIM*
PACO*
*The roles of FR. EPHRAIM and PACO can be played by the
actors who play TATÍN and JULIO.

PLACE

The action takes place in and around the Rabel's house in Santiago
de Cuba during one week in July, 1979

Spanish Words:
Abuela, Abue: Grandmother
Tía: Aunt
Natilla: A custard dessert
Ay: all-purpose exclamation
Mar Verde: Green Sea, the name of a beach
Dulce Coco: coconut sweet
Mantilla: lace shawl
Compañera: Comrade
Doña: Madam, title of respect to elderly matrons
Señor: Mister, sir
Tío: Uncle

PROLOGUE

Stage in complete darkness. At the stage right hand corner we see a light that looks like the light that would be cast by a round stained glass window of an old church in the noonday sun. In the shadow there is a wooden chair in which FR. EPHRAIM *sits wearing a white cassock. We should not see him clearly, but we should realize that he is an old man and he seems to be asleep.* PAYE *enters and puts down a suitcase and shoulderstrap tape recorder. He looks at the darkness, steps into the light. He sees the old priest, but is afraid to wake him, so he waits.*

EPHRAIM: (*Clearing his throat as he speaks.*) What is it?
PAYE: Startled. What?
EPHRAIM: What can I do for you?
PAYE: I'm looking for the priest.
EPHRAIM: You have found him.
PAYE: Father Ephraim?
EPHRAIM: Yes?
PAYE: It's Carlos. Carlos Rabel. The one they called Paye. Carmela Santos and I were the ones who printed those fliers against the banning of sermons ... ?
EPHRAIM: My sister Carmela wanted to marry a colored man, but mother would not allow it. Later when Mama was blind she married him. Darkness is a great equalizer. Pause.
PAYE: I used to be an altar boy.
EPHRAIM: Remembering suddenly. Once you were trying to light the top candles last and you set your sleeves on fire ... !
PAYE: Delighted by the recognition. Yes, that was me!
EPHRAIM: I'm sorry. I fell asleep on my meditation.
PAYE: I thought the church was empty.
EPHRAIM: I was dreaming of dust. Everyone was dust and the wind was blowing us away. I was supposed to be meditating on the five glorious mysteries. Sighs. I fell asleep
PAYE: Maybe I could come back another ...
EPHRAIM: You're back?
PAYE: For a visit.
EPHRAIM: Ah!
PAYE: I live in Toronto. Canada.

EPHRAIM: Canada! (PAYE *nods*.) The church hasn't changed
    any, has it?!

PAYE: It's too dark, Father. I can't really see.

EPHRAIM: It hasn't changed. La Placita has changed. It's changed
    a lot since you left.

PAYE: Yes, and the new monument is ...

EPHRAIM: I say Mass on that monument every thirtieth of
    November in memory of your uncle. It's the most at-
    tended Mass ... next to Palm Sunday.

PAYE: Palm Sunday is still a favorite?

EPHRAIM: Everyone wants palms to hang behind their door. It's
    more of a superstition than a holy rite, but it's nice to
    have church full.

PAYE: Not many people come to church anymore?

EPHRAIM: Not many people come to church ever. It's the per-
    petual malady of Catholicism in Latin America; devotion
    without participation. Off on a tangent. When the Car-
    dinal was here from Spain we had the altar covered in
    jasmines. The smell of jasmines goes well with mantillas
    and incense. I can't stand up anymore, you know. My
    knees are too weak to hold me up.

PAYE: There's no priest to assist you?

EPHRAIM: I was praying you'd have a vocation, no? What do
    you do?

PAYE: I'm a playwright, but ...

EPHRAIM: A playwright. Pity. I thought you might have had a
    calling.

PAYE: To the priesthood?

EPHRAIM: You might have been a Cardinal. Are you famous?

PAYE: No. Not at all. Not yet.

EPHRAIM: Carlos ... Carlos Rabel. A Cuban writing plays in
    Canada. Laughs. Canada, right?

PAYE: Yes, Father.

EPHRAIM: Tell me, Paye, have you written a play about us?

PAYE: No. I ... I haven't.

EPHRAIM: You should. You should write a play about an old
    priest who's resigned to the fact that his church will be
    dark and dusty forever. I would like to be in your play.
    Quotes. "The whole world is a stage and the people are
    the players." Shakespeare, the bard of Avon. (*Coughs*.)
    Is your mother still as beautiful?

PAYE: Yes.

EPHRAIM: Raphael is a good painter. You like Raphael?

PAYE: Yes.

EPHRAIM: Your mother was a convert, you know. (*Silence.* PAYE *comes close to the priest and looks closely into his eyes.* EPHRAIM *does not see him.*)

PAYE: Father?

EPHRAIM: Yes.

PAYE: Do they still censor your sermons?

EPHRAIM: (*As if not hearing.*) Tell me Paye, when you become famous, will you be a famous foreign playwright or a famous Cuban in exile?

PAYE: I don't know.

EPHRAIM: (*Slowly.*) You must resign yourself to being either foreign or at best a Cuban *"in exile."* It is a title you will have to bear just as I wear my robes.

PACO: (*Entering.*) Father! Who's there? (*He stays out of the light.*)

EPHRAIM: Ah, Paco. I have a visitor. From Canada. Carlos Rabel. Paco Gómez. (PACO *and* PAYE *shake hands.*)

PACO: Julio's cousin?

PAYE: Yes.

EPHRAIM: Paco is the caretaker cum sacristan. But he thinks he is my guardian angel.

PACO: It's dark in here.

EPHRAIM: My friend will understand. You see, Carlos, my eyes have become sensitive to the light.

PACO: The truth is he prefers the darkness.

EPHRAIM: Darkness is a great equalizer.

PACO: You must excuse Father Ephraim, but he must take his siesta now.

PAYE: Yes, I ... (PACO *picks up the priest in his arms.*)

EPHRAIM: Tell your mother that I still remember her as one of Raphael's madonnas.

PACO: Pleased to meet you, Rabel.

EPHRAIM: And put me in one of your plays. I would like that. (PACO *begins to exit with* EPHRAIM.)

PAYE: Yes, I will.

EPHRAIM: Thank you for coming to see me. God bless you, Carlos.

PAYE: Yes, Father, goodbye. (*Looks around at the dimly lit stage, genuflects and exits.*)

ACT I

From the black after PAYE *has exited, the stage lights come up to reveal some pillars and railings to indicate a verandah, and four large archways through which we see a kitchen,* AMELIA'*s bedroom,* CACHA'*s bedroom and the rest of the house beyond. The stage floor should be painted so that these rooms seem to be around a small square patio. There are steps leading from the corner stage right onto the verandah. There we see a suggestion of a door which leads into the house.* PAYE *comes up the steps, feeling the heat, carrying the suitcase and shoulder-strap tape recorder. He looks through the open door, but does not go in. Instead he comes around to the corner of the verandah which will be down stag center. He looks to the left, to the rest of the verandah which stretches to the stage left corner. The walls between the verandah and house through which we see the patio and the rooms surrounding it are non-existent, but must be respected as walls and therefore there is another entrance at the stage left side of the verandah, which can be indicated by a hanging piece of tiled roof.* PAYE *looks at the house and speaks directly to the audience from the corner of the veranda center stage.*

PAYE: (*Addressing the audience.*) My grandparents' house is a big square house which they rented until the Revolutionary Government passed a law giving the deed to the property to tenants who had paid rent for a period longer than twenty years. It is an old house, a Spanish colonial house, one of the oldest in the city of Santiago de Cuba. I was born in this house and I spent my childhood riding a tricycle on this verandah with assorted cousins—all boys! My grandparents' house has seen weddings and wakes, nine children, twenty-six grandchildren, fires, earthquakes, hurricanes, revolutions, departures and reunions. Now behind the door there is a little plaque stating the ownership of the occupants with the headline "Thank You, Fidel." (*He picks up the suitcase and enters the house through the stage right door.*)

PAYE: Abue! Good morning! Abuela! (PAYE *moves into the patio. There are clothes on the line. A towel has fallen. He picks it up and is about to hang it when* AMELIA *enters. Alarmed by his presence, she grabs a mop and cocks it in mid air.*)

AMELIA: Drop it!

PAYE: (*Startled.*) What?!

AMELIA: (*Calling.*) Dilia! Cacha!

PAYE: I ...

AMELIA: Somebody! Quick!

PAYE: Wait a minute!

AMELIA: Thief! Thief!

PAYE: No. You got it all wrong!

AMELIA: Dilia! (*Swings the mop at him.*)

PAYE: Wait! (AMELIA *throws the mop at him and as* PAYE *ducks, she grabs him from behind in a bear hug.*)

AMELIA: I got him! (DILIA *enters.*) I got him!!

DILIA: Amelia, let him go, he'll hurt you.

AMELIA: I'll kill'im first!

PAYE: It's me.

AMELIA: Call somebody! (*Begins calling out "thief" repeatedly. From this point on everyone speaks at once, saying their respective lines without waiting for any cue. The effect should be a jumble of everyone screaming and shouting until* CACHA *screams "shut up.» At that point everyone stops.*)

DILIA: Amelia, don't be crazy, let him go!

PAYE: I sent a cable ... (AMELIA *bites him on the neck.*) Ouch!!

CACHA: (*Entering.*) What in the world ...

ANA: (*Enters.*) What is it?!

DILIA: A thief!

PAYE: Abuela (*Breaks loose.*)

DILIA: Look out!

ANA: Amelia, are you sure he's a thief?

PAYE: It's me, Tía!

ANA: Let the man get out!

DILIA: Look out, Mama.

ANA: Here, Amelia. (*Gives* AMELIA *the bat.*)

PAYE: Listen, it's me, Paye. Abuela!

AMELIA: I'll knock'im out!

ANA: (*Taking up* AMELIA'*s repeated cry of "thief."*) Thief! ...

PAYE: It's me. Paye!

CACHA: Paye? Shut up all of you! It's Paye!

DILIA: Paye? (*Rushes over to turn off the radio.*)

CACHA: It's Paye! (*Opens her arms to him.*) Paye, my Paye. (*They embrace.*)

AMELIA: (*After a long pause.*) Jesus, I nearly bashed his head in! (*Picks up her mop and exits.*)

VOICE: (*Off.*) Is everything okay, Doña Cacha?

CACHA: Yes, Beto. It's Tato's son, Paye; he's come home. (*Blackout. Afro-Cuban drums are heard. People chattering as*

*they get into places. Laughter. As the lights come up we
find* CACHA *seated in one of the rocking chairs.* PAYE *is
seated on the arm of* CACHA'*s chair with his arm around
her.* DILIA *and* ANA *are gathering the clothes off the line
as they speak.*)

DILIA: But the carnival is not till next week!

ANA: You haven't changed a bit!

CACHA: Ay, Paye, what a surprise!

DILIA: The last we heard, you were coming for the carnival!

PAYE: They just changed my flight!

ANA: I would have picked you out in a minute!

DILIA: We weren't expecting you till next week.

CACHA: It doesn't matter. The main thing is that you're here. I
thought that I would have to close my eyes for good and
never see you again, Paye. (PAYE *kisses her.*) I've missed
you and Tato and ... all of you.

DILIA: You didn't recognize us, eh, Paye?

PAYE: Sure I did.

CACHA: Older. Much older!

PAYE: Abue, you look terrific.

DILIA: Huh, don't let her fool you.

CACHA: What are you trying to do, make me out an invalid? (*To*
PAYE.) I'm over eighty years old, and I have my own
teeth, I cut my own food, I bathe and dress myself, and I
haven't lost control of my bowels. (PAYE *laughs.*)

DILIA: Ah, Mama, Paye's come hundreds of miles, he doesn't
want to hear about your bowels! Ay, Paye, how long has
it been?

PAYE: Seventeen years?

DILIA: I bet you miss it plenty.

PAYE: Yes.

DILIA: What's Canada like? Not like here, is it?

PAYE: No.

ANA: Nothing's like her, they say. Perucho's son, you remember
Perucho?

DILIA: Who?

ANA: Long time ago. Perucho.

PAYE: I remember.

ANA: (*To* DILIA.) He used to sell corn fitters at La Placita.

PAYE: Greasy little blobs! He had a glass eye and wore a raincoat
regardless.

CACHA: Ay, what a memory!

PAYE: It's hard to forget a man with a glass eye.

DILIA: I did.

ANA: Well, his sister is a good friend of Gaetana, the lady that used to sew for Mirta, next door to my sister Somalia. Anyway, Perucho's son left for New York, and he had a terrible time with English and the cold. He *hated* it there. So he moved to Miami because everyone told him it was just like Cuba. But no. The place was crawling with Cubans, sure enough, all pretending they were still in Havana. But Havana's not Santiago, and it wasn't the same, not at all.

DILIA: Ay, Ana, this is taking too long.

ANA: Wait, I'm just getting to it. Paye knows what I'm talking about, don't you, Paye?

PAYE: Yes. I guess.

ANA: Anyway, Paye, he moved from Miami to Puerto Rico because they say that San Juan is *just* like here. But, no sir. His father got a letter from him just last New Year's ... he said that *nothing* was like Santiago! Now he wants to come back!

DILIA: (*Totally disinterested in* ANA's *story.*) I wonder where Tatín's got to?

ANA: He said he'd be home before lunch.

CACHA: Oh, he's going to be surprised!

ANA: He said he'd be home before lunch.

CACHA: Oh, he's going to be surprised!

ANA: He'll be glad we came to Santiago early this year.

DILIA: Ay, Ana, are the boys going to get here before Paye leaves?

ANA: I don't think so ... we made arrangements for them to be here next week ... we thought that ...

DILIA: Ay, Tatín'll be so disappointed.

ANA: So will the boys.

PAYE: Where are they?

ANA: Ernesto's got a scholarship to a special course ...

DILIA: One of the best schools on the island!

ANA: And Adrián's at a boys' camp near Havana. It's on a farm. We arranged for them to come for the carnival. They've asked a lot about you and the rest of the family abroad.

CACHA: Adrián looks a lot like you when you were that age!

AMELIA: (*Enters more groomed.*) I hope I didn't miss anything important.

DILIA: Ay, here's the one who nearly broke his skull! (*Laughs.*)

CACHA: This is my grandson, Carlos. Paye, this is Amelia. (*They shake hands.*)

AMELIA: Pleased to meet you.

CACHA: Amelia's living here with us while she goes to school in
      Santiago.

PAYE: Where are you from?

AMELIA: Oh, you never heard of it. It's up in the hills. Near
      Baracoa. It's a village called Alan.

PAYE: Alan?

AMELIA: It used to be a coffee plantation and the American who
      owned it named the village after himself.

CACHA: It's *way* up in the hills.

AMELIA: You can see the coast line when the clouds lift. Maybe
      you would like to go?!

DILIA: Ay, Amelia, Paye's not a tourist. He's here to see us!

CACHA: Ay, yes! And we want to see him. Wait till Clara sees
      you!

DILIA: You better run down to Tía Clara's or she'll accuse us of
      keeping him all to ourselves!

CACHA: Clara's waited seventeen years, a few more minutes won't
      hurt.

DILIA: You forget how Tía Clara is when it comes to Paye?

ANA: (*To* PAYE.) Your Godmother, no?

PAYE: Yes.

DILIA: Clara has two gods, Jesus and this one! (AMELIA *laughs.*)

PAYE: I should go and see her ...

ANA: Why don't I go and tell her he's here ... she'll come ...

DILIA: Ana, tell her that he just arrived. This very second.

VOICE: (*Off stage.*) Hello, Doña Cacha.

CACHA: Hello Graciela.

DILIA: (*Under her breath.*) You should see Graciela. The girl's a
      cow!

CACHA: Alpidio's daughter, you remember her, Paye? I think she
      went out with Tatín.

DILIA: Only one, Mama. Tatín was going out with Ana when Paye
      left.

CACHA: Dilia doesn't like her because she went out with Tatín.

DILIA: The girl was vulgar. She would cough and spit like a lizard.

PAYE: I'm glad Tatín married Ana.

CACHA: Oh, yes.

DILIA: She's all right.

CACHA: It's not easy being married to Tatín. Mr. Perfect!

DILIA: He has high standards, and that's good.

CACHA: Too high. Ernesto and Adrián are terrified of him. And
      Ana, she lives trying to keep things smooth.

DILIA: Tatín hasn't been given everything on a silver platter, and he expects everyone to strive just as hard ...

CACHA: See, Paye, no one can say a word about Tatín in front of your Aunt Dilia.

PAYE: Has he ... ? (*Gets up.*) It's hot, isn't it?

CACHA: Paye, you all right?

DILIA: You want some water? (DILIA *motions to* AMELIA *who goes but looks puzzled.*) It's the heat. He's not accustomed to this heat.

CACHA: Paye?

DILIA: You hungry? I bet you haven't eaten.

PAYE: I'm fine, Tía.

DILIA: I'll go get lunch ready, right away! (*Exits.*)

AMELIA: (*Hands* PAYE *a glass of water.*) Here.

PAYE: Thanks. (*Drinks.*)

DILIA: (*Shouting from the kitchen.*) Amelia, will you give me a hand in here!

AMELIA: Coming!

PAYE: (*Giving* AMELIA *the glass.*) Thank you, Amelia. (AMELIA *exits.*)

CACHA: You all right, Paye?

PAYE: Abue, I'm not sure if I have forgotten my feeling against Tatín. He hurt me.

CACHA: You hurt him a lot too. You refused to speak to him— even to say goodbye.

PAYE: Abue, you think that Tatín, that he still ...

CACHA: (*Taking* PAYE's *hand.*) When I was a little girl, Paye, my mother had a friend, Nenita. She was a beautiful lady; always powdered and combed. She used to visit us often. Then suddenly she stopped coming, and I asked why. My mother told me that Nenita had been in a fire and that she had been badly scarred. I cried, and I burst into tears on the spot! But as time went on, one day she came to visit us again. I heard her voice from the other room and I knew it was Nenita. I got nervous. I was afraid to come out. But they called. When I walked into the room and I saw her, I burst into tears again. She looked so lovely, just as lovely as ever, though her dress was cut high around her throat and her sleeves were long. I felt like such a fool. You see, Paye, Nenita had learned to cover her scars for her friends. (*Pause.*) Tatín is your brother, and if he has scars, he's learned to conceal them. You must do the same, Paye. You see?

PAYE: (*Almost in tears.*) Yes, Abue, I see. (*They sit in a long silence.* CLARA *enters followed by* ANA.)

CLARA: Where is he? Where's ... ay, my Paye.

PAYE: (*Meeting her.*) Tía!

CLARA: Oh, look at you. Oh, my Paye. (*Covers* PAYE's *face with kisses.*) Let me look at you. (*Stands back.*) Oh, God in Heaven! (*Throws herself at* PAYE *again.*)

PAYE: Tía, please. (*Comforts her.*)

CLARA: Isn't he beautiful, Cacha?

CACHA: All my grandchildren are beautiful.

CLARA: And look at me. I must be a fright!

PAYE: You look fine, Tía. Pretty as ever!

CLARA: Go on. I don't even have any face powder, and I'm all sweaty. And my hair! I was going to tint it this evening. I'm all grey you know, almost white! Ay, there was a time when I couldn't get a bottle of dye even for American money. Everyone thinks I'm too vain for my age, but I say they can all go fart into the wind. But, look at me now. I'm not even dressed and here you are! Oh, Paye. My little Paye, all grown up! (*Cries.*)

DILIA: (*Entering.*) Ay, Tía, let him breathe!

CLARA: You shut up, you've had Tatín all these years. My Paye's here now, and I ... (*Cries.*)

PAYE: Tía.

ANA: I wonder what's keeping Tatín?

CLARA: (*Blowing her nose on the hem of her dress.*) I'm so proud of you. Your father, he keeps us up to date on your plays and ... things.

PAYE: Papa tends to brag a little ...

CLARA: I've always known you were the one in the family with the real sentiment ... (*Kisses* PAYE.)

DILIA: Did you know Tatín got a medal from the Hispanic Academy?

PAYE: Yes, yes.

CLARA: A writer needs real sentiment!

DILIA: First prize!

CACHA: First time a Cuban's held that honor since 1948.

DILIA: (*Correcting her.*) '38, Mama. He's been published in Mexico and Chile and ...

CLARA: Will you stop talking abut Tatín! I want to hear about Paye!

CACHA: How's lunch coming?

DILIA: The rice is on.

CACHA: Tell me about Sylvia; how's your mother?

PAYE: Fine.

DILIA: Mama, if you want to bathe, you better go do it now before the water shuts off for the day.

CACHA: I'll bathe later.

DILIA: There won't be enough in the tanks later. If Amelia does the dishes! That girl refuses to realize that on the days the water shuts off, whatever is in those tanks is all we have for the rest of the day. I'm always running out.

CACHA: Well, talk to her.

DILIA: I can't talk to her. You invited her here.

CACHA: I'm not the one who keeps running out of water.

DILIA: Never mind. I'll see about getting the tanks fixed myself.

CLARA: What's the matter with them now?

DILIA: They don't fill up properly.

CLARA: They never did. Ever since I can remember, those tanks ...

DILIA: And what am I supposed to do, climb up on the roof myself?! I asked Fito to have a look at them, and Roberto was supposed to have fixed them, and he couldn't be bothered to look at them again! And Nando's useless! Sometimes my brothers make me sick. They live only a few blocks away and they only come here to tell me what I'm doing wrong in the caring of their mother!

CLARA: Dilia, please!

DILIA: And Mama thinks they're all saints!

ANA: All right, Tía.

CLARA: Ay, Dilia, we don't want Paye to think that the whole family's falling apart.

DILIA: Who said anything about falling apart?!

CLARA: It's the way you complain about everyone.

DILIA: I have reason to complain, Tía.

CACHA: Enough!

DILIA: I don't know what Tía Clara's accusing me of. Paye knows the family. What are we supposed to do, pretend we always get along like nuns on a bus ride? (PAYE *laughs.*)

CACHA: (*Getting up.*) I'll go take my shower ...

DILIA: (*Exiting.*) Luck will be another twenty minutes. Hurry up, Mama! (CACHA *follows* DILIA *off to the interior of the house.*)

CLARA: You musn't pay your Aunt Dilia any attention. Age doesn't agree with her. (*Looks around to see if they're alone.*)

ANA: I'll go give Tía a hand with lunch. (*Exits.*)

CLARA: Come, let's sit and talk for a minute. (CLARA *leads*
     PAYE *to the rocking chairs.*) When I heard you were here,
     I couldn't believe it. My heart jumped to my throat. Ana
     couldn't keep up with me running up the hill. I kept walk-
     ing out of my shoes. These lousy things! (*Shows them.*)
     Come from Rumania, or something. They melt in the
     heat!! Soles come right off on the sidewalk!! Ay, Paye, if
     we had only known back then that it would turn out like
     this. Everyone here at the house still thinks that Fidel is
     Christ our Saviour! If I open my mouth in front of any-
     one here, they'd have my head on a skewer! I don't say a
     word up here. Out of respect for Cacha. I'm not afraid of
     anyone! I've put Tatín in his place a few times and good!
     Once I made a reference to the day he slapped you during
     lunch, and he said that he would do it again. And I said
     to him, "Thank God, Paye's not here because, if you did
     it again, I would slap you silly, Señor Tatín." I gave him
     such a piece of my mind ... He's never said another word
     to me since.

PAYE: You and Tatín don't speak to one another?

CLARA: Yes, we do. But he knows just where to draw the line.
     In front of me, he doesn't even praise Fidel! But, Paye,
     don't you open your mouth, please! God in Heaven! If
     anything happened to you on this trip your mother would
     never forgive us.

PAYE: Nothing is going to happen, Tía.

CLARA: You remember Niko the Turk? (PAYE *nods.*) They picked
     him up about a month ago. He was saying atrocities about
     the committee!

PAYE: He's half mad anyway, no?

CLARA: Exactly! He's even worse since you left! Half the time he
     runs around with a load of shit in his pants! Ay, Paye, you
     have no idea what it's like! Imagine a shortage of oranges
     in Cuba!

PAYE: Well, that's because of the trade with Russia.

CLARA: Oh yes, that's what they say, but all I know is that during
     capitalism we had oranges!

PAYE: (*Laughs.*) You haven't changed a bit, Tía!

CLARA: Now tell me, tell me all about Canada and ... Oh your
     postcards! I got your postcards from all over Europe. I
     keep them in an album. I feel as if I've been to all those
     places! But you're so thin, Paye. Don't you have anyone

to cook for you? We'll have to fatten you up. You'll have to come down to my house. I'll make some natilla for you. But, here I'm talking and talking and you should be the one who should be talking.

PAYE: I'd rather hear about you.

CLARA: Me?! What's there to tell. I go from my house to church and from church to my house and that's it. A widow's life can be pretty desolate sometimes. Especially when she doesn't have any children. Your uncle and I ... (*Makes the sign of the cross.*) ... we never had any children. Of course you knew that. It would have been good to have a few children. But ... *I* couldn't.

PAYE: Tía, I didn't know ...

CLARA: Naturally no one speaks of it anymore. It doesn't come up in conversation or anything, but there was time when everyone in the family felt sorry for your uncle for having married a barren woman. Oh, but that was before donkeys learned to bray! Beside I have my Paye here with me again! Oh, we're going to have such fun! It'll be like the old days. Like when I used to celebrate your birthdays! You remember? (PAYE *nods.* TATÍN *enters from the street.*)

TATÍN: Ey, Tía!

CLARA: Tatín! (TATÍN *advances in their direction, eyeing* PAYE.) You'll never guess ...

TATÍN: Paye? (PAYE *stands up.*)

CLARA: That's right! (*They stare at one another in silence.*)

TATÍN: Paye? Are you speaking to me now? (PAYE *advances tentatively.* TATÍN *wipes his sweat.*)

PAYE: (*Locked in* TATÍN's *embrace.*) Tatín ... (DILIA *and* ANA *enter from inside and stand watching.*)

DILIA: He didn't recognize him!?

CLARA: He did. Right away!

TATÍN: Paye, you remember Ana.

ANA: Yes. He did.

DILIA: He got here by surprise!

PAYE: They got my visa all mixed up.

CACHA: (*Entering.*) Is Tatín here yet?

DILIA: Yes, Mama.

CACHA: Well, our Paye's here early!

CLARA: My Paye! (PAYE *and* TATÍN *try to speak at once. They laugh.*)

TATÍN: Paye-Paye!

PAYE: It's nice to be called Paye again!

DILIA: What do they call you ... ?

PAYE: My friends, Carlos.

CACHA: Ay!

TATÍN: Should we call you Carlos?

PAYE: No! No! Paye's fine. It's just fine. It's just that no one's called my Paye in so long. Even the family in Jamaica. Once when I was there for Christmas, Papa called me Paye by mistake and Alexandra nearly choked on her milk. She thought it was the funniest thing since Aunt Sophie fell into Uncle Solomon's grave. (TATÍN *looks puzzled.*) They were lowering him in. Oh, you should've been there! She had been wailing: "Solomon, take me with you! Don't leave me, Solomon!" Then as she fell, she started screaming, "Draw me out! Will you get me outta here!" (*Everyone bursts into laughter but* TATÍN.) Everyone was laughing so hard they didn't have the strength to get her out of the hole. And Uncle Elías, he slipped in the mud and fell in too! (*More laughter.*)

TATÍN: Why do you still make up these lies? (*A moment of tension.*)

CACHA: (*To* DILIA.) How's lunch coming?

PAYE: (*Softly.*) It's the truth, I swear.

DILIA: I was waiting for you to start frying. (*Exits.*)

PAYE: Ay, Tatín, I brought a tape recorder for you. (*Looks around for his suitcases.*)

CACHA: Amelia put your things in your room. Your old room.

PAYE: I brought something for you too, Abue, and for you, Tía. (*Starts to exit.*)

CLARA: (*Following him.*) What is it?

PAYE: (*Off.*) Your favorite! Yardley's Violets.

CLARA: (*Off.*) Ay!

ANA: (*To* TATÍN.) Don't be so hard on him.

TATÍN: (*Looking toward* CACHA *to see if she heard.*) Ana, please!

CACHA: Go see what Paye brought for you. (CLARA *gasps with delight.*) You've been wanting a recorder for a long time, no?

TATÍN: Yes. Don't you want to see what he brought for you?

CACHA: I'm old. I can wait. Go. Go on! (ANA *and* TATÍN *start off.*) Tatín. (*They stop.*) He's here for one week ... I want everything to be nice for him ...

TATÍN: Yes, Abue.

CACHA: Paye. (ANA *and* TATÍN *exit to* PAYE'*s room.* CACHA *sits in her rocking chair and fans herself. She speaks to the audience.*) It's a funny thing with names! Take Tatín; when he was born Tato did not want to name him Carlos after himself. That was too much like everybody else. So he named him Nelson after the Englishman. (*Smiles and shakes her head.*) Well, since he didn't inherit his father's name, he ended up inheriting even worse, his father's nickname, and from Tato he got Tatín. (PAYE *and* TATÍN *laugh off.*) When Paye was born the whole family was expecting a girl. Well, imagine, I already had ... (*Counts.*) ... five grandchildren, and all of them boys. Tato had an armful of girls's names picked out. All of them foreign; after some duchess in Sweden or a lady writer from France. None that I would be able to pronounce. But when the midwife put him in my arms and said, "It's another boy," we were all stumped. So I named him Carlos, like his father and my husband. That's a sensible name. How he got to be called Paye is rally quite a simple story. As a baby, Sylvia took him to visit her family in Jamaica, and there he learned to say "Bye-bye" and wave his little hand; in English! It was real cute. But his cousins who had no idea of what he was saying, started calling him "Paye-paye" and it stuck. (*Laughs.*) The third one was named Aramis after the Three Musketeers, (*Raises an eyebrow.*) and no nick-names were allowed. Well, Ari for short. (*Smiles.*) Tato's always been one for foreign airs! I believe he named his daughter after a Russian princess. Alexandra. (*Pause.*) I never met Alexandra. I never held her in may arms. I've held all my grandchildren at birth. They were all born in this house and the midwife passed them directly into my arms. All my grandchildren, except one. Tato sent us a cable when Sylvia had Alexandra, and I held it, the little piece of paper ... I held it next to my cheek and I cried. (*Rocks gently in her chair, fans herself and is silent. After a long pause,* AMELIA *calls from the kitchen.*)

AMELIA: Lunch! Doña Cacha! Tatín, Paye. (TATÍN, PAYE *and* CLARA *laugh offstage.*) Lunch! (*Lights fade as* CACHA *gets up and exits. Lights up on* TATÍN. *The inside of the house is in darkness. He sits on the downstage railing.* PAYE *enters from the interior of the house wearing jogging shorts and an open shirt, bare feet, stands behind* TATÍN *and yawns.*)

TATÍN: Where do you think you are? Miami Beach? You don't wear things like that in Santiago.

PAYE: I couldn't sleep. (*Pause.*)

TATÍN: Me neither. (*Pause.*) The heat?

PAYE: Yea, the heat. (*Pause.*) Ana sleep?

TATÍN: I guess. (*Pause.*) Time?

PAYE: Almost five. Tatín ... ? (*Pause.*) Want to talk some more?

TATÍN: Sure. What did I say?

PAYE: You told her I was a "noteworthy Cuban playwright" and ...

TATÍN: Aren't you?

PAYE: I was surprised at the adjective.

TATÍN: Noteworthy?

PAYE: No, Cuban. (*Silence.*)

TATÍN: An orange is an orange because it comes from an orange tree. (*They look at one another.*) They get oranges in Canada, no? (PAYE *smiles. Silence.*) Very few of our writers write for the theater. At the last writer's conference I met a young woman who wrote plays, but they were really for television. I myself have a few scenarios that might be best served by dialogue, but between my radio broadcast and lecturing I hardly have enough time to write all the things I want. (*Smokes.*) Besides, I really felt more at home in prose. I don't have a flair for the dramatic. I'm working on a story about a man who's on trial because his neighbors accuse him of manufacturing butterflies out of thin air. I want to finish it for an anthology. I'm really quite excited about it. (*Pause.*) And you, are you working on anything?

PAYE: (*Shaking his head.*) I try. I sit at the typewriter with my finger perched ... and nothing. I haven't written anything in nearly two years.

TATÍN: You're wasting time.

PAYE: You remember that poem I wrote when I was eleven? "Ode to the Triumphant Revolution." (TATÍN *nods.* PAYE *smiles.*) I remember when it came out in the paper, Tía Clara read it out loud, and everyone was so proud, even Tía Dilia ... everyone. I remember, you took the newspaper, glanced at my poem, and without even looking up went on to read the news of the day. Why must you always put me down?

TATÍN: I don't always put you down.

PAYE: Yes, you do. You call me a liar. Because I'm having difficulty writing, you say I'm wasting time.

TATÍN: You are wasting time. The first act of the play you sent was light weight.

PAYE: I was trying to come up with a comedy. Serious plays don't sell. (*They are beginning to raise their voices.*)

TATÍN: Serious plays become literature.

PAYE: (*Shouts.*) I know the people in that play. I write about people I know.

TATÍN: Then you should denounce the people you know.

PAYE: (*Shouts.*) I don't want to write propaganda. (DILIA *enters wearing a light housecoat.*)

DILIA: (*To* PAYE.) Shhh! Do you want to wake up your grandmother? (PAYE *turns brusquely and walks into the house.* DILIA *walks to* TATÍN *and caresses his head.*) What's the matter? There's something the matter, isn't there?

TATÍN: No.

DILIA: I know you well, Tatín. There's something brewing inside of you. I'm hurt that you won't talk to me. (TATÍN *doesn't answer. Pause. She kisses him on the cheek.*) Come on. You should get some sleep. (*Lights fade as they enter the house. Cuban music comes up. Daylight comes up on* ANA *seated at the table. She cleans stones from a bowl of beans. The Rabel household is occupied by* DILIA *in the kitchen,* PAYE *and* CACHA *getting up from their respective beds.* CACHA *and* PAYE *go through the archway that goes to the interior of the house.* PAYE *is carrying a towel.* CACHA *is still in her nightgown. While* ANA *speaks,* DILIA *fixes a tray comprised of a large expresso coffee pot and a pot of hot milk. She enters the interior of the house shortly after* PAYE *and* CACHA *pass by. Music volume cuts to half.*)

ANA: The Rabel family is quite the important family. Cacha's youngest son died fighting for Fidel. The whole family was up to their eyeballs in the fight against Batista, and when Fidel took power, naturally the Rabels took their place in the ranks of the revolutionary government. (*Music fades to nearly nothing.*) Paye turned against the revolution with a vengeance. The Jesuits really had their claws in him. But still, imagine what a shock it was when Tato Rabel, the eldest of the Rabels, decided to leave Cuba. No, no, no, it was unbelievable. (*Music has faded ... Pause.*) I've heard a hundred times how in 1942, Tato Rabel came back from Jamaica married to Sylvia. He had been working in the consular office in the island, that's where he learned to speak English; and he came back married to a fifteen-year-old English Jewess, with the face of an angel! Sylvia had to convert to everything. To Catholicism. To Spanish. To pesos. To the Rabel family. She gave up everything for her husband and for twenty years she was more Cuban than sugar cane. But in '62, Tato and Sylvia took Paye and Aramis and went back to Jamaica. Tatín refused to leave. Paye was delighted to take his father away. (*Blackout. We hear a radio playing Cuban music. Lights come up on* PAYE *and* TATÍN *sitting on the patio in rocking chairs. No one else is seen. As lights come up, music fades to background.*)

PAYE: I was so surprised when your letter came, the first one. What made you sit down and actually write to me?

TATÍN: I don't know. (*Offers* PAYE *a cigarette.*)

PAYE: No. thanks.

TATÍN: (*Lighting up.*) I think it was a letter Papa wrote to Abue saying he was concerned with your involvement in the Anti-Vietnam movement in university.

PAYE: (*Smiling.*) And you figured there was hope for me yet?!

TATÍN: Something like that. (*They chuckle.*) And you, why did you write back?

PAYE: I don't know. But when your letters would come talking about your work and the family and the carnival ... (*Sighs.*) You know, I have your letters all filed by date and once in a while I go through them. My favorite is one you wrote around the time Adrián was born. You talked about every one of the cousins, what they were like, what they were doing ... I read that one often. I've wanted to be here so many times. (*Looks up the street.*) I was really hoping to be here for the carnival.

TATÍN: That would have been nice.

PAYE: Tatín ... ? (*Pause.*) You ever think about going abroad?

TATÍN: Why? Should I want to?

PAYE: No. I suppose not. (*A persistent jeep's horn is heard from the street.* JULIO *enters from the jeep.*)

TATÍN: You remember your cousin Julio?

PAYE: Not looking like that.

JULIO: (*Shouting.*) Paye!

DILIA: (*Rushing out.*) What's going on?

JULIO: Paye, put it there!

DILIA: It's only Julio, Mama.

CACHA: (*Joining them.*) At this hour ... ?!

PAYE: Julio! Jesus, look at you!

JULIO: (*Flexing his arm.*) Just a little exercise. You look good for an old man your age! Whiter than salt pork! I got the jeep to take you to the beach.

PAYE: The beach?

TATÍN: We haven't been to bed yet.

JULIO: *You* go to bed, who invited you?

DILIA: Don't say hello to us.

JULIO: Ooops! (*Kisses DILIA.*) Abuela. (*Kisses CACHA.*)

CACHA: How's the baby?

DILIA: Julio's wife just had a baby.

CACHA: A month ago.

JULIO: A boy.

CACHA: Eduardo.

JULIO: What about you? You married yet?

PAYE: No, not yet.

JULIO: Christ, I'm on my third.

CACHA: It's nothing to brag about.

JULIO: Why not? Not many men can get a really good looking woman, let alone three.

DILIA: Not many men can get two women to divorce him in such a hurry!

PAYE: You've been divorced twice?

JULIO: Sure, we're a modern nation.

AMELIA: (*Enters. still dressing herself.*) Julio!

JULIO: Hey big mamma! (JULIO *takes* AMELIA's *face in his hands and shows it to* PAYE.) You ever seen anything as ugly as this anywhere?

AMELIA: Get out! (AMELIA *slaps* JULIO *around.*)

JULIO: (*Trying to pat her ass.*) Well, at least you have something to fall back on. (*Pats her.*)

AMELIA: Get your hands off.

JULIO: Only teasing.

AMELIA: See what I have to put up with at every rehearsal?

JULIO: See what Abuela saddled me with?

CACHA: And I intend you to watch out for her.

JULIO: You kidding! With that face who'd bother her?

CACHA: Ther're a lot of drunks in the carnival and ... ?

JULIO: They'd have to be plastered! (AMELIA *hits* JULIO.)

DILIA: Did you hear. Paye can't stay for the carnival?

JULIO: That's what he thinks. You think you're getting on a plane before July 25th, you're even stupider than me!

PAYE: Well, the main thing was to see the family.

JULIO: This year's dance is going to knock the judges on their asses. It's the best La Placita has ever done. One of the guys playing the bongos just came back from Angola.

AMELIA: And he's got some rhythms that are going to make the conga *hot!*

PAYE: I wish I could, Julio.

JULIO: Well?

DILIA: His visa's only for one week.

JULIO: What the hell does he need a visa for?!

PAYE: Next time, Julio.

JULIO: So, you'll miss the carnival. We'll have to have a party AT LEAST. How about it, Tía? Let's roast a pig!

DILIA: Where are we supposed to get a pig from?

JULIO: I'll get a pig. How about Saturday?!

CACHA: (*Lowering her voice.*) Julio, I don't want you getting into any trouble ...

JULIO: Don't worry, Abue. The pig's as good as roasted.

AMELIA: Ay, a party!

JULIO: Okay! Them that's going to the beach, let's go. I only got the jeep for a few hours.

DILIA: Before you go, Julio, I want you to look at the water tanks.

JULIO: Right now?

DILIA: Just look at them now; it'll only take a second ... (JULIO *begins to exit with* DILIA.)

JULIO: Get your towels and wait for me in the jeep. These old women are going to drive me crazy!

AMELIA: That Julio!

PAYE: He's certainly changed. I remember Julio as a skinny little shrimp with no teeth and always scratching himself! (AMELIA *laughs and exits.*)

CACHA: I guess you all grow up. Are you going to the beach?

TATÍN: I don't know, I ...

CACHA: Why not? You're young! (*Exiting.*) I'll get your towels and things. Ana!

PAYE: The beach! A party! A roast pig! This pig Julio's talking about; where's he going to get it?

TATÍN: I don't know. He probably knows a man who raises pigs.

PAYE: Is that allowed?

TATÍN: Raising pigs?

PAYE: No. Knowing a man.

TATÍN: This is still Cuba, Paye. Sure you're not tired?

PAYE: Of course I'm tired, but I couldn't sleep now.

ANA: (*Enters.*) Paye, Abue can't find your bathing suit.

PAYE: Oh, its's still in my duffle bag. I'll find it. (*Exits.*)

ANA: Are you really going to the beach?

TATÍN: Yes, why?

ANA: No, nothing. Remember you have to prepare two radio broadcasts for when you get back.

TATÍN: Have I ever needed reminding?

ANA: No ... How are things going with you and Paye?

TATÍN: Fine.

ANA: You know, he reminds me of Adrián. (TATÍN *laughs cynically.*) What's the matter?

TATÍN: Nothing.

ANA: What did I say?

TATÍN: Now I know why I lose patience with Adrián. He is like Paye.

ANA: You didn't lose patience with Adrián until recently.

TATÍN: Well, he gets so vehement when anyone in the house complains about shortages or anything like that. He doesn't respect me anymore. He talks back.

ANA: That's true maybe. But it's also you. You have been in a foul mood for months. And when I ask you what's the matter, you always say nothing. Is it me? (*Moves after him.*) Are you unhappy with me?

TATÍN: (*Sharply.*) It's not you! It has nothing to do with you!

JULIO: (*Offstage.*) No sweat. I'll fix it Saturday. (TATÍN *moves away from* ANA. *She stares at him silently.*) Here we go! Abue's packing us breakfast, we better get outta here before she decides to pack a bed!

CACHA: Here! (*To* JULIO.) Make sure they're back before lunch.

JULIO: (*Shouting over* CACHA's *line.*) To the beach! And don't anyone fart in the jeep, the floor boards are real loose! (*They exit noisily.* CACHA *waves.* ANA *stands perfectly still.*)

CACHA: You all right, Ana?

ANA: Yes. I just didn't sleep well. I worry when Tatín isn't in bed with me.

CACHA: There's nothing to worry about. They'll get some sleep later on. Now he's too excited to sleep. You can't imagine what Paye's visits means to him, to all of us.

ANA: I don't know what to imagine, what to expect.

CACHA: There's nothing to worry about, you'll see. (*Exits. Blackout. Music from the radio is heard.* DILIA *is busy in the kitchen stirring in a double boiler.* PAYE *enters from the street, shouting.*)

PAYE: (*Entering.*) Abue!

DILIA: (*In lowered voice.*) She' resting.

PAYE: Oh. (*Stands there for a moment with nothing to say.*)

DILIA: I'm making something special for you. Natilla.

PAYE: For me?

DILIA: Don't you like it anymore?

PAYE: Yes, I love it.

DILIA: Used to be your favorite.

PAYE: Oh, yes!

DILIA: Good! I've been skimming the top of the milk every day when I scald it. I wasn't going to say anything until I was sure I had enough.

PAYE: For the party?

DILIA: No, it's for you. I didn't want you to go back without something to remember me by. (*Silence.*) Where's Tatín?

PAYE: He went over to La Placita; someone called him over ...

DILIA: He has quite a following here in Santiago; never comes often enough. (*Silence.*) How about something cold to drink? (*Pours him a glass of lemonade.*)

PAYE: It's hot, isn't it?

DILIA: Yes, unbearable.

PAYE: Doña Rosario said it was earthquake weather.

DILIA: Tch! What the hell does she know? Some people always have something to add to the confusion. As if it wasn't enough with the heat. (DILIA *watches* PAYE *drink.*) Tell me if it needs more sugar.

PAYE: It's fine Tía.

DILIA: We haven't had a chance to talk, you and me. I know you probably haven't thought kindly of me ... (PAYE *tries to speak.*) No, no. It's only natural. I ...

PAYE: Tía ...

DILIA: I never had much time for anyone else but Tatín. (*Pause. The radio D.J. blurts out the word "carnival."*) It's a pity you couldn't stay for the carnival.

PAYE: Do you still go out, Tía?

DILIA: Me. No! I'm too old for that. I like to watch ... see them go by and wave and clap. There has to be someone to watch! (*Silence. Turns the radio down to almost nothing. Looking down.*) I don't know you've noticed on this trip

... Tatín and I aren't like we used to be. I find out things about Tatín's life by reading them in the papers. I'm ... another aunt. Mama always said that I was a stupid, self-ish woman. Sometimes when the stakes are very high, you have a good hand, but you end up playing the wrong card and losing everything. Why do you live all the way up in Toronto?

PAYE: Because in Jamaica, there's very little theater.

DILIA: Yes, but you see your family only once a year.

PAYE: That's as much as I can afford. And Papa pays half.

DILIA: Is there anything else you would do instead?

PAYE: Than playwriting? I've thought about it often.

DILIA: Why don't you get married and have children?

PAYE: (*Laughs.*) I couldn't support a wife, let alone have children. Besides, knowing a playwright's income, no woman would marry me.

DILIA: I still think that you should move to Kingstown.

PAYE: If I could live under communism, I would live in Santiago.

DILIA: I am not a communist, Paye. I'm too old and too stupid to understand socialism. I'm a Fidelista because I am a Rabel. I'd never heard of Karl Marx. The fact of the matter is that my life hasn't changed that much one way or the other. I still get up at six-thirty every morning to scald the milk, make the coffee, butter the bread, fry the bacon. The revolution was not for me. It was for Tatín. He and his sons will see the Cuba that Fidel is building ... I'm not campaigning. But that is why Tatín had to stay. Tato couldn't take him. I begged him. Tatín's place was here. He *understands* the revolution. He had a right to stay?! He was all I had.

PAYE: (*Putting his hand on* DILIA'*s shoulder.*) Tía ...

DILIA: Tatín's life here ... is a good life. He's *someone.*

PAYE: Oh yes, Tía. Tatín has everything. I envy him, Tía, if you want to know the truth.

DILIA: Do you? Really?

PAYE: Yes. Yes I do. (*They stare at one another.* DILIA *smiles.*)

DILIA: (*Stirring her mix.*) You have to keep stirring or it'll sepa-rate. (*Tastes it.*) I think it needs more vanilla.

PAYE: (*Handing her the bottle.*) Here. You know, I love natilla!

DILIA: Good! I'll warn you, it's not as good as Mama's, but she's my teacher, so it can't be too bad. (*Offers him a taste off the mixing spoon.*)

PAYE: Hmmmmmmmmm! It's delicious.

DILIA: (*Smiles.*) Stay, I'll let you lick the bowl. (*Music swells. Blackout. Exit. Lights come up on* PAYE *in his room changing shirts.* AMELIA *stands by the dresser dressed in a militia uniform. She reaches into the bottom drawer and takes out a belt-holster.*)

PAYE: Thank you for giving me your room, Amelia.

AMELIA: It's your room.

PAYE: (*Laughs.*) Yea. (AMELIA *has put on the holster.*)

AMELIA: It's a good thing you got some sun?

PAYE: Why?

AMELIA: When you arrived you looked whiter than a Polish sailor. (*Slight pause.* AMELIA *sits at the edge of the bed.*) Doña Cacha is so happy since you arrived. She seems younger somehow. She doesn't even seem tired. (PAYE *sits down, takes off his running shoes and socks.*)

PAYE: You are very good to her, Amelia. I've noticed.

AMELIA: Doña Cacha has been good to me. I was only little when the revolution built the first schoolhouse in my village. It was named Tony Rabel after your uncle. Doña Cacha came up and I was chosen to present her with a bunch of flowers. She said that the future of Cuba was in the hands of us children. She didn't let got of my hand. I was so proud. I wrote to her often. I told her about the monument to her son and how I polished the plaque. When I graduated, I wrote her that I had been offered a scholarship to study in Santiago but that my father didn't have the money to send me. Doña Cacha wrote to my father and told him that she would take me into her home while I studied in Santiago. (*She stands up.*) Doña Cacha has been good to me. The revolution has been very good to me and my family. I work hard and I study hard because I want to reflect the values of the revolution. I know first hand that these values are good and true for our people. (*They are standing at either side of the bed.*)

PAYE: (*Bursting into a rage.*) Bullshit! We've traded one tyrant for another. (TATÍN *stands within earshot.*)

AMELIA: (*Shouting.*) Things have improved!

PAYE: Improved?! Improved from what? All we needed was an honest government—and a market for our sugar, coffee, tobacco and rum!

AMELIA: How about the literacy program?

PAYE: Yeah, sure, learn to read so that we can better indoctrinate you! Read the news! It tells you how great Fidel is.

AMELIA: He is great! I would lay down my life for him.

PAYE: Well, I hate him, and I would gladly see him dead! (*Pause.*)

PAYE: When I left Cuba, I never dreamed it would be for good—an exile. I thought Fidel wouldn't last. But he closed the borders. He decides who can go and who has to stay. He stole my birthright to *my* country. He set up a dictatorship and taught you to say "Thank you, Fidel." (*Pause.*) For what?! He sold us to the Russians for a chance to stay in power forever.

AMELIA: Doña Cacha warned us not to discuss politics with you. She was right.

PAYE: I'm sorry I blew up at you—it's not you I'm angry with.

AMELIA: (*Changing the topic abruptly.*) Is it true they have penguins in Toronto?

PAYE: Sure. They have them as pets; walk them around on leads—a friend of mine has one; bit me here, once. See!

AMELIA: I don't think I could live in a place that had penguins!

PAYE: No.

AMELIA: I've got to run now—or I'll be late! (*She exits.*)

PAYE: (*Angry at himself.*) Jesus Christ! (*He flops on the bed crying. Blackout—slow fade on* TATÍN. *Lights up as* TATÍN *is dragging both rocking chairs onto the verandah.* CACHA *follows him slowly. A newspaper is on one of the rocking chairs.* TATÍN *places the chairs near the railing and he sits on the stage right chair.* CACHA *sits in the stage left chair. She is carrying her fan.* TATÍN *opens the newspaper and begins to read.*)

CACHA: Paye's quite the young man! (*Silence.*) It's nice to see you two, you and Paye. (*Silence.*)

TATÍN: (*Reporting from the paper.*) They're going to make it easier for exiled Cubans to return for a visit. They are no longer being considered as traitors. Fidel is urging everyone to treat the visitors with "greatest respect" ...

CACHA: Yes. I'm glad you spoke highly of Paye's work in front of Amelia. Paye needed to hear you say all that. He's waited a long time for it. (*Sighs.*) Now, whether you mean it or not ... Paye will only be home a few more days. (*Silence.* CACHA *rocks and fans herself.* TATÍN *reads the paper.*) I miss your father. Don't you?

TATÍN: Yes. (*Silence.*)

CACHA: When your Uncle Tony died, I thought that I would never recover. But death is very final and ... in time ... (*Pause.*) Having a son in exile never ends. A son. A father. A

brother. Paye's missed too much. Exile is a terrible pun-
ishment. For everyone. (*Pause.*)

VOICE: (*Off.*) Good evening, Doña Cacha.

CELIA: (*Off.*) Yes, I know. They say he weighs sixty-eight pounds!

CACHA: Paye?!

CELIA: No, the pig! (CLARA *and* PAYE *enter laughing.* TATÍN
gives his seat to CLARA *and sits on the railing reading.*)

CACHA: What's so funny?

CLARA: (*Controlling her laughter.*) Just as we were walking up
the hill, the Chinese couple that moved into Dr. Pera's
house come running out into the street. The man came
out followed by the wife beating him over the head with
a half-plucked chicken and screaming in Chinese. And a
herd of children running behind like Chinese New Years.
(CLARA *and* PAYE *laugh again.*)

TATÍN: Tía, in the first place, they're not Chinese. They're Korean. Remember Korea? Where the war took place in the
fifties?

CLARA: Ay, no wonder there's war in the world. There was a time
when a Chinaman was a Chinaman no matter where he
came from! This heat! (*Fans herself.*) It doesn't get this
hot in Canada, eh Paye?

PAYE: No.

CACHA: (*Under her breath.*) It snows.

PAYE: In winter.

CLARA: Don't stand there like a flag pole. I'll fan you. Come.
(PAYE *moves next to her.*) Come, Paye, sit on my lap like
when you were my little boy.

PAYE: Tía, I'm too heavy! (*He does.*)

CLARA: Ay, snow! What's in Canada, Paye? Is that where Canada
Dry comes from? (*She fans* PAYE. PAYE *and* TATÍN
laugh. TATÍN *closes the paper and gives it to* CACHA,
who opens it.)

TATÍN: I've always had a rather picturesque image of Canada. Sort
of like Peyton Place; leaves on the sidewalk, picket fences
and always a neighbor named Billy, with freckles.

PAYE: Leaves on the sidewalk gets a definite yes, the picket fence is
iffy and the neighbor kid is more likely to be called Enzio
or Pasquale.

TATÍN: What do you like about Toronto?

PAYE: In twenty words or less?! Oh ... Toronto is like a pubescent
girl. It's got everything, but it doesn't know what to do
with it. (CLARA *laughs.*)

CACHA: (*Putting the paper aside.*) Well, that's that.

CLARA: She can only read the headlines without her glasses.

PAYE: Can I get you your glasses, Abuela?

CACHA: No, no. I really don't need them. I only read the headlines anyway. If something is important enough, it'll come up in conversation.

CLARA: (*Whispering.*) She's too vain to wear her glasses.

CACHA: Nonsense! I don't like to wear them because they distort everything. I can see. I don't see as well as I used to, but it's gone gradually and I've become accustomed to how I see things. I know my world. Then they gave me those glasses and I didn't know what was what. One minute the wall's over there, the next minute it's closer. If I look up I see you, if I look down I see only your nose!

TATÍN: They're bifocals.

CACHA: They're infuriating! I like to see things equally. If I have to give up reading little letters, it's a small price to pay to keep my world in perspective. (CLARA *fans* PAYE.) I see you got a little color. (PAYE *looks at his forearms.*) Maybe Julio can take you to Mar Verde again. I hear it's really beautiful.

PAYE: It is. You've never been?

CACHA: (*Laughing.*) Me?! Your grandfather used to take me to the beach. He used to go to Ciudamar on Saturday afternoons.

CLARA: Ay, yes!

CACHA: In those days, the beaches were not all public and there was a section, fenced off so that Batista's military men could swim. A diving board, a pavilion, lawn chairs and umbrellas. They had everything. The rest of us had to share two showers and a stretch of sand no bigger than a sandbox. In the private part there were always matrons looking like Eva Perón, covering their porcelain skin from the sun. No negroes were allowed there. (*Laughs.*) But they say that when a black man takes revenge, he does it with style. (*Giggles.*) You know what they used to do? They used to wait for the current to be flowing from the public section to the military and they'd swim over to the rope fence that divided even the water, and they'd shit and wave their load goodbye to the other side! (*Laughs.*) Once your grandfather was floating on his back out in the deep water, when the current suddenly reversed and all the turd kept coming back. He felt something bobbing by

his feet; a shark?! No! It was a turd the size of a sausage.
(*They're all laughing. The lights start to change slowly into
a sunset effect.*) He never went to the beach again. That
was in nineteen ... forty-four. I haven't been to the beach
since.

PAYE: You should come with us next time. The sea air will do you
good!

CACHA: I'm afraid Mar Verde's not for me.

PAYE: Mar Verde's for everybody. It is paradise! It's beautiful.
Abue, it's *so* beautiful. (*He stands at the edge of the verandah. Silence.*)

CACHA: They say that when Columbus landed in Cuba he said:
"This is the most beautiful ... "

PAYE: (*Finishing the quote.*) " ... beautiful land that human eyes
ever beheld."

CACHA: No one is quite certain where Columbus landed, but
wherever it was, he certainly summed it up quite nicely.
(*The sunset glows for a few seconds. Blackout.*)

ACT II

Lights come up on a barrel in the middle of the patio. JULIO
*sings "Quiéreme Mucho" from inside the barrel. He stands up and
reveals his bare chest.* PAYE *enters.* JULIO *sings to him ...*

JULIO: Remember that one?

PAYE: (*Applauding.*) I'm surprised *you* remember it.

JULIO: I always think of you when I hear that song. You sang it
at Abuelo's sixtieth birthday. (PAYE *smiles, embarrassed.*
JULIO *climbs out of the barrel.*)

PAYE: Is that it? Fixed?

JULIO: (*Wiping his chest and flexing his muscles.*) Yes. The out-
going pipe was jammed with dirt. Well, that ought to hold
it for a while. Now, you gotta help me get this sucker back
up on the roof!

PAYE: Okay, let's go.

JULIO: Wait a minute! Let me cool off a second at least. Where's
Tatín?

PAYE: He's writing something for his radio broadcast. I'll get'im.

JULIO: No, no. Leave him be. He doesn't have to get sweat on
his back. Neither do you, really.

PAYE: In this heat you can't help but sweat.

JULIO: Not like this. You guys have brains. You guys don't ever have to exert your muscles. Not like me. All I got is muscles. (*Flexes with pride.*) Nice, no? It drives the women crazy. (*Flexes into another pose.*) I don't have any brains.

PAYE: I'm sure you do.

JULIO: No. None to speak of. You guys, you got the brains in the family. I'll cut sugar cane every season and work out with the militia, and that'll be it for the rest of my life.

PAYE: What would you rather do?

JULIO: You really want to know.

PAYE: Yeah, tell me.

JULIO: What I'd really like to do? I'd like to have a steady sit-down job in an office with a big window to stare out of, like in Havana. And drive a car; one of those little sports cars. Red.

PAYE: Julio, you're an aspiring playboy.

JULIO: What's that?

PAYE: A playboy? It's like a gigolo, but independent.

JULIO: Oh, yes, I could live with that.

PAYE: Have you ever thought of leaving ... ?

JULIO: No. If you don't have brains, no matter where you go, you still end up shoveling shit. (PAYE *laughs.*) You make lots of money?

PAYE: Me? No.

JULIO: (*Surprised.*) How come?

PAYE: Playwrights don't get to make lots of money.

JULIO: Is that right? (*Stretches his back muscles. Dries himself off once more.*) You don't mind not making lots of money?

PAYE: Me? Yeah, I mind. I'm miserable about it.

JULIO: You didn't want to be a doctor like Ari?

PAYE: No.

JULIO: And you're still outside?

PAYE: What do you mean?

JULIO: Well, if I was going to be something that didn't make lots of money ... if I was going to be miserable and broke, I'd rather do it in Cuba. Now, you, you got brains. You could be rich! If I had brains, I might consider going abroad and getting rich ... but then I'd only be miserable outside of Cuba. Twice as miserable. (*Thinks a moment.*) I would have to be *very* rich. I can't understand being abroad and not being rich. There isn't much consolation

in that! (*Silence.*) You remember the time you set Tatín's
bed on fire?

PAYE: And I threw a bucket of water on him! (*They laugh.*) I
locked myself in the bathroom. and when I thought it
was quiet enough and everyone was back in bed, I came
out ... Papa was there, with the belt. (*They laugh. Music.
Blackout. Lights come up on* AMELIA *on the verandah.*)

AMELIA: (*Shouting.*) Rosario! Ah, compañera. Doña Cacha
wants to know if we could borrow some of your chairs
for the party?

VOICE: Ay, yes, of course. I have six cane-back ones, four with
the chrome legs, the one from my vanity and ...

AMELIA: How about the long bench?

VOICE: Ay, that's so tough!

AMELIA: It's tougher standing up! There's going to be such a
crowd!

VOICE: I've been thinking about the pig all day!

AMELIA: (*Trying to exit.*) I got to run now, I got to run down to
Clara to borrow her tablecloths!

VOICE: Ay, Amelia! I only have five cane-backs. I forgot. Graciela
busted the other one last week!

AMELIA: She can stand up! (*Blackout. Lights come up on* Tatín
*sitting on the railing center. Smoking. There are party
noises in the background. Dance music. Voices. He addresses the audience.*)

TATÍN: Paye's letters were always full of all the wonderful things
that are out there. He'd mention steaks he had when there
were real shortages here. He'd bring up his trip to Europe and things he'd seen there, and remark too bad you
couldn't see this or that. It was as if we wanted to hurt
me.

ANA: (*Enters.*) So here you are. (TATÍN *looks.*) It's cooler out
here. (*Sits beside him.*) The pork was good, wasn't it?
(TATÍN *nods.*) I'm sorry Tía Cuca put sauce all over your
rice. I know you don't like it that way. (*There is a burst
of laughter from inside.*) Listen to that! Too bad the boys
didn't get to come. They should have come, you know.
(*Pause.*) I suppose it would have made it harder for you
and Paye to talk.

TATÍN: (*Butting a cigarette.*) You were dancing with Paye.

ANA: Yes. He was telling me about seeing Baryshnikov at an open
air amphitheater. (*Pause.*) Did he tell you he was unhappy
living in Toronto?

TATÍN: Why? Why do you ask?

ANA: I don't know. I always thought that ... you know ... but from the way he speaks, I get the feeling he feels ... dissatisfied.

TATÍN: He's having a bad time of it right now.

ANA: Did he tell you that?

TATÍN: In dribs and drabs.

ANA: He still manages pretty well.

TATÍN: He works at a lot of other things.

ANA: Ahh! (TATÍN *looks at* ANA.) You know the shirt he's wearing. It's silk. Bought it in India. He spent three months in India.

TATÍN: Yes, I know.

ANA: He's been everywhere.

TATÍN: Yes I know. He gets the Sunday *New York Times* and he's met Lillian Hellman. He has an electric typewriter, a private phone and everything Paul Simon ever recorded. (*Pause.*)

ANA: You wish you were in his shoes?

TATÍN: I wish I were in anybody else's shoes.

ANA: Tatín ...

TATÍN: What about you? Whose shoes do you wish you were in?

ANA: I ... I don't know ...

TATÍN: Come on, just off the top of your head.

ANA: (*Thinks.*) I guess I still wish that I was Kim Novak.

TATÍN: Kim Novak?

ANA: When I was a little girl I always wanted to look like Kim Novak. Now, Paye tells me she's not even a star anymore.

TATÍN: You asked Paye about Kim Novak? (*Laughs.*)

ANA: Well, why not? (TATÍN *laughs heartily.*) You're making me feel stupid. (*Starts to smile.*)

TATÍN: Kim Novak!!! (*They both burst out laughing.*)

ANA: (*As laughter subsides.*) Tatín ... I know what's the matter ... why you've been acting like you've been acting. (TATÍN *looks at her attentively.*) I thought it had to do with Paye ... His visit and memories and ... but, it really has to do with the radio broadcasts, doesn't it? It does, doesn't it? (*Applause from inside. Voices. As* DILIA *and* CACHA *enter* TATÍN *jumps to attention as if he'd been discovered.*)

DILIA: C'mon you two, the party's inside!

TATÍN: Abue! Tía! (*They walk up stage but sit at the patio.*)

CACHA: You should be inside dancing!

TATÍN: We were getting some air.

CACHA: Ah, yes, it's cooler out here.

DILIA: You should see Tía Clara!

TATÍN: She must be boiling over in that dress.

DILIA: (*To* TATÍN *as if gossiping.*) She's been trying to match up Amelia with one of the Moreno boys. Manolo.

TATÍN: Is he the one with the gold tooth?

DILIA: No, he's the one with the warts. (*Points to her chin, her cheek, and her eyebrow. Laughs.*) I think Tía Clara's had too much to drink.

TATÍN: You're not too sober yourself, Tía.

DILIA: Drunk? Me?!

TATÍN: I saw you swig back Tío Nando's beer at the table. More than once!

DILIA: Tch! That much won't even take the itch from a bee sting! (*Laughter and cheers from inside.*)

CACHA: Listen to that! (CLARA *enters. She is wearing an overly fancy 50's cocktail dress.*)

CLARA: Ay! The queen of the carnival is here! I've been dancing and dancing ...

CACHA: You better sit ...

CLARA: And I'm still in one piece! I'm putting the young girls to shame. (*She sits.*) Ay, to be eighteen again!

CACHA: Or fifty. (*All laugh.*)

CLARA: Ay, no! No, Cacha, not me; if I'm going to dream, I want it all beautiful: eighteen, technicolor, violins and blonde hair! I'm glad I got all dressed up! (*Blows down the front of her dress.*)

ANA: Can I get you a drink, Tía?

CLARA: Ay, Anita, you know I don't drink. But be an angel and get me my fan. It's on the table by the gramophone. (ANA *exits.*) I'm just a little hot, but as soon as I cool off ... Ay Cacha, I didn't take a break! (*Laughs.*)

CACHA: Clara, remember Monday's wash day.

CLARA: I may not even wash this Monday. (*Music changes to a conga.*)

DILIA: Conga! (DILIA *exits dancing.*)

ANA: (*Entering.*) I think Julio's drunk, he keeps trying to lift Tía Carmen. (*Gives* CLARA *her fan and ice water.*)

CLARA: You'll know he's drunk when he tries to lift Graciela! (TATÍN *laughs.*)

CACHA: You should laugh, you used to go out with her.

ANA: Before he was married.

CLARA: Before she was fat!

PAYE: (*Off.*) Tía Clara! Conga!

CLARA: Ay, a request! A request!

CACHA: Slow down Clara ...

CLARA: (*Hurriedly trying to put on shoes.*) I'm fine Cacha ... (*Suddenly screams.*) Anhhh! My bunion! I can't get my shoes back on! (*All laugh.*)

ANA: Sit this one out, Tía.

CLARA: Not on your life! I'll have to dance barefoot.

CACHA: Clara, tomorrow, you'll ...

CLARA: (*Getting up.*) Tomorrow, I don't care if they amputate! (*Hobbles off, waving her shoes in the air.*)

ANA: She's crazy!

CACHA: Ay, no, Anita. Clara's wearing her party dress, that's all. I'm glad Julio got the pig—and that we've all made it like the carnival for Paye. (DILIA *laughs from inside.*) When your grandfather was alive, there'd be parties in this house till noon the next day. Your uncles... when they were young, they used to dance like they had an itch in their groins from the inside out. Your Uncle Pucho used to spend the three days of the carnival dancing. Even when he came by for a clean shirt in the afternoons, he'd be congaing through the house singing, "If I don't dance, I lose the beat, if I don't dance, I lose the beat," over and over and over.

DILIA: (*Entering.*) You should see Paye dancing. He hasn't forgotten that he's Cuban! And Tía Clara! You know she's dancing barefoot? (*Takes* CLARA'*s fan.*)

ANA: I've never seen Tía Clara like this.

DILIA: Two weeks ago, all she could talk about was her hemorrhoids! Poor Tía Clara! Having to do without Paye all these years.

CLARA: (*Enters.*) The room's spinning in there.

DILIA: Tired, Tía!

CLARA: No! I just wanted the young girls to have a crack at Paye. Give me my fan. (*Sits.*)

DILIA: You're going to have to give away that dress after tonight.

CLARA: It'll wash.

ANA: Tía, you should get a new one.

CLARA: And where is one supposed to get this kinda material in ...

DILIA: Don't get her started, please. (*Cheers are heard from inside.*)

CLARA: Listen to that! It sounds like the old days. Ay, if Sylvia
   and Tato could only be here tonight. (*To* ANA.) Sylvia
   used to have such a good time at these things. Once she
   had two drinks in her, she didn't know if she was talking
   English, Spanish or Jew. (*To* DILIA.) You remember the
   time she was trying to tell Father Ephraim that he hit the
   nail on the head and she wound up telling him that he
   really knew how to screw! (*All laugh.*)

PAYE: (*Enters holding a beer.*) So the party's out here.

DILIA: Look at him, he's soaking wet!

CACHA: Isn't he beautiful! Why don't you change your shirt,
   you'll ...

PAYE: I just have the stet I'm leaving with tomorrow.

CACHA: What did you do with the others?

TATÍN: He's leaving some to me.

PAYE: And Julio, and Roberto and so on and so on.

CACHA: What are you going to do, run around Canada naked?

PAYE: How's everybody doing out here? (*All mumble "fine" or "all
   right," except* CLARA *who is staring into space.* PAYE
   stumbles.*)

DILIA: You're drunk, Paye.

CLARA: Everybody's drunk to you, Dilia. It's a pity you never
   had a husband, then you'd know what drunk really was.

DILIA: Let's not start on that one!

AMELIA: (*Enters wearing her full carnival costume.*) Where's Paye?

CACHA: Ay, Amelia!

DILIA: See, Tía, Amelia couldn't stand to see you the only one all
   dressed up.

CLARA: Turn around, let's see.

AMELIA: I promised Paye I'd try it on before he left.

PAYE: It's superb!

AMELIA: La Placita's going to take first prize this year.

DILIA: As always! (AMELIA *exits.*)

CACHA: Having a good time, Paye?

PAYE: The time of my life. (*Raises his drink.*) To La Placita!

CACHA: Tonight we're all happy, Paye.

DILIA: You'll have a lot to tell them when you get back.

CACHA: Ay, yes, look at him; he's even got some color. (CLARA
   fans PAYE, *who has put himself within reach of the breeze.*)

DILIA: A few more days at Mar Verde and he'd really start looking
   like a Cuban again!

PAYE: (*Suddenly standing up.*) I have something to say. (*A shrill
   scream from inside.*)

DILIA: I better go see ...

PAYE: No, no, Tía, sit down. I want everyone to hear. (*Kisses her.*) You know, I used to be afraid of you. (*To all.*) Now I find out that Tía loves me after all.

DILIA: Ay, Paye, you're drunk!

PAYE: (*Raising his beer.*) To my Tía Dilia! (*Tries to stand on a chair.*)

ANA: (*To* TATÍN.) I think he's had too much to ...

CLARA: Ay, yes, Paye, sit down.

PAYE: (*Kissing* CLARA.) No, no, Tía. Now that everyone is here. (*Looks around.*) Well, the main ones ... my family (*Pause.*) I want to return to Cuba for good! (*There is a momentary silence.*)

TATÍN: He's drunk!

PAYE: No, I'm not. I want to come home. If you'll have me?!

TATÍN: You're crazy! (*There are voices rasied from inside. A girl screams.* PAYE *and* TATÍN *shout over the voices.*)

PAYE: What's so crazy about it? It happens ...

AMELIA: (*In a panic.*) Dilia, come quick. It's Julio; he's drunk!

TATÍN: You don't know what the hell your're saying! You couldn't live here!

VOICE: (*Off.*) Julio!

VOICE: (*Off.*) Get somebody, quick, get Dilia! (DILIA *exits.*)

TATÍN: It's not as simple as that!

VOICE: (*Off.*) What the hell is he doing?!

PAYE: What's the matter, don't you want me here?!

TATÍN: No!

PAYE: It's my home!

AMELIA: Dilia, hurry!

VOICE: (*Off.*) Don't let'im! Grab him!

VOICE: (*Off.*) Go around!

VOICE: (*Off.*) Stop him!

TATÍN: You're thinking of no one but yourself! Well I got news for you. Life in Cuba isn't like you've seen here this week. There isn't always a party.

VOICE: (*Off.*) He's had too much to drink!

PAYE: And you think I have everything given to me on a silver platter!

VOICE: (*Off.*) Don't, Julio!

AMELIA: Dilia, he's taking off everything!

VOICE: (*Off.*) Stop it Julio! (*The voices from inside have increased in urgency. Screams.* JULIO *appears stark naked.*

AMELIA *and* DILIA *run after him.* DILIA *stops at up-stage door.*)

JULIO: Adiós, Abuela! (PAYE *and* TATÍN *ignore the chase and get into a screaming match of their own.*)

TATÍN: You wouldn't be happy here!

PAYE: Julio is!

TATÍN: You're not Julio!!! (TATÍN *climbs on the table.*) I have an announcement too. I'm leaving Cuba for good!

ANA: On what boat?

DILIA: That is the most preposterous ...

ANA: What about us, your wife and your kids?

TATÍN: Why is it with the goddamned Cubans that they won't listen and they all want to speak at once?

PAYE: Well, you'll have to put up with me because I intend to apply to come back.

TATÍN: I will do everything in my power to stop you.

PAYE: You hateful son of a bitch, what power do you have?!

TATÍN: You don't think I heard what you said to Amelia! I'll report that ...

PAYE: You stinking commie bastard—you'd betray your brother to get your way ... You hate me that much.

TATÍN: Bullshit!

PAYE: Yes, it's hate—and I hate you back. You have the heart of a cockroach. (PAYE *goes wild scraming.*) I hate you! I hate you! I hate you!!! (TATÍN *slaps* PAYE. PAYE *slaps him back. Silence.* PAYE *bursts into tears and falls into* TATÍN's *arms.* DILIA *notices that* CACHA *is having difficulty breathing.*)

DILIA: Mama! (*To* ANA.) Water!

CLARA: Take mine. (*She does.*)

PAYE: Abuela?

CACHA: I'm okay. I'm okay.

DILIA: (*To* ANA *and* CLARA.) Help me get her to bed. (PAYE *goes to help.*)

TATÍN: No. Stay. (*Trying not to be heard.*) I don't hate you, Paye. I don't want you here because if I could I'd leave myself.

PAYE: (*Loudly.*) You! You want to leave Cuba! (ANA *and* DILIA *turn to look at* TATÍN. PAYE *sits.*)

TATÍN: If I could get my wife and my sons out—all at onec—I'd take the next plane, boat, raft out of here.

PAYE: What?

TATÍN: This is a mess. We're sending troops to Angola, we're buying arms from Russia. My radio show is being censored.
My writing is being questioned ...

PAYE: In the six days that I've been here, you've been leading me
to believe ...

TATÍN: You believed what you wanted to believe. (ANA *enters.*)

ANA: Is that what it is, Tatín?

TATÍN: Yes. (ANA *crosses to him and puts her arms around him
in support.*)

PAYE: How is she?

ANA: All right. The shock, her age. She's breathing fine now.

TATÍN: Do you want to leave, Ana?

ANA: I'm not the one who's being censored.

TATÍN: Could you leave?

ANA: My needs are simple. A ballet bar and a bunch of kids doing
demiplies—anywhere. But if we leave, Tatín, we all leave
together. You, me, the boys. All four of us. Paye, you
have a plane to catch tomorrow. I'm glad you came. It
doesn't take much to live in Cuba. Just blind faith. Either
you have it or you don't. (*She hugs* PAYE.)

PAYE: (*Returning the embrace.*) Thank you. Ana. (ANA *exits. To*
TATÍN.) What are you going to do?

TATÍN: Leaving Cuba is a slow, tedious process at best.

PAYE: You know, Tatín, I never felt like I belonged anywhere as
much as I do here. I have been living in exile all these
years. And you're right, I'm not writing. And I don't care
if I ever write again.

TATÍN: You don't mean that.

PAYE: Yes, I do. I only write because I'm lonely. Because I'm
seeking approval from total strangers in the dark, because
...

TATÍN: You have something to say. You have imagination.

PAYE: Up there, in the winter, people bundle up and cast their
eyes on the sidewalk. Ice is slippery. It's a way of life.
You don't look up. You don't see who you're passing on
the street.

TATÍN: Here, the committees are becoming more powerful. Now
that my work is getting noticed abroad, what I write becomes scrutinized. I'm asked what things mean by people
who learned to read ten years ago.

PAYE: Surely you knew there'd be censorship?

TATÍN: Of course. It is understood that until stability is reached,
censorship is necessary, and that under seige, the mili-

tia must be armed to the teeth. Our neighors must be watched. Our people must be indoctrinated so that they can learn to cope with the new way of life. (*He lights up a cigarette.*) But, that has become the new way of life. You see, Paye, I am a disillusioned man. And it makes me sad.

PAYE: So what will you do?

TATÍN: I have two sons who know nothing but this and who beieve fervently the lessons they've been taught. And in a few years, they'll be of military age and won't be allowed to leave. (*There is long silence.*) Paye, stay abroad. And write.

AMELIA: (*Enters.*) We found Julio! (*Giggles.*)

TATÍN: Shhh! Abuela's in bed.

AMELIA: (*Suppressing her laughter.*) He was sitting on the pitcher's mound on a nest of red ants. (*She laughs.*)

TATÍN: It's not funny.

AMELIA: His balls are swollen like pineapples! (*She exits.*)

PAYE: I'll envy you the carnival.

TATÍN: (*Shrugging his shoulders.*) Euphoria for the masses, a little something to ease the pain. What time is your plane? (*Before* PAYE *can reply,* DILIA *enters.*)

DILIA: Paye, Mama wants to see you. She is afraid she'll fall asleep and you'll leave without seeing her. Tatín, you wouldn't leave, would you? (*Almost in tears.*) When Mama dies, what will I do? (TATÍN *bursts into tears in* DILIA's *arms. Lights fade. Lights come up in* CACHA's *room.* PAYE *is sitting on the edge of the bed under the mosquito net.*)

PAYE: Abuela?

CACHA: Paye?

PAYE: Tía said ...

CACHA: I've been waiting for you. They gave me something, I think to make me sleep, but I've been waiting ... I must talk to you, Paye.

PAYE: Yes, Abue.

CACHA: Here, sit close to me. (PAYE *moves closer.*)

CACHA: I'm not going to die, Paye. Not yet. I ... I'm waiting for everyone to come home. They have to come. Because I'm waiting. (*Touches* PAYE's *hand lovingly.*) Tomorrow ... I will have to speak to Julio. And Tatín! Tell them. I will speak to them tomorrow.

PAYE: Yes, Abue. Now rest ... (*Starts to get up.*)

CACHA: (*Holding him back.*) Tato is my son. You are my grandson. You were born in my arms! (*SILENCE.*) This is your
home, Paye. No one can turn you away. You understand,
Paye?

PAYE: Yes, Abue.

CACHA: Even after I'm dead ... this is your home. You were born
in my arms, Paye. In this house.

PAYE: Abue ...

CACHA: You will come back, Paye. I know it. Maybe not soon,
but you will come back. You will all come back. (*Reaches
out for him.*) My little Paye.

PAYE: (*Controling his emotions.*) Sleep now, Abuela, tomorrow
...

CACHA: Yes. Tomorrow. Tell Tato I'm fine. I'm not going to die.
Tomorrow, Paye ... Paye-Paye. (CACHA *is asleep.* PAYE
*kisses her. Music comes up softly. Blackout. Lights come
up on* DILIA, ANA *and* TATÍN *facing front on the verandah.* CACHA *joins them. They clap and wave as though
the carnival were passing by. There is carnival music. On
the stage right corner, a light comes up on* PAYE. *He is
speaking into a tape recorder.*)

PAYE: It is coming around to winter again real soon. The trees all
over the city are a carnival of color; though in my mind
they'll never compare to the carnival I missed that time.
I shall never stop misssing it. It and everything else I left
behind. No matter where I am, I guess a part of me will
always be there. My home. (*Pause.*) I miss you, Tatín. I
think of you all the time. I think of what we said to one
another and what we left still unsaid. (*Pause.*) I never
quite managed to tell you that ... that I love you, and that
neither miles, nor long silences, will ever alter that. It's a
pleasant thought that makes my exile less cruel, easier to
bear. Enough said and not enough. Mama and Papa are
trying all they can through the Jamaican Embassy. Mama
knows the counsel well and she seems hopefull that he'll
get you and your family out. A million warm and gentle
kisses for you and the whole family ... from your brother
who awaits you, Paye. P.S. I am enclosing a copy of my
play. I hope you like it. (*As he speaks the last few words,
everything goes wild with color and light. The music swells
and confetti pours from the sky. Suddenly the music stops
and all freeze in a tableau as the confetti falls slowly as in
a glass enclosed souvenir shaker. As the last of the confetti*

falls, lights fade to black.)

Once upon a Dream

by

Miguel González-Pando

Once upon a Dream
About the Author

It has been within that space flanked by conflict, contradiction and passion that Miguel González-Pando has existed, even before leaving Cuba as a teenager. By then, his "love of country" had already compelled him to take a stand against the Batista dictatorship, as he led a student walk-out that forced the government to close down every high school in the country. Because of that action, he was indicted for "conspiring against the powers of the state" and was forced to flee into exile for the first time. A political amnesty in 1958 made his return possible. Soon after Castro came to power, González-Pando became disenchanted with the Revolution for the same reasons he had opposed the Batista regime: lack of freedom and disregard for human rights.

It was time again to take a stand. Still a teenager, González-Pando enrolled in the Bay of Pigs Invasion, landed in Cuba and was captured. Sentenced to a term of thirty years, he was released after only two years in Castro's infamous prisons. Then came his third exile which has lasted to this day.

In the United States, even as he continued to participate in covert operations against Castro, González-Pando attended the University of Miami and later won a scholarship to Harvard's Graduate School. He completed all course work for a doctorate in economics, but family demands prevented him from finishing his dissertation.

At Florida International University, where he has been a faculty member since 1973, González-Pando became a pioneer in bilingual education and refugee assistance. He also founded the University's Center for Latino Education, which served as a locus of community and educational activities for Hispanics.

Despite his violent past as a freedom fighter, González-Pando has forged the public image of a man of peace. In 1978 he accepted Cuba's invitation to participate in the controversial *diálogo*, a negotiation between Castro and a group of exiles selected by the communist government. The event, denounced by Miami's more conservative ranks, did serve to open up the island to travel by Cuban exiles and to obtain the freedom of thousands of political prisoners. Nevertheless, it became clear that Castro had orchestrated it to improve his deteriorating international reputation. Much to the dictator's astonishment, González-Pando challenged Castro to his face and later denounced that very process as a self-serving charade staged by the Cuban government.

Criticized and maligned by his former Bay of Pigs comrades-in-arms for his liberal views, González-Pando turned to writing in both English and Spanish: plays, short stories, essays and political articles for local and national publications. For years, his bi-weekly column in *El Nuevo Herald*, the Spanish-language newspaper of *The Miami Herald*, has brought him praise as well as censure. His once-solitary search for a peaceful democratic transition in Cuba has lately gained more acceptance among the exile community, and in 1990 González-Pando was among the founders of the *Plataforma Democrática*, a coalition of ideologically diverse parties that have renounced violence as a means to liberate the island.

Although better known as a political activist, González-Pando's dramatic production reflects a similar passion and boldness. "Once Upon a Dream" is the author's fifth play. Two others, "La Familia Pilón" (1982) and "The Torch" (1987), have been produced in Miami. Still unstaged and unpublished are two other plays, "The Great American Justice Game" (1986), a hilarious yet provocative satire about the English-Only Movement, and a more conventional work, "Había una Vez un Sueño" (1987), which was a finalist in the prestigious Letras de Oro literary competition.

"Había una Vez un Sueño" was revised in 1990 and retitled "A las Mil Maravillas." It received a dramatic reading by Teatro Avante in 1991. The author then rewrote it in English as "Once Upon a Dream," a modern tragedy set in New York's harsh environment.

"Once Upon a Dream" splits the marginal reality of Hispanic exiles and refugees into polar contrapositions. In the play, the adult world moves regressively to a lost paradise, a pastoral *locus amoenus* that suggests its Caribbean origins—even the characters' speech reveals traces of their native Spanish syntax. All conception of what is to happen seems shaped entirely by the idealized past where nostalgia and wishful thinking intertwine in a combination that nullifies all notion of current reality. The widowed mother dreams of herself as a youthful wife, not as the mother of teenagers living in a very different dimension. For its part, the adolescent world is markedly picaresque, concerned with the real need to fulfill all necessities in a ruthless environment. To the mother's contrived reality one must add her children's own fantasies, which assume the possibility of escaping not only notice, but also retribution or consequences.

It appears obvious that González-Pando's idea of a northern American city may suggest New York or any such urban area. Probably, however, that notion of city life took shape during his years in Boston. To that notion one must contrast the "other" place, a place absent of real people, populated only by ghosts from times gone by: yesterday's Havana or any other Latin American city.

As they must, seers of the past become blind observers of the present and cannot anticipate the outcomes of living away from responsibility. Already the nineteenth-century Spanish novelist and playwright Benito Pérez Galdós had discovered that those Spaniards who insisted on living in the past, longing for the glory that was the Spanish Imperial Golden Age, were killing the present. His neat formula (the past is death, the present is life) always served to show how the past can and does stifle the present. "Once Upon a Dream" captures, dramatically, the juxtaposition of pastoral and picaresque, adulthood and adolescence, past and present, northern blight and tropical light. In short, life and death.

CHARACTERS

DOLORES, the mother, a widow.
LOLITA, the daughter, fifteen years old.
MACHITO, the blind son, twenty years old.
TONY, a neighbor and friend of Machito.
FATHER MARTÍN, a priest, a friend of the family.
ÁNGELA AND CARMEN, friends of Dolores.

TIME

The action takes place at the present time in New York City.

ACT I

.... First Scene: The Dreams ....

The stage is completely dark. A blue spotlight begins to illumi-nate LOLITA's *face.*

LOLITA: (*Matter-of-factly.*) "The web of our life is of a mingled yarn, good and ill together. Our virtues would be proud if our faults whipped them not, and our crimes would despair if they were not cherished by our virtues." *All's Well That Ends Well,* by William Shakespeare. (*As the blue spotlight dims, the stage illuminates, revealing the living-dining-kitchen in a small third-floor apartment in New York's barrio, where thousands of refugees and Latin American immigrants hold on dearly to their dreams as a way of transcending the everyday reality of their marginal existence. It is daytime. The walls are completely cov-ered with posters of musical extravaganzas, old photos, re-ligious paintings and other memorabilia, giving the home the melancholy air of a monument to nostalgia. Lolita, a girl of fifteen whose face denotes the wisdom gained by having grown up too close to the grim reality of life, is try-ing on a long formal gown; her mother, Dolores, an intense woman who moves quickly as if she were trying to keep one step ahead of her destiny, comes out of the bedroom obliv-ious to Lolita's words and sits at the sewing machine to fit the gown on her daughter; the figure asleep on a small sofa in the corner is barely noticeable.*)

DOLORES: (*Softly, but with great excitement.*) A narrow sash of pink velvet around the waist ... and that's it. You're going to look like a princess, a real princess. If only your father could see you now ... !

LOLITA: I liked the pattern I had chosen better.

DOLORES: This one is more traditional, Lolita. Good taste never changes.

LOLITA: You are the one who never changes.

DOLORES: Remember that I got my dressmaker's certificate—back in my country, where everything was done by hand.

Come on, raise your arms to see it fits comfortably. (DO-
LORES *begins humming the melody from "Blue Danube"
while she takes* LOLITA *by the hand as if to dance.*)

LOLITA: (*Pulling away.*)   This fashion has already gone out of
fashion ...

DOLORES: Your late father always insisted that I design and sew
everything he ever wore on stage. That's why I can take
credit for his success.

LOLITA: (*Complaining loudly.*) Those were different times, Mama!

DOLORES: Shh ... your brother is asleep.

LOLITA: It's two in the afternoon ...

DOLORES: (*Kneeling to measure the length of the gown.*) Don't
pick an argument with him, darling—let's see ... let's see
... let me see the length ... (*In a mechanical tone, as
if fully aware that she has said this before.*) You know
that your poor brother hasn't been feeling very well lately.
Besides, he's upset about your party.

LOLITA: (*As if play acting.*)   Perhaps he needs a well-deserved
vacation after his very long rest.

DOLORES: Ah, if only your father were alive ...

LOLITA: I've told you as far as I'm concerned, you can forget
the stupid party. I can't see the point in wasting all that
money ...

DOLORES: (*Busy fitting the dress.*) You get to be fifteen only once.
When you grow up and have children, you'll understand—
don't be so ungrateful. At least, you could try to respect
your father's last wish—God rest his soul.

LOLITA: This is so ridiculous! We live in this dump, full of roaches
and rats, and as far back as I can remember, all you cared
about, all you talked about, all you ever planned to do
was show off at my fifteenth birthday party!

DOLORES: Yes!   Show off!   You said it: everyone will know
that the daughter of Macho Santiago and Dolores Jiménez
celebrated her fifteenth birthday in style, like her father
wished on his deathbed! Now, stop complaining and keep
still ... I've got pins in my hand ... And don't you argue
with me, young lady!

LOLITA: And what about after, Mama?

DOLORES: After?

LOLITA: Yes, after the party—what then? The next day, the next
month, the next year, what then, Mama? Who's going to
remember?

DOLORES: (*Stunned.*) Everyone will! Your father's family, your father's friends, all those who knew and admired your father since we came to this country ... Your father was an extraordinary man, Lolita. Years will go by, you will have children, and people will still remember the great Macho Santiago, because he made history and left a trail ...

LOLITA: Mama, what family and friends are you talking about?

DOLORES: Everyone, child. Those who filled St. Patrick's the day your father and I got married ... and those who said your father was the best percussionist in the world and they would follow him wherever he played ... (*Leaning on the dresser, on the verge of tears.*) And those who stopped traffic on Fifth Avenue to accompany your father's remains, walking in the rain, all the way to the cemetery on that ugly morning of September four, 1976. (*Takes a photo album from a drawer and opens it.*) Here, here are the pictures and the newspaper clippings ... (*Pauses, glancing at the photos absent-mindedly.*)

LOLITA: And where are all those people now, Mama? Where are they? Have they ever called you to see if you needed something, have they ever come to visit us in this dump, full of roaches and rats? Have they, Mama? When has his own family even so much as answered your Christmas cards? Almost fifteen years have gone by, Mama. Don't you realize that for those people we no longer exist?

DOLORES: (*Confidently.*) On your fifteenth birthday, everyone will be present, like when your father was alive. And on that day, you'll truly learn to honor the memory of that great man the Lord carried off to His glory at the peak of success. You'll see ... you'll see ... Everything's turning out just perfect—here, take a look, did I show you the tiara I ordered? (*Shows her a magazine.*) It goes perfectly with the lace gown ... Everybody will think they are seeing a true princess waiting for her prince.

LOLITA: Mama, stop it: this is not "Cinderella!" (*Throws away the magazine.*)

MACHITO: (*From the sofa-bed.*) Be quiet, dammit!

DOLORES: (*In a soft voice.*) There, now you woke up your poor brother ... (*Sweetly.*) I'm sorry, Machito, I dropped something ... (*Gently, to* LOLITA.) Now, go change your dress ... (*The telephone rings and* DOLORES *rushes to answer.*) And hang it carefully so it won't wrinkle. (*On the tele-*

phone.) Ángela? (*Listens.*) I was expecting your call. Listen, did you remember to speak with the printer? (*Delighted.*) They are pretty, eh? And how much will he charge for the five hundred invitations? (*Listens.*) No, no, I expect more than five hundred—the ballroom holds up to eight hundred guests—and I'm sure everyone is coming. As a matter of fact, I'm going to the Palace to order the buffet tomorrow ... Enough for one thousand!—I don't want people to say later that there wasn't enough food ... (*Covering the telephone as* LOLITA *comes out of the bedroom.*) Pick up your shoes and hurry so you can get to the store in time to get me the pink velvet sash ...

MACHITO: (*Sitting up on the sofa-bed.*) Can't even sleep in this place. This stinking party is driving you crazy ... !

DOLORES: (*Hurrying, still on the telephone.*) Well, I've got to hang up now—Machito just got home from work and I have to serve him lunch. (*Listens.*) Yes, yes, of course he's working ... And don't forget the invitations ... and also remember to drop in tomorrow so you can try on your dress. (*Hangs up and addresses* MACHITO.) I'll get your coffee right away. (*Heads toward the kitchen.*) Didn't you sleep well?

MACHITO: With all the street noise and your damn chatter, who can get any sleep in this house? And you well know I need a sound sleep so I can wake up relaxed and not forget my dreams ...

DOLORES: (*Serves him breakfast.*) What if you try going to bed a bit earlier ... ?

MACHITO: (*Putting on a sequined robe like musicians wear on stage.*) Are you ready to start screwing up my day with that damn lecture? How many times do I have to tell you my best dreams happen around noon? When I dream at noon, I get it right, Mama! Get it into that crazy head of yours: I must take advantage of that exact time for my dreams ... Or is it you want me to be a blind bum forever? (*Feels his way to the dining table confidently and sits down.*)

DOLORES: (*In a softer tone.*) And did you manage to dream ... ?

MACHITO: (*Eating his breakfast, while staring off into an imaginary horizon.*) I was riding a handsome black mare, so shiny ... and I could see a field full of flowers of all colors ... (*Sips his coffee.*) In the distance, you could clearly see three mountains covered with a green forest ... (*Takes another sip.*) And we start galloping up hill through the forest, but about halfway, the mare begins to slip and to resist my commands—you know how things seem so weird in a dream. Then I try spurring her on, but she still pays no attention to me, and I sink my spurs into her side, but she keeps on slipping and slipping ... and I sink them in again and again until her guts burst out full of shit, and I keep on spurring her harder and harder, and then the mare stands on her hind legs and falls on top of me and covers me with all the shit that's bursting out from her guts, and then the hill turns into a whole bunch of shit, and I sink and sink deep into that hot shit ...

DOLORES: For God's sake, Machito, what kind of a dream is that?

MACHITO: What kind of a dream ... ? The kind that pays off easy cash at the betting window, Mama. Don't you get it? "Shit and horses"—why, it's clear, clear as day. Shit in dreams always means money, just ask Tony. Look, Mama, you gotta lend me fifty bucks ... I got up today with the itch in the palms of my hands—every time I get that itch it brings me good luck. I'll bet you anything today we're gonna win at the horses.

LOLITA: (*From the bedroom, sticking out her head.*) "I talk of dreams, which are the children of an idle brain, Begot of nothing but vain fantasy ... "

MACHITO: Aw, come on, quit pissing me off with your shitty little poems at a time like this!

LOLITA: (*Teasing.*) *Romeo and Juliet* by William Shakespeare!

DOLORES: (*Pleading.*) Machito, don't talk to your sister like that, she's got to learn those verses for her drama class ... Remember that Lolita is her father's daughter, she was born to be a great artist.

MACHITO: An artist? Come on, Ma, this kid has the same chance of winning that scholarship as me winning first prize in the Lotto without buying any tickets ... All the "artists" I know end up going hungry or becoming hookers ...

DOLORES: Machito!

LOLITA: (*Acting.*) Let him be, dearest Mother—when I get to be a famous Hollywood star, he'll come feeling sorry ... and of course, begging for some gambling money.

MACHITO: (*Still eating breakfast.*) Hasn't Tony called?

DOLORES: No one has called. Come on, calm down and finish your breakfast, now ...

MACHITO: And if he tried to call, the line was busy. I'll bet you were glued to the phone, babbling on about the party. (*Feels his way to the fire escape window, sticks his head out, and calls to the floor above.*) Tony! (*Louder.*) Tony!!

TONY: (*His voice comes from the floor above.*) What?

MACHITO: Come on down, gotta go to the racetrack ... Awesome dream, bro'! And hurry up—I woke up with the itch in my hands. (*Kisses the palms of his hands, plays a couple of beats on the conga drum that stands by the window and walks toward the bathroom.*) Come on, Ma, get me that money fast—gotta get there in time for the third race. (*Stumbles over the shoes* LOLITA *forgot to pick up and kicks them with a curse.*)

DOLORES: Child, I told you to pick up your shoes! (*Picks up the shoes and puts them on the dresser, then takes out her purse.*) All I can lend you is this ... (*Places a bill in* MA-CHITO's *hand.*)

MACHITO: (*Holding his mother by the arm while feeling the bill.*) How much is it? How much is it?

DOLORES: Ten *pesos.* (*Tries to shake herself free from* MACHITO.)

MACHITO: Ten stinking *pesos.* Shit, what the hell do you think I can do with ten stinking bucks? Come on, loosen up, loosen up: we gonna win today, and tonight I'll treat you out to dinner to celebrate. (*Kisses her and pinches her behind.*)

DOLORES: Machito, you know how it is. You know perfectly well how expensive things have got in this country. The little money I manage to make with my sewing is not enough for the rent, the phone, the utilities, the food ... (*Sweetly.*) Look, Machito, what you have to do is look for any odd job to help with your expenses—anything will do ... Father Martín promised to find you something ... I'll never understand why you had to quit that job he found you— God knows we needed the money ...

MACHITO: (*From the bathroom, washing his face.*) You keep trying to piss me off, eh? That's what you really want: to screw up my day. How the hell am I gonna waste my time working when my best dreams happen right around noon? Haven't I told you a thousand times it's got to do with the position of the Sun and the Moon? Besides, you can't expect me to work for the shit money they pay

helpless blind people, particularly when I been given this
special gift for seeing things in my dreams and knowing
what they mean?

DOLORES: But Father Martín promised me ...

MACHITO: That priest just feels sorry for me, Mama, and I'm not
going to spend my whole life living off anyone's charity
... You know very well it wasn't "my" fault I lost my sight
... and that gambling's all I'm good for any more. Why
can't you understand that? (*Begins to shave, leaning out
the bathroom door.*)

DOLORES: But I can't go on paying for your gambling, Machito
...

MACHITO: You speak as if I never won. Don't you remember last
Christmas I had this dream where I saw Father Martín,
and I placed a bet on the number thirty-three—that stands
for "the age of Christ" in the numbers game—and I won
three hundred dollars? Shit, and if you'd lent me more,
I'd won thousands, Mama. Thousands!

DOLORES: But the next day you lost everything on another one
of your bets.

MACHITO: Dammit, you only remember the times I lose. Can't
always win, Mama! My dreams don't lie—sure, sometimes one can't get their meaning right ...

DOLORES: Machito, my love, get this through your head: the
problem is that I'm alone, and what little money I make
slaving at that damn sewing machine all day isn't enough
to make ends meet in this house ...

MACHITO: (*Interrupting violently.*) But you sure got enough to
throw away fifteen thousand dollars on a shitty party—
and I can go fuck off, as usual!

DOLORES: (*Pleading.*) My darling, you've got to understand ...

MACHITO: What's there to understand? That Papa left fifteen
thousand dollars for my sister's party, and I had to settle
for the "relics of the Great Macho Santiago": this robe he
was wearing the day he dropped dead on top of his conga
drum, and his old razor ... ?

DOLORES: Don't talk that way about your father's things: I made
that robe with my own hands, and it's full of memories,
and when I see it, it's as if he were here.

MACHITO: Money is what I want. And because of your selfishness
...

DOLORES: Selfishness? But I live only for you and your sister.
Since your father died I've devoted myself to both of you,

body and soul. Never once thought of myself in these fifteen years—everyone knows it—and with that money, I'll never get one single thing for myself. Not a blouse, not a lipstick I ever got myself with that money. No one will ever say that Dolores Jiménez used her dead husband's life insurance money for her own pleasure.

MACHITO: And can you imagine what people will say if the son of Dolores Jiménez, the poor blind kid, gets caught stealing because his mother refused to lend him fifty fucking bucks while she's got fifteen thousand stashed away in the bank?

DOLORES: (*Imploring.*) That money is sacred!

MACHITO: I'm not gonna keep on being a poor, pitiful blind bum all my life. One way or another, I gotta strike it rich! Or is that what you really want: for me to become a criminal? Can't you see you're forcing me to become a criminal, Mama? For the last time, I'm warning you!

DOLORES: Machito, how can you say that? Why do you torture me this way? How many times have I explained to you that your sister's party is something sacred? Nobody can touch the money your father left for that! Don't you think, in all these years since your father died, how much I had to go without? When we couldn't keep up with the payments for the house he left us, not you nor anyone else ever saw me take one penny of that money ... God knows it wasn't easy—I didn't want to leave our home. Or do you think it doesn't matter to me when people see us living in this filthy place ... ? (LOLITA *comes out of the bedroom.*)

MACHITO: And all for a shitty party for that kid!

LOLITA: No, no, no, no! Not for this kid: for the rest of the world! (*Confronting* DOLORES.) And for you, Mama, this stupid party, above all, is for you! To satisfy your crazy pride, you're turning into some kind of weird monster.

DOLORES: (*Slapping her daughter's face.*) You can't talk like that to your mother, not yet! (*Crying,* LOLITA *slams the bedroom door behind her;* DOLORES, *upset, rummages inside the dresser for her purse.*) Here: take these forty *pesos* and make sure your horse wins this time, because I don't plan to go on supporting your filthy habit ... (TONY *comes in through the window.*) For God sake, Tony, you scared me! I didn't hear you!

MACHITO: (*Showing* TONY *the palms of his hands.*) Look-look-look-look! The palms of my hands are burning with that lucky itch ... ! And I dreamed of shit—shit and horses!

What do you make of that?

DOLORES: (*To* TONY, *collecting herself.*) And how's your mother, Carmen? (*Elated, without waiting for a reply.*) I've got her dress ready for Lolita's party—the pattern we chose is so chic ... (*With childlike excitement.*) Tell me, Tony, tell me, what did Carmen say when she learned the party would be at the Palace Hotel? (*Loudly, to* LOLITA, *who remains in the bedroom.*) Come on, Lolita, get going so you can get me the velvet ribbon before they close ... (*To* TONY, *teasing.*) And do you know where we're going tomorrow? To pick out the canapes for the buffet—the canapes at the Palace are famous, the best in town. And not just because I say so: even the newspapers say it. Well, of course, the Palace will always be the Palace—I used to stay there all the time with my late husband, God rest his soul. It was there he made his debut when we first came to the city. Just think, even Ricky Ricardo, Lucy's husband, came to celebrate with us. And if you don't believe me, look, here I have all the pictures and the newspaper clippings to prove it ... or ask your mother: Carmen must remember—everyone must remember! (*To* LOLITA, *opening the bedroom door.*) Let's go, Lolita! (*To* TONY.) Well, as I was saying, first thing tomorrow, we're going to the Palace to pick out the canapes. (*Looking for* LOLITA *from the bedroom door.*) Hurry, Lolita, they're about to close the shop ... !

MACHITO: (*To* TONY, *coming out of the bathroom.*) She's crazier than a goat ... Throwing away fifteen thousand bucks on a shitty party for this stupid kid ... And for me, "Fifty *pesos* is all I can give you ... "

TONY: Fifteen thousand!

MACHITO: Hell, I sure could use that kind of money ...

LOLITA: (*To* MACHITO, *as she comes out of the bedroom.*) Why don't you try working for it, then ... ?

DOLORES: (*Following* LOLITA.) Let your poor brother alone ...

MACHITO: (*To* LOLITA.) Yes, that's easy for you to say: you've never done a day's work in your life, and look how healthy you are ... If you were like me ... (LOLITA *ignores him and leaves the apartment.*)

LOLITA: *Adiós* ... Ta-Ta ...

DOLORES: She's just a kid, Machito ... just a schoolgirl ... She was born to be a big star, like her father, the great Macho Santiago, the best percussionist of his day ... (MACHITO *and* TONY *prepare to leave through the fire escape window.*) And don't put yourself down like that: you only have a ... a little inconvenience ... Right, Tony? Here in the United States there are special programs for the ... the ... people like Machito. (TONY *takes no notice of her.*) Help him, Tony, those stairs are so very dangerous ... (*Calling out the window through which they have just left.*) Listen, tonight I'm making your favorite pumpkin *flan* for dessert, so don't come home too late—I'll wait up for you. (*Walks back to the table, takes a photo album, and starts leafing through it; the lights dim slowly.*)

CURTAIN

.... Second Scene: The Celebration ....

The same room as in the previous scene. It is about 3:00 a.m. TONY *is sitting on the fire escape window sill; at his side, almost with his back to* TONY, *is* MACHITO, *balancing precariously on a chair leaning against the wall. The apartment is dark, except for the flashing blue light of a neon sign coming through the window and directly illuminating* MACHITO's *face. Both are drinking beer.*

TONY: (*Laughing.*) ... and just when I was beginning to think it was hopeless and we'd laid down our last buck on a lame horse—I swear, Machito, I'd just about given up— then, wow! from way back, number one, our Pretty Baby, suddenly seems to wake up as he comes out of the last turn ... (*Sips his beer.*) Hell, then he really took off like the wind!

MACHITO: (*Imitating the race announcer and pretending to ride a horse.*) " ... And on the final stretch, number one, Pretty Baby, catches up with Bet on Me and begins to gain on the two leaders, Blue Grass and Canonero ... and with a quarter-mile to go, it's Canonero first, Blue Grass second, followed by Pretty Baby in third place ... " But our Pretty Baby advances and fights for second place with Blue Grass ... "and now, it's Canonero first, followed closely by Blue Grass and Pretty Baby ... " (TONY, *"riding" on the window sill, cheers Pretty Baby on.*) "And Pretty Baby finally catches Blue Grass, and with just a few yards to go, it's

Canonero and Pretty Baby running neck-to-neck ... " (*Increasingly excited,* TONY *keeps cheering Pretty Baby on.*) "Canonero and Pretty Baby ... Canonero and Pretty Baby ... and at the post it's ... "

TONY: (*Raising his arms in the air like a victorious jockey at the finish line.*) ... The winner by a nose, number one, Pretty Baby ... making us fucking rich! (*Drinks from his beer can.*)

MACHITO: Did I tell you or what?

TONY: Man, you practically never miss ...

MACHITO: (*Proudly.*) The magic formula can't fail: dreaming at noon ... shit ... horses ... the itch in the palms of my hands when I wake up ... What else could that little horse of mine do but win?

TONY: Hey, Machito, about that dream ... how did you figure it out?

MACHITO: The formula ... the magic formula: one horse and three mountains—the number one horse in the third race ...

TONY: Maybe it was the other way around: the number three horse in the first race?

MACHITO: (*Hiding his amusement at* TONY'*s naivete.*) Tony, how the hell could it be the first race, when we didn't get to the racetrack until the end of the second race ... ? Don't you see?

TONY: Hell, you're right, what a dumb question ... !

MACHITO: It's easier than it looks ... when you have this magic power, of course ... Want another beer?

TONY: I'll get it ... I'll get it ...

MACHITO: (*Going to the refrigerator.*) Better let me do it: you may stumble in the dark and wake up the old lady, then we'll end up having to listen to that stupid nagging of hers: "What are you doing still up in the middle of the night?" (*Opens the refrigerator and takes out two beers.*) Talk to me!

TONY: What ... ?

MACHITO: Catch! (*Hurls a can of beer towards* TONY.)

TONY: Hell, you sure are something, bro'!

MACHITO: (*Faking a mysterious tone.*) That's another of my supernatural powers: finding beer cans in the dark— they don't call me the Wizard of Darkness for nothing. (*Laughs.*) Check this out! Check this out—with my eyes closed ... (*Runs around the room confidently, then gets*

back to the chair; sits down and opens the can of beer.)
Am I the Wizard of Darkness or what ... ? (*Takes a sip
of beer, amused.*) And you ain't seen nothing yet: you
gotta see me shave with the razor my father left me.

TONY: (*Raising his beer can.*) Let's drink to Pretty Baby, number
one in the third race! (*Drinks.*)

MACHITO: Here's to Pretty Baby, number one in the third race!

TONY: ... and how did you know it was the Belmont Racetrack
and not the one at ... ?

MACHITO: (*Pretending annoyance.*)   Hey, enough of that!
Whatcha trying to do—steal the secrets from the Wizard
of Darkness? (*Holding back his laughter.*)

TONY: (*Naively.*) No, no, Machito, I swear I'm not, I swear I'm
not!

MACHITO: Look, you better stick to counting the money: I'm the
one with the magic powers around here, okay?

TONY: Five hundred dollars ... five hundred fucking dollars ... !

MACHITO: And if only the old lady had lent me a hundred instead
of fifty fucking dollars, we'd still be counting, bro' ...

TONY: A thousand, Machito! We could've won a thousand!

MACHITO: (*Breathing deep.*) A thousand dollars ... (*Drinks.*)
And what would you do with a thousand dollars, Tony?

TONY: I don't know, I don't know ... I gotta think about it. (*Takes
a sip of beer.*) Ah, now I know: I'd get drunk every day
for a whole year. (*Laughs.*) No, no, no ... better still ...
I think I better buy me ... a Cadillac convertible. Second
hand, but a real Cadillac! (*Takes a sip.*) What about you,
Machito?

MACHITO: Me? Easy—I'd bet it all on my next dream.

TONY: You mean that, Machito ... ? Wouldn't you like to get
yourself a Cadillac ... ?

MACHITO: What the hell would I do with a fucking Cadillac when
I ain't got the money to pay for a driver?

TONY: I'll drive it for you ... we'll buy it between the both of us,
so I can keep on taking you around.

MACHITO: (*Pause.*) You really expect me to settle for just one
thousand? Not for one thousand, not for ten thousand
... not even for a hundred thousand ... ! (*Pressing the
cold beer can against his brow.*) I got ambitions, Tony ...
big ambitions, much bigger than you could guess—and
my dreams are gonna take me all the way to the top. To
the very top—no stopping, no looking back, like my old
man did.

TONY: You bet, Machito!

MACHITO: (*Standing on the chair and raising the beer can high.*) And when fortune carries me to the highest peak, then I'll be ready to buy all the fucking Cadillacs I want, and hire me a bunch of dames with great big tits to drive me around.

TONY: No, Machito, no, I'm your driver. You gotta give me your word that I'll drive your Cadillac ... I'll be the one to tell you what's going on around you ...

MACHITO: (*Sits down again, thoughtfully, sipping his beer.*) Wanna know the truth? Things like that don't turn me on that much. But when I hit it big no one will ever feel sorry for me any more, no one will give a fuck about my being blind or a Spic with an accent. (*Takes a sip.*) Then I can buy the old lady a house to get her out of this fucking place and really show her who I am ...

TONY: (*Fantasizing.*) Wow!—you and me driving all over the *barrio* in our Cadillac convertible. (*Proposing a toast.*) Here's to the Wizard of Darkness ... !

MACHITO: (*Raises his beer can, but remains lost in his own thoughts for a moment.*) All I need is one good dream ... (*Talking to himself.*) Just one good dream, and lots of money to bet on it ... (*Takes a sip, thoughtfully.*) You believe in miracles, bro' ... ?

TONY: Miracles? Like a dog learning to sing ... ?

MACHITO: The real miracle is for the dog to bark, bro' ... Check it out: we already got birds to do the fucking singing.

TONY: There ain't no fucking miracles, man ...

MACHITO: Some lucky son-of-a-bitch hits the big jackpot every day. Ain't that a miracle?

TONY: (*Unaware that he is reading* MACHITO's *mind.*) Machito, just think, all the dough we could've won if we'd bet your old lady's fifteen thousand ...

MACHITO: (*Feeling found out,* MACHITO *his balance and topples over, chair and all, making a loud noise; both young men remain speechless.*)

TONY: You okay?

DOLORES: (*Turning on the light as she comes out of the bedroom, still half-asleep.*) Ay, you scared me to death! For God's sake, do you know what time it is? It's three o'clock in the morning! What are you doing still up? No, no, no ... you don't have to tell me: you're getting drunk.

MACHITO: We're celebrating!

TONY: Making a toast!

MACHITO: (*Loudly, raising his beer can.*) Here's to Pretty Baby, number one in the third race ... !

LOLITA: (*Coming out of the bedroom, alarmed at the noise.*) What's wrong?

DOLORES: Can't you guess? Just those two, getting drunk at three o'clock in the morning. You can tell they don't have to get up in the morning to earn their daily bread like the good Lord says ...

MACHITO: Ain't this better than bread? (*Extends his open hand, palm up, toward* TONY.)

TONY: (*Placing the five bills, one by one, in* MACHITO's *hand.*) One, two, three, four and five hundred dollars ... !

DOLORES: (*Almost disappointed at* MACHITO's *unexpected success.*) Okay, okay, so this time you won ... I hope now you'll know what to do with that money.

MACHITO: (*Aware that he is annoying her.*) Gamble it away, all of it ... just as soon as I have another magic dream ...

DOLORES: What do you mean, gamble it away! (*Yawning and plainly bored,* LOLITA *goes back to bed.*)

MACHITO: Mama, what good did your advice ever do to me? (*Mimicking her.*) "Machito, why don't you take the medicine the doctor prescribed to make your eyes better?" ... "Machito, when are you going to learn Braille, so they can teach you to read with your fingers and you can make a future for yourself?" Well, the future is already here, and so what? What good were the gallons of medicine you made me take, ain't I still blind as a bat? Even got sores in my fingertips from so much reading! What good was all your advice, Mama? Good for nothing! For nothing at all!

DOLORES: Don't say that: it kept your hope alive ...

MACHITO: My only hope is a good dream.

DOLORES: Go ahead and gamble it away if you like, but don't count on me later ...

MACHITO: Count on you! (*Takes another sip of beer.*) I never could count on you, or Papa either. My dreams are all I can count on. You won't give me my eyes back ... only my dreams can light up this endless darkness. Don't you worry, I'm not counting on you ...

DOLORES: (*Disgusted.*) I can't even talk to you any more. It's no use—you're so full of anger ... Can't you see I'm telling you this for your own good? (*Approaching her son and ca-*

ressing him.) Machito, my darling, my darling, gambling is a vice ... You've got to stop it ... what are people going to say?

MACHITO: (*Affectionately.*) Of course I'll stop, Mama, but this is not the right time. Can't you see I've got to quit right after one good lucky break? Can't you see, after losing and losing so much, I'm on to a a winning streak ... ? It was about time my luck changed, just ask Tony—ask anyone who knows anything about gambling: luck comes and goes. And now it's coming back to me ...

DOLORES: Coming back? How often have you told me that?

MACHITO: But this time I'll be ready—I'll hit it big, I can feel it: I can see it in my dreams, Mama! It's all so clear in my dreams!

DOLORES: (*Upset.*) I don't know what will become of you ... Remember I'm warning you! (*Tidying up the room and throwing away the empty cans.*) Well, I better get some sleep now: tomorrow I have to get up early to pick up the invitations ... and I also got to go over to the Palace to choose the canapes. (*From the threshold of the bedroom door.*) Machito, at least get yourself a good suit for your sister's party with some of that money ... Remember, after playing your father's record, I want the two of you to start the party with a waltz, and everybody will be watching ... (*Returns for a moment.*) And look at that pumpkin *flan*, after I worked so hard to make it, you haven't even tasted it ... (DOLORES *disappears into the bedroom while the lights slowly dim.*)

CURTAIN

.... Third Scene: The Die Is Cast ....

The following afternoon. The same room as the previous scenes. It is raining, and evening is already falling. The flashing blue light from the neon sign slips in through the window. DOLORES, *more agitated than usual, is fitting the dress on her friend* CARMEN, *who is looking at herself in the mirror.*

CARMEN: They're pigs, darling. The electric chair is what they deserve. See how they left this arm of mine when they ran off with my purse. And I still work the rich folks' area, around the theaters. As if one didn't have to work hard enough to make a few bucks ... Drugs, crime, muggings ...

DOLORES: (*Elated, oblivious to* CARMEN'*s story.*) You're going to look fabulous at the party in that dress. Everything is turning out just great ... Just think, the main ballroom at the Palace—have I told you my husband, Macho, God rest his soul, made his debut in that very same ballroom when we first came here? (*Without waiting for a response.*) Yes, yes, of course I've told you, why, even Ricky Ricardo, Lucy's husband, came to see the Palace show that night ... Well, it's the same ballroom, and they're going to decorate it with white lilies—fresh lilies, of course, they're more expensive, but I won't have people say afterward that Dolores Jiménez skimped on her daughter Lolita's fifteenth birthday party.

CARMEN: (*Insists.*) And what about sex ... free sex ... free and easy? I'm telling you, it's not fair: these women of today will sleep with anyone for drugs, and not even charge for it, darling ...

DOLORES: Oh!—I forgot the most important thing—the Palace orchestra, in full evening dress and everything, they'll play a waltz first so Lolita can dance with her brother, and then they'll go on playing until midnight ... I have it all planned: of course, to open the ball, we'll have a minute of silence in memory of the Great Macho Santiago, and we'll listen to the record of his greatest hit. (*Nostalgically.*) I can't wait. All I do is think how happy Macho, my husband, is going to feel when he looks down from heaven at his children dancing the waltz in the main ballroom at the Palace ... Because if anyone is in heaven, it's Macho—that man was a saint.

CARMEN: (*Taking off the dress, under which she is wearing a too-revealing blouse and a very tight mini-skirt.*) You never gave yourself away like that in my time, no way ... (*Touching herself lewdly.*) This pussycat sure can purr, but she never gave it away or sold herself cheap ... A girl has her professional pride.

DOLORES: It's hard to be a physiotherapist ...

CARMEN: A "physio" what?

DOLORES: Physiotherapist: that's what they call a professional masseuse.

CARMEN: Ay, darling, one gets called so many names ...

DOLORES: (*Picking up the dress.*) Just look at the time! It's already too late to go to the post office. If I hurry, I still have time to pick up the invitations at the printer's. Ángela's coming with me, she'll have to close the beauty shop early if she wants to come along ...

CARMEN: I should have become a manicurist ...

DOLORES: (*Opening the bedroom door.*) Lolita!

CARMEN: (*Prepares to leave.*) Perhaps Ángela could give me a part-time as a manicurist at her shop ...

DOLORES: All right, Carmen, don't worry, I'll fix everything for you and I'll have the dress all ironed out and ready for you tomorrow—you can pay me then. (CARMEN *leaves.*) Lolita!

DOLORES: (LOLITA *comes out of the bedroom, and* DOLORES *hands her a small notebook and a pencil.*) Come and help me with the numbers ... (*Both sit down at the table.*) Add it up: the ballroom is five hundred, and three thousand for the orchestra ...

LOLITA: Three thousand!

DOLORES: Yes, three thousand! Don't argue with me and add up the numbers! Plus seven thousand for the buffet and another three thousand for the champagne ... How much is that? How much is it?

LOLITA: You've already got ... thirteen thousand, five hundred ...

DOLORES: (*Picking up and checking the notebook.*) Ay ... ! And one thousand for the decorations and one hundred for the invitations ... let's see, let's see ... (*Hands the notebook back to* LOLITA.) How much will the stamps be for the five hundred invitations?

LOLITA: Well, Mama, we could hand deliver some of the invitations.

DOLORES: We'll do no such thing! You either do things right or not at all! You figure it out: stamps for five hundred invitations! (*Rises and looks for something inside the dresser.*)

LOLITA: One hundred and twenty-five dollars for the stamps, plus fourteen thousand six hundred ... Fourteen thousand seven hundred and twenty-five!

DOLORES: Then we still have money left over for the photographer. I want pictures, pictures and more pictures to fill up another album at least! (*Uses her keys to open the top drawer.*) Did you happen to see where I left the checkbook? When I went out this morning, I was sure I had left it in the drawer where I keep important things ...

LOLITA: It's got to be there: in the top drawer, where you always keep it locked away. (*Rising to help her.*)

DOLORES: (*Now searching inside the refrigerator.*) It's not there, it's not there, I already looked. And it's not here either—sometimes I hide it in the freezer when ... My God, could someone have sneaked in while we were out?

LOLITA: No one was here when I got home from school.

DOLORES: (*Anxious.*) And wasn't Machito still asleep?

LOLITA: He was already gone ... too early ... for Machito ...

DOLORES: (*Nervous as she empties her purse on the table and continues searching.*) Maybe Tony came to pick him up—I don't like that Tony one bit. (*Increasingly agitated.*) Haven't you noticed, you can never hear him come in? He's like a ghost, you know he's there, but you can't hear him come in—he gives me the creeps ... (*Putting things back in her purse.*) That checkbook—where the devil can it be?

LOLITA: Maybe Machito put it somewhere else ...

DOLORES: For the love of God, child, how can you even think that?

LOLITA: (*Not understanding.*) Think what, Mama?

DOLORES: (*Goes to the telephone and dials with shaking hands.*) Where could those two have gone now? (*Waits.*) Ay, Tony, it's you—I'm glad I found you. Is Machito with you? (*Pause.*) Yes, please, tell him to come down for just a minute ... help him down the stairs ... (*Hangs up the telephone and looks inside the dresser once more, while she keeps on babbling.*) Your brother, the poor thing, he may have his faults, but everyone knows that the family of Dolores Jiménez and Macho Santiago is poor but honest. You've never seen any bad examples in this house. Let them ask all the neighbors, from the butcher to the owner of the laundry where I used to work, or the people who knew your father, God rest his soul ... or let them ask Father Martín, let them ask about the reputation that ... (*Stands frozen in front of the dresser.*) Come here, Lolita. (*Finds the checkbook in the middle drawer, looks it over, and shows it to her daughter.*) Are you sure you didn't touch this checkbook? Without thinking, absent-mindedly, didn't you leave it here, in the middle drawer?

LOLITA: No, Mama, I ...

DOLORES: (*Interrupts violently.*) Now, you concentrate before you answer! Think, Lolita! Think! I left it locked in the top drawer with the important things ... didn't you put it some other place? Are you sure you didn't touch it? (*Seeing that* MACHITO *and* TONY *are coming in through the fire-escape window,* LOLITA *does not answer, merely looks at* MACHITO. DOLORES *then becomes aware of her son's entrance.*)

DOLORES: (*Trying to control herself.*) Machito, my love, tell me that you didn't touch the checkbook ... By all that's most dear to you—on the memory of your father, God rest his soul—swear to me that you haven't touched this checkbook ... Swear it to me, Machito!!

MACHITO: I haven't touched anything, you can ask Tony ...

DOLORES: And what does Tony have to do with all this? (TONY *disappears through the window, saying nothing.*)

LOLITA: Without Tony, you can't ...

DOLORES: Shut up, Lolita! (*Again examines the checkbook.*) There's a check missing here, Machito. Tell me you didn't take it, my love ... Look at me, please ... Don't turn your face away. Look at me straight in the face—I can guess the truth in your eyes. Look at me and tell me you didn't take it! (MACHITO *avoids his mother's eyes.*)

LOLITA: Tell her, Machito. Tell her! Look her in the face and tell her you haven't taken it ... !

MACHITO: (*To* LOLITA.) I already told her ... how many times do I have to tell her again?

DOLORES: But I want you to say it looking straight to my face.

MACHITO: The blind cannot look!

LOLITA: He can't look you in the face, Mama, because he's a liar and a thief, and you've always spoiled him—"your poor brother this, your poor brother that ... " Between your madness and his dreams, I don't even know which one is crazier ... That's why I can't wait to run off to Hollywood or China, or any place, away from this madhouse pasted over with lies ...

DOLORES: (*Leaning on the table to avoid collapsing.*) Dear God, how many more trials? Are you also going to give me a thief for a son, who steals from his own mother? How much longer, my God? How much longer? (*Sobbing.*) Why did you take it, Machito? Why? Why have you made me break the promise that I made to your father on his deathbed?

MACHITO: Damn you!! (*With his back to his mother.*) It's just

that you ... you don't understand. You'll never be able
to understand. You know nothing about the power of
dreams. I only wish you could, for one single night or one
single hour ... if only for an instant, you could feel that
revealing ... that supernatural force ... that takes over
all my senses and gives me back my sight. (*Very calmly.*)
Ay ... and this was such a clear dream—I'd never had a
dream that was so revealing. I could see everything clearly
... the slightest details of the train that carries me to the
racetrack—the number fifteen train, painted bright red
like the sound of a trumpet ... the other passengers—I
could still describe their smiling faces as they encouraged
me ... and then the tunnel, cool like marble. In the distance I could see the station lights—the same racetrack
station, only now it looks different than Tony had always
described it ... (*Almost in a trance.*) The lights keep coming closer, more and more slowly, until the train stops at
last ... (*Pause.*) The doors open and suddenly I can see
him clearly—no, it's not a vision, it's him! It's him! My
own father is there to meet me ... And I can see him writing the number fifteen on the wall in front of me, and then
he disappears up the stairway that leads to the racetrack.
As I don't want to trust my own sight, I go to the wall,
close my eyes, and feel what my father has just written.
(*His hands follow the action that he is describing.*) The
number one is unmistakable, straight as an arrow aiming
at the sky ... and then my fingers slowly trace the curves
of the number five. Yes, it is fifteen! The number fifteen
again, and now I can no longer doubt.

DOLORES: My God ...

MACHITO: (*Tenderly.*) It was ... it was a loan, Mama. I only
borrowed it. The day after tomorrow, when I win the
bet, I'll give it back to you, down to the last penny ...
don't worry ... Can't you see, Papa had come back, and
now he was taking care of everything? He has come back
with a gift—the number that'll bring me the lucky break
I been waiting for—I always knew he would return and
take care of everything ... Now you see, he came back,
and he was giving me this chance. No one ever gave me
a gift like that, Mama ... No one ever gave me nothing!
How could I blow this chance when it was my own father
who was giving it to me?

DOLORES: Machito, how could you do this to me ... ?

MACHITO: (*In an effort to make his mother understand.*) Don't worry. I'm telling you: Papa came back to take care of everything. He hadn't forgotten me, can't you see? On the fifteenth of the month ... Lolita's fifteenth birthday ... the number fifteen on the train ... and the fifteen thousand dollars ... The number fifteen four times—I can't think why I didn't see there was too much coincidence ... But, of course, it wasn't a real coincidence, and he came back so I knew it was no coincidence.

DOLORES: Machito, you know—everyone knows!—the sacrifices I made for you, the pain I suffered day after day. I can't take it any more ... I carry so much pain in my heart, I feel like every day I'm giving birth to you again.

LOLITA: (*Embraces her mother.*) Don't cry, Mama.

MACHITO: (*To* LOLITA.) She doesn't want to understand that I had to listen to my father, I had to trust him ...

DOLORES: (*To* MACHITO.) Since the night of your accident, my pain never stops ...

MACHITO: (*With sudden cruelty.*) What never stops since that night is your guilt.

LOLITA: Machito!

DOLORES: (*Defensively.*) Guilt? What guilt? For going with your father to a New Year's Eve party?

MACHITO: You left me alone!

LOLITA: Don't blame her ... !

DOLORES: I left you with the neighbor who used to look after you. Your father ...

MACHITO: (*Interrupting her.*) Papa sure didn't plan to go out that night, but, of course, you didn't want to miss that party ... you always loved to parade yourself. He didn't want to come along with you—he would've chosen to stay home and play with his son—but you insisted. He protested: "I never have time to play with my son"—he sure told you that. You argued ... he complained ... you got angry ... and you got your way. (*Pause.*) Two hours later, while you were dancing in your blue-dyed shoes to the sound of a waltz at the Copa Club, the light went out for that boy you left behind to parade yourself in front of people ...

DOLORES: Shut up!

MACHITO: While you had fun in front of strangers, the blue sea that little boy fell into, head first, washed away the light from his eyes forever, like an endless night without hope of day ...

DOLORES: Stop it! Stop it! I'm begging you!

MACHITO: You didn't even bother to put away that big pail of blue dye where you'd tinted your shoes ...

DOLORES: Stop torturing me!

MACHITO: And since that endless night, that boy stopped being his father's pride and joy ...

DOLORES: It wasn't like that. What happened was that your sister was born ... (LOLITA *starts sobbing and runs into the bedroom.*)

MACHITO: Of course, and she wasn't blind, and you took better care of her than you ever did of me, so you could have at least one healthy child you could feel proud of, one child you could bring out into the world without having to feel ashamed in front of all those people you care so much about ... (LOLITA *can be heard weeping in the bedroom.*)

DOLORES: It was not like that! It was not like that!

MACHITO: And since I didn't count any more, before he died, my father thought only of his healthy child ... (*Amid their shouting,* LOLITA *can be heard throwing objects at the bedroom wall.*)

DOLORES: Don't torture us any more ... We got word at once— they had already taken you to the hospital, and the doctors wasted no time in trying to save your eyes.

MACHITO: If you stayed home that night, I could be looking into your eyes right now.

DOLORES: It was an accident, can't you see? You fell in the dye by accident, those things happen because God ...

MACHITO: God has nothing to do with that, Mama. It wasn't God who made my father go to the dance. It wasn't God who insisted, it was you! It wasn't God who left behind that big pail of blue dye, it was you! It was you! Dammit, it was you!

DOLORES: Every day I pray to God for a miracle. (*The uproar continues in the bedroom.*)

MACHITO: The only miracle you can expect from God is to be forgiven—but first you must repent ... admit that my blindness is your fault and yours alone. That it was your fault I lost my sight, it was your fault my father stopped loving me, and now you are guilty again: guilty of denying me a few stinking bucks, and this time you're blowing my last chance to make something of the rest of my life.

LOLITA, *hysterical, comes out of the bedroom, pounces on her*

*party dress that hangs from the mannequin and tears the garment
in two. The lights go out.*

CURTAIN

ACT II

.... First Scene: The Betrayal ....

*The stage is dark. The blue spotlight begins to illuminate the
face of* LOLITA, *who appears seated at the dining room table.*

LOLITA: (*Without much feeling.*) "That she may feel How sharper
than a serpent's tooth it is To have a thankless child."
King Lear, by William Shakespeare. (*The blue spotlight
goes out as the stage lights rise, illuminating the same
apartment as in the first act. Day is breaking.* DOLORES
*comes out of the bedroom and sits down at the dining ta-
ble, where* LOLITA *is addressing the envelopes for the invitations,* DOLORES *maintains her usual enthusiastic air
contrasting with her daughter's depressed manner.* MA-
CHITO *is asleep on the sofa.*)

DOLORES: (*Softly, so as not to waken* MACHITO.) Come on,
princess, smile and stop complaining, for the love of God
... You'll see that everything will turn out just perfect.
And do your best with those invitations ... make sure it's
your best handwriting.

LOLITA: (*Complaining.*) But I've got so much homework to do,
don't you think it's plain silly to waste all this time over
a bunch of invitations for a party that's not even ... ?

DOLORES: (*Ignoring her daughter rather than interrupting her on
purpose.*) The party comes first! Can't you get it through
your head that it's a sacred promise I made to your father,
God rest his soul! (*Amused, in a confidential tone.*) And
what a party! Just think, Carmen told me that everyone's
so excited about the invitations ... even Ángela, you had
to see the way she ran out of her beauty shop when I
passed by yesterday afternoon ... Guess what she said:

she says—with that superior air she's put on after buying
the shop, so now she's not just another hair stylist any
more—she says, "Dolores, since practically everybody's
made an appointment for the day of the party, I took the
liberty"—she "took the liberty," I swear those were her exact words—"I took the liberty of making an appointment
for each of you first thing in the morning." Everybody's
made an appointment—did you hear that? Everybody ...

LOLITA: But, Mama ...

DOLORES: (*Interrupting her.*) No buts about it ... (*Annoyed, she
gets up and paces around the table.*) You've got to have
faith—these are nothing but trials, Lolita ... I've always
believed God never sends you more trouble than you can
handle. Can't you see how the printer let us pick up the
invitations on credit? And what about your gown? Didn't
I mend it like nothing happened to it? And even at the
Palace, didn't they say we could make the deposit day
after tomorrow? And you know the Palace is the Palace,
not just any old place ...

LOLITA: (*In disbelief.*) The day after tomorrow! And where will
you get the money the day after tomorrow? The last thing
we need now is for you to start believing in Machito's
dreams!

DOLORES: The last thing is to lose hope ... ! These are just trials,
Lolita. Trials God sends you ... (*Almost to herself, with
a slight touch of doubt not previously apparent.*) After so
much sacrifice and so much suffering, there's no doubt in
my mind that God can't fail us. (*In a tone so delicate that
she seems removed from reality, while her absent glance
follows her raised hand.*) A little bird does not fall from
the sky unless the hand of the Lord intervenes ... (*Smiles
tenderly.*) Father Martín gave such a beautiful sermon last
Sunday ... (*In her own world.*) A little bird does not fall
from the sky unless the Lord's hand intervenes ... Ah,
that St. Thomas, such a wise man ...

LOLITA: (*Sharply.*) It was St. Matthew who said that, Mama.

DOLORES: (*Unable to get back to reality.*) Eh ... ? What did you
say?

LOLITA: (*Intentionally ironic.*) It wasn't St. Thomas who said that
about the little bird.

DOLORES: Aw, come on, be quiet and get on with those envelopes.
(*Sits down, restless.*)

LOLITA: (*With bitter mockery.*) And of course, the mailman is go-

ing to deliver them without stamps ... (*Mimicking* DO-
LORES' *tone and gesture.*) A little bird from the sky is
going to take them from door to door ...

DOLORES: (DOLORES *stands up hesitantly and, trying to close
the conversation, takes the fox stole from its hanger. Showing* LOLITA *the stole.*) I've saved it for your fifteenth
birthday ever since Macho, your father, passed away ...
He gave it to me for a present when he made his debut in
Las Vegas and we traveled there together ... Have I told
you this before? (*Seeing* LOLITA'*s bored expression.*) Yes,
of course, I have. (*Pauses to dig into her memory.*) But
now I can't remember exactly if it was Las Vegas or Atlantic City. (*Looking at herself nostalgically in the mirror.
*) Well, it really doesn't matter now, does it? We used to
travel so much ... Doesn't it look as good as new? (*Pa-
rades herself.*)

LOLITA: (*Reluctantly.*) It's beautiful, Mama.

DOLORES: Lolita ... Come on, do try on your gown for a minute.
Let me see how it looks on you once again ... just to see
how it turned out.

LOLITA: Right now? What about the invitations ... ?

DOLORES: Please, princess, do it for me ... Come on, I need to
see how it looks on you with the tiara and everything ...
for a second, just a second ... You can finish all that later
...

LOLITA: (*Walks reluctantly to the mannekin where the dress is
hung and begins to undress.*) "A fool, a fool, I met a fool
i'th' forest, A motley fool—a miserable world!—As I do
live by food, I met a fool, Who laid him down and basked
him in the sun, And railed on Lady Fortune in good terms,
In good set terms, and yet a motley fool." *As You Like It,*
by William Shakespeare.

DOLORES: (*Hangs up the stole again and feels it with her hand
as if caressing a memory.*) Macho, your father, took me
everywhere—just think, they were always inviting him to
parties with important people, even movie stars—and,
naturally, he always insisted I come along. I still keep
a newspaper clipping where it says your father was going
to be the next Ricky Ricardo. Can you believe that? I
could've been like Lucy, Ricky Ricardo's wife ... I would
look so good as a redhead ... (*Looks at the fox stole one
more time and lets out a brief sigh.*) Those were real parties! (*With renewed vigor, leaving nostalgia behind.*) And

how are those invitations coming? (*Goes back and gath-
ers up the invitations stacked on the table.*) But, child, are
you still on the letter "C"? At that rate, you won't finish
before the day of your *quince* party.

LOLITA: But didn't you want me to try on the dress, Mama?

DOLORES: (*More to herself than to* LOLITA, *while checking the
invitations mechanically.*) After so many trials, so many
sacrifices, so much suffering, God can't possibly fail us
now ... (*Once more she raises her hand slowly and follows
it with her glance.*) A little bird doesn't fall from the sky
unless the Lord's hand intervenes ...

MACHITO: (*With a terrified shout, from his bed.*) Papa! Papa!
(MACHITO *throws himself violently from the bed, trips
over a small table, falls down, gets up, and, as though mad,
begins to stumble around the apartment, knocking down
several chairs.* LOLITA, *her party dress still unbuttoned,
seeks refuge in a corner of the room;* DOLORES *drops the
invitations and runs to* MACHITO's *aid.*)

DOLORES: Oh, my God! Oh, my God!

MACHITO: (*Desperately.*) Papa! Papa! Papa!

DOLORES: (*Puts her arms around* MACHITO *from the back.*)
Dear God, Machito, what's the matter with you now?

MACHITO: (*Ignoring his mother, in a trance.*) Papa, why do you
make fun of me? Why, Papa? (*His voice fades away as he
sinks slowly on the window sill.*) Papa ... Papa ... Papa
... (DOLORES *tries to hold him, but* MACHITO *keeps on
slipping down until both end up on the floor:* MACHITO
*huddles in his mother's arms and goes on repeating, "Papa,
Papa."*)

DOLORES: For God's sake, Machito, it's just a nightmare ...
(*Turning nervously to* LOLITA.) Do something ... ! Get
your poor brother some water ... ! (MACHITO *begins to
sob;* LOLITA *brings him water. Bringing the glass to* MA-
CHITO's *mouth.*) There, there, now ... it's all over, it
was just a nightmare ... There, take a drink ... it's over,
it's all over ... (MACHITO *takes the glass in his shaking
hands and drinks;* DOLORES *kisses him tenderly as she
wipes away his tears.*)

MACHITO: (*Oblivious, between sobs.*) You lied to me ... Papa,
again you lied to me ... You came back only to lie to me
again ...

DOLORES: (*Keeps on kissing him.*) There, there now ... It was
nothing but a dream ... a bad dream ... (*The two women*

    manage to prop him up in the chair.)
MACHITO: (*Oblivious.*) It's the exact same red train ... same
  bright red, like the sound of a trumpet ... it stops very
  slowly ... the doors open again ... and again Papa is
  waiting for me ... Again he writes the number fifteen on
  the wall, and then he disappears up the stairway leading to
  the racetrack, like he did before ... I close my eyes and
  feel the wall to make sure, I feel the numbers, wet and
  sticky like honey ... I glance at my fingers ... and they're
  full of blood—I didn't know blood could be so red ...
DOLORES: (*Softly.*) Now, now ... it was only a dream ...
MACHITO: I take the stairs and run, shouting, "Papa! Papa!
  Papa!" ... (*Begins to get excited.*) I come to a large ballroom ... it's crowded ... the music stops, and everybody
  turns to me, and they begin to laugh at me and to make
  fun ... Why are they laughing? Why are they making fun
  of me? Why? Why? I close my eyes, but I keep on seeing
  their faces ... and I put my hands over my eyes, but I can
  still see their smirks ... and I don't want to see them any
  more ... (*Shouting.*) Damn them, I want to stay blind
  forever! (*Suddenly calms down.*) And it's then I realize
  that I'm stark naked and I have his razor in my hand ...
DOLORES: That's enough, Machito! Stop it, will you? Don't go
  on, don't go on.
MACHITO: (*Accusing.*) And there you are, having the time of your
  life ... and Lolita too ... and the long dress she's wearing
  is made out of my sequined robe—my sequined robe!—
  the same one Papa left me ... (*Getting excited again.*)
  Papa! Papa! I found you at last! Tell them to give me
  back my sequined robe! Tell her it's mine. (*Very violently.*)
  Papa! Papa, don't laugh, Papa! Don't laugh! Don't make
  fun of me! Papa! Papa!! (*Begins to weep uncontrollably.*)
  And I had to do it ... I had to do it with his own razor
  ...
DOLORES: (*Soothing him.*) It's nothing ... Come on ... Don't
  worry ... don't worry—it was just a dream ...
MACHITO: (*Coming out of his trance.*) Just a dream ... ? Can't
  you see ... what this dream ... means to us ... ? (*Recovering.*) Are you so dumb you can't you see? Can't you
  see that the bet ... ?
DOLORES: (*Tenderly putting her hand over his mouth.*) Nothing,
  nothing, nothing ... Don't let it matter ...
LOLITA: (*Removing her mother's hand.*) See what, Machito? See

what?

DOLORES: (*Annoyed at* LOLITA.) Leave him alone now, you silly
    girl! Let him get over it ...

LOLITA: (*Insisting.*) What's going to happen now, Machito? What
    did the dream tell you?

DOLORES: How can you be so cruel! Can't you see your poor
    brother is not well? (*To* MACHITO, *very tenderly.*) Don't
    try to speak now ... Wait till you feel better ...

LOLITA: (*Giving her mother a challenging look.*) No, Machito ...
    no! You got to tell her! What did the dream mean?

MACHITO: Papa didn't come back to take care of everything like
    I thought. He came back to make fun of me again ...
    I saw him with my own eyes, making fun of me—I kept
    hearing his hateful laughter even after I closed my eyes
    ... that's why I had to do it ... yes, I did him in with his
    own razor ...

DOLORES: Don't say that again! You couldn't ...

LOLITA: (*Insists.*) But what did the dream mean to you, Machito?
    Tell Mama what it all meant to you.

MACHITO: Papa tricked me ... (*Returning to reality.*) We're
    gonna lose everything, can't you see?

DOLORES: (*Stunned.*) Everything, Machito ... ? All the party
    money ... ?

MACHITO: Papa fooled me ... He came back to fool me, you
    know what I mean? That's why I had to get even with the
    son-of-a-bitch ...

DOLORES: (*Looking up to heaven.*) Dear God, dear God, what
    have I done for You to abandon me like this? I, Dolores
    Jiménez, Your most faithful servant! When You took my
    husband, I accepted Your will ... When my son had the
    accident, I said it was only a trial ... When I lost my
    home, I resigned myself ... I never lost hope. But now
    this! What curse have you laid on this poor family? What
    fate stronger than my faith are you placing in our way?
    Why do you reward my devotion with such cruel punish-
    ment? Why do you always ignore my prayers? Why, dear
    God? Why?

LOLITA: (*Beginning to cry.*) Mama, don't worry ...

DOLORES: And what am I going to do now? (*To* LOLITA.) What
    will people say? Now that everyone—everyone!—is wait-
    ing for an invitation ... and how can I ever pay for the
    Palace buffet, and the orchestra and the champagne, and

the photographer, and the lilies—the fresh white lilies ...
?

MACHITO: (*Stumbling up to the window, sticks his head out, and begins to shout.*) Tony! Tony! Tony! (*Turns toward his mother.*) I have to withdraw the bet ... Maybe there's still time to get the money back ...

DOLORES: (MACHITO *keeps calling for* TONY.) Can you still do it, Machito? Ay, dear God, help us—I must keep this promise! (*Since* TONY *does not answer, she turns to* LOLITA *desperately.*)

LOLITA: (*Frightened.*) No, no, Mama, don't let him go ...

DOLORES: (*Imploring.*) Machito, can you still do it ... ? Isn't it true that you can still get back the party money? (MA-CHITO *calls for* TONY *again.*)

LOLITA: (*Desperate.*) Mama, I'm scared! (*To* MACHITO.) Ma-chito, please don't go. Don't go! (MACHITO *calls for* TONY *again.*) It's not worth it, Machito: the dream ... the razor ... (MACHITO, *confused, remains with his back to the window.*)

DOLORES: (*Interrupting violently.*) Are you out of your mind, child? (*To* MACHITO, *pulling at his arm.*) Help me, for the love of God ... Help me keep my promise!

LOLITA: Forget the party, Mama! It's not worth it! (*To* MA-CHITO.) Don't go, Machito, I'm too scared ... (MA-CHITO, *agitated and confused, finds himself torn between his mother and his sister.*)

DOLORES: (*Taking* MACHITO's *face in her hands to make him listen only to her.*) Machito, my love, only you can help me now to keep my sacred promise ... Tell me I can count on you!

LOLITA: Why do you send him to find his nightmare? Can't you see that this is our last chance to get back to the real world ... ? No, don't go, Machito! Stop this madness, Mama! (*Takes* DOLORES' *hands off* MACHITO's *face.*)

DOLORES: (*To* LOLITA.) And why do you go against me at a time like this?

LOLITA: His dream is loaded with violence, Mama! Don't let him go ... (MACHITO *remains standing, still not know-ing what to do;* DOLORES *walks toward the door, trying to avoid* LOLITA, *but her daughter follows her.*)

DOLORES: (*Desperate, to* LOLITA, *justifying herself.*) But he says there's still time to get it all back. Isn't it true, Machito, that you still have time?

LOLITA: (*Pleading.*) No, Mama, don't let him go ...

DOLORES: Leave me alone!

TONY: (TONY *appears in the window, but stays outside when he sees what is happening. To* MACHITO.) You woke me up ...

DOLORES: (*Surprised at* TONY's *arrival.*) Ay, dear God, I can never hear him coming ... !

MACHITO: (*Very agitated, putting on his pants.*) Tony, we have to take back the bet ... (*Gropes for his shoes*)

LOLITA: Stop him, Mama! Don't let him go! Don't let him go! (MACHITO *goes toward* TONY, *fastening his pants, but then stops, goes into the bathroom for a moment and comes out again, concealing the razor in his pocket;* LOLITA *tries to get in his way, but* DOLORES *prevents her from doing so.*)

DOLORES: (*Harshly.*) Let him do what he's got to do! (MA-CHITO *leaves through the window where* TONY *is waiting, and both go down the fire escape.* LOLITA, *shaking herself free of her mother, runs over to the window with the intention of calling to him, but gives up.*)

LOLITA: (*From the window, turning toward her mother.*) If something happens to him ... (*Pauses.*) ... this time it will really be your fault! (LOLITA *goes to the telephone and dials a number;* DOLORES *remains oblivious.*) Father Martín, please! (*Listens.*) This is an emergency! An emergency! (*Listens again.*) And can't you interrupt him? It's matter or life or death! (*Hangs up the telephone violently, watches her mother angrily, and runs out the door.* DOLORES *remains alone, confused; she slowly closes the door and begins to pick up the invitations still scattered on the floor; the lights dim until only the flashing blue light remains, slipping in through the window.*)

CURTAIN

.... Second Scene: The End ....

A few hours later. It is now evening. The apartment is dark and in shambles, as it was left at the conclusion of the previous scene. The flashing blue neon sign intermittently lights MACHITO's favorite chair, which is now empty. DOLORES, who seems to have *lost all her energy, lies despondently on the easy chair. She is almost invisible. The telephone rings insistently, but she does not answer it. Once the phone stops ringing, we hear the anguished sound of sirens in the distance.*

MACHITO: (*Out of breath, enters through the window.*) Mama? Mama? Are you here, Mama? (DOLORES *does not answer.*) Mama? (*Shouting.*) Mama!!

DOLORES: (*Softly.*) Don't shout, remember the neighbors ...

MACHITO: Mama! (*Goes toward her.*) Mama ... I brought you the money ... I got it back. (DOLORES *remains still.*) Here it is, look ... look, here it is! (*Kneels in front of the easy chair where* DOLORES *is sitting and shows her the money, but since she does not react, he places it in her hands.*) Take it! Take it! I got it all back, just like I told you ... (DOLORES *remains silent.* TONY, *from the fire escape, begins to call* MACHITO.)

MACHITO: (*Turning toward the window.*) Here's the money, Mama ... So you can keep your promise ... so you can have the party for Lolita ... (MACHITO *goes to his bed, finds his father's robe and rolls it up to take it with him;* TONY *is heard again calling him from the stairway;* MACHITO *returns and kneels before his mother once more.*) Gotta run now. They're calling me. Did you hear me, Mama? Are you listening?

DOLORES: (*Very softly.*) What happened, Machito?

MACHITO: (*Nervously.*) I already told you, I already told you: they gave back all the money. Go ahead, count it! Count it! It's all there. (TONY *calls him again.*)

DOLORES: Tell me what happened.

MACHITO: (*Evasively.*) Nothing ... Nothing happend, Mama ...

DOLORES: I'm sick of your lies ...

MACHITO: But didn't you want the money back?

DOLORES: How did you manage to get it back? (TONY *calls again and, for the first time in this scene,* DOLORE's *expression hardens.*) My God, it's like the voice of the devil himself calling you ...

MACHITO: (*To* TONY.) I'm coming! I'm coming! (*To* DOLORES.) Gotta run now ...

DOLORES: (*Holds on to* MACHITO.) Before you "run," tell me how you got the money back ...

MACHITO: You wanted the money—and here it is! What more do you want from me?

DOLORES: The truth. Tell me the plain truth this time at least
... Don't you forget I brought you into this world, and
you are my own flesh and blood ... (TONY *insists.*)

MACHITO: I really gotta go now ... ! (*Breaks away.*)

DOLORES: Dear God, have mercy on us! (TONY *keeps on calling.*)

MACHITO: The important thing is you got the money to keep your
promise ... (*Frightened.*) You see, Mama, it was only a
loan ... ? (*From her easy chair,* DOLORES *turns on a
lamp and watches as her son collects some belongings and
wraps them in his father's robe.* TONY *calls again and
MACHITO hurries.*) I'm coming! I'm coming! (*To* DO-
LORES.) I'm going ... I'm going away, Mama ... (MA-
CHITO *tries to leave, but she steps in his way.*)

DOLORES: What have you done, Machito? What have you done
now? (*He starts sobbing and tries to get away, but she
grabs his arm.* TONY *is heard once again.*)

MACHITO: (*Trying to get away.*) Let me go! I have to go! (*In
the struggle,* DOLORES *pulls at the robe that MACHITO
is carrying, and the bloody razor falls to the ground. DO-
LORES picks it up, but drops it, horrified, upon realizing
that it is spattered with blood. She then rises slowly, staring
at her own hands in shock.*)

DOLORES: (*Lets out a shriek.*) Blood! My God, Machito, what
have you done? What have you done to me now? (TONY
calls him again. MACHITO *turns toward the window but
does not answer.*)

MACHITO: (*Trying to make his mother understand.*) I had no
choice ... (*To* TONY.) I'm coming, I'm coming! (*To* DO-
LORES.) He didn't want to give me the money back ...
(*Agitated and confused.*) The music stopped and everybody began to laugh at me ... make fun of me ... Papa
was laughing too, like he did in that nightmare: the same
voice, the same hateful laughter that drove me mad ...
(*Almost submissively.*) And I had to do it ... (*Violently.*)
Can't you see that son-of-a-bitch came back just to lie to
me and make a fool of me? Can't you see I just had to do
it?

DOLORES: Do it? But for God sake, Machito, what did you do?

MACHITO: (*At the top of his lungs.*) I killed my own fucking father,
dammit!!

DOLORES: You couldn't ... (MACHITO *gets away from his
mother and exits through the window;* DOLORES *remains*

still, as if frozen; the telephone rings incessantly, but she appears not to hear it. She finally answers it, absent-mindedly, in a very low voice.) Yes ... ? (*She listens.*) The party ... ? (*She stares at the phone as if surprised and leaves it off the hook.*) I almost forgot the party ... Is it time already ... ? (*Suddenly the door opens and* LOLITA *bursts in, still wearing her long gown, followed by* FATHER MARTÍN.)

LOLITA: (*Throwing herself into her mother's arms.*) Mama! (DOLORES *means to return the embrace, but on seeing* FATHER MARTÍN, *she recoils, tries to hide her tears, and nervously fidgets with her dress and hair.*)

DOLORES: (*Recovering her enthusiasm, she now takes on a demented look.*) It's the excitement of the party, Father ... you know how young people are ... (LOLITA *looks to* FATHER MARTÍN, *seeking an answer.*)

LOLITA: But Machito ...

DOLORES: (*Interrupts.*) Machito is on his way home ... (*To* FATHER MARTÍN,) He went to get his new suit so he can dance the first waltz with Lolita ... This is the happiest moment of my life ... Father, you can understand what this moment means to me better than anyone else ... (ÁNGELA *and* CARMEN *enter; they are very agitated.*)

CARMEN: (*Overly sad.*) Ay, Dolores, my poor darling, we rushed over as soon as we heard ... (*Even more solemn upon realizing* FATHER MARTÍN *is present.*) Good evening, Father. (*To* DOLORES, *aware that* FATHER MARTÍN *is watching her.*) At a time like this, the Catholic faith is our only comfort ...

DOLORES: (*Watching* FATHER MARTÍN.) What time is it? But isn't it still too early for the guests? (*She puts on the fox stole and admires herself in the mirror.*) What do you think of my fox stole? You know I have saved it especially for this occasion since my husband gave it to me when we went to ... (*Turns to* LOLITA.) Was it Boston or Atlantic City ... ? (*To* LOLITA.) Or perhaps it was Las Vegas, I'm not sure now ... (*Turns to* CARMEN *and* ÁNGELA.) Macho, my husband, always insisted I go with him everywhere ...

LOLITA: Mama, Mama! What's the matter with you? (*She tries to embrace her but* FATHER MARTÍN *stops her.*)

DOLORES: (*To* LOLITA.) Didn't I tell you ... ? Don't you see everyone is coming? (*Euphoric.*) Carmen, Carmen,

Carmen ... (*Goes toward* CARMEN *and embraces her giddily.*) Carmen and Ángela ... my two best friends had to be the first to arrive ... But come and try the Palace's canapes, they're the best in town, and not just because I say so, mind you, even the newspaper says it. Well, the Palace ... (*To* FATHER MARTÍN.) Father, did you know that Macho, the children's father, God rest his soul, made his debut with his orchestra in this very same ballroom—everyone came: Ricky Ricardo and even the Mayor, though he was American ...

LOLITA: (*Dejected.*) Father ... ? Explain to her ...

FATHER MARTÍN: (*Interrupting her.*) Leave her alone. Don't say anything ...

DOLORES: (*Putting on a record.*) Come on, put on a happy face, young lady, didn't I tell you everything was turning out just perfect ... ! (DOLORES *once again addresses* ÁNGELA *and* CARMEN *enthusiastically, as the guaguancó record begins to play.*) How do you like the decorations? The white lilies are fresh—they are more expensive, of course—but no one will say later that Dolores Jiménez skimped on her daughter's *quince* party ... And remember that I want pictures, lots of pictures, enough pictures to fill at least another album ... (DOLORES *continues to babble about the party; as the lights begin to dim so does her voice, while the other characters remain frozen and the room itself fades into darkness. Only* LOLITA's *face remains visible, lit by the flashing blue light that slips through the window.*)

LOLITA: (*Emotionless.*) " ... Our revels now are ended. These our actors, As I foretold you, were all spirits, and Are melted into air, into thin air; And like the baseless fabric of this vision, The cloud-capped towers, the gorgeous palaces, The solemn temples, the great globe itself, Yea, all which it inherit, shall dissolve; And, like this insubstantial pageant faded, Leave not a rack behind. We are such stuff As dreams are made on, and our little life Is rounded with a sleep." *The Tempest,* by William Shakespeare ... (LOLITA *steps back away from the light and the stage is now bare; the blue neon light that slips in through the window continues to flash on* MACHITO's *favorite chair for a few more seconds; the anguished sound of sirens is heard in the distance.*)

CURTAIN

BIBLIOGRAPHY

Aguirre, Yolanda. *Apuntes sobre el teatro colonial.* Havana: Cuadernos Cubanos de la Universidad de La Habana, 1968.

Arrom, José Juan. *Historia de la literatura dramática cubana.* New Haven: Yale University Press, 1944.

Castellanos, Isabel. "Lengua y sociedad en el teatro bufo cubano del siglo XIX". *Turia. Revista Cultural* Instituto de Estudios Turolenses de la Diputación Provincial de Teruel 13 (1990), pp. 34–47.

Castellanos, Jorge & Castellanos, Isabel. *Cultura afrocubana.* I y II, Miami: Ediciones Universal, 1988 y 1990 [vol. III forthcoming].

Cortina, Rodolfo J. & Moncada, Alberto, eds. *Hispanos en los Estados Unidos.* Madrid: Ediciones de Cultura Hispánica (Colección Hispana), 1988.

Escarpenter, José & Madrigal, José A. "El teatro popular cubano hasta 1869". In *Perro huevero aunque le quemen el hocico* by Juan Francisco Valerio. Boulder: Society of Spanish & Spanish American Studies, 1986, pp. 9–46.

Fernández, José B. & Fernández, Roberto G. *Bibliographical Index of Cuban Authors (Diaspora 1959–1979).* Miami: Ediciones Universal, 1983.

Figueroa, Pablo. *Teatro: Hispanic Theatre in New York City, 1920–1976.* New York: El Museo del Barrio, 1977.

Greenbaum, Susan. *Afro-Cubans in Ybor City.* Tampa: University of Tampa and Sociedad Martí-Maceo, 1986.

Kanellos, Nicolás. *A History of Hispanic Theatre in the United States: Origins to 1940.* Austin: University of Texas Press, 1990.

————, ed. *Biographical Dictionary of Hispanic Literature in the United States: The Literature of Puerto Ricans, Cuban Americans, and Other Hispanics.* New York, Westport & London: Greenwood Press, 1989.

————, ed. *Hispanic Theatre in the United States.* Houston: Arte Publico Press, 1984.

————. "Towards a History of Hispanic Literature in the United States." In *Images and Identities: The Puerto Rican in Literature*, ed. Asela Rodríguez de Laguna. New Brunswick, N.J.: Transaction Books, 1987.

Leal, Rine. *La selva oscura.* Havana: Editorial Arte y Literatura, 1975.

_____ . *Breve historia del teatro cubano.* Havana: Editorial Letras Cubanas, 1980.

Mardis, Robert Francis. "Federal Theatre in Florida." Ph.D. dissertation, University of Florida, 1972.

Miller, John C. "Hispanic Theatre in New York, 1965–1977." *Revista Chicano-Riqueña* 7, 1 (Winter 1978):40–59.

_____ . "Contemporary Hispanic Theatre in New York." In *Hispanic Theatre in the United States,* ed. by Nicolás Kanellos. Houston: Arte Publico Press, 1984.

Montes Huidobro, Matías. *Persona, vida y máscara en el teatro cubano.* Miami: Ediciones Universal, 1973.

_____ . *Teoría y práctica del catedratismo en "Los negros catedráticos" de Francisco Fernández.* Miami: Editorial Persona, 1987.

Mormino, Gary. *The Immigrant World of Ybor City.* New York: Statue of Liberty, Ellis Island Centennial Series, 1987.

Palls, Terry L. "The Theatre in Revolutionary Cuba: 1959–1969." Ph.D. dissertation, University of Kansas, 1975.

Perrier, José Luis. *Bibliografía dramática cubana.* New York: Phos Press, 1926.

Pottlitzer, Joanne. *Hispanic Theater in the United States and Puerto Rico.* New York: Ford Foundation, 1988.

Poyo, Gerald E. *With All and for the Good of All: The Rise of Popular Nationalism in the Cuban Emigre Communities, 1848–1898.* Durham: Duke University Press, 1989.

Robreño, Eduardo. *Historia del teatro popular cubano.* Havana: Oficina del Historiador de la Ciudad de La Habana, 1961.

Watson Espener, Maida. "Ethnicity and the Hispanic American Stage: the Cuban Experience." In *Hispanic Theatre in the United States,* ed. by Nicolás Kanellos. Houston: Arte Publico Press, 1984.

_____ . "Teatro, mujeres hispanas e identidad." In *Hispanos en los Estados Unidos,* ed. by Rodolfo J. Cortina and Alberto Moncada. Madrid: Ediciones de Cultura Hispánica (Colección Hispana), 1988.

_____ . *Cuban Exile Theatre* (Gainesville: University Presses of Florida, forthcoming).